Sociological Thought

From Comte   To Sorokin

**MARX · SPENCER · PARETO
DURKHEIM · SIMMEL · WEBER
· MANNHEIM ·**

Francis Abraham
& John H. Morgan

Wyndham Hall Press

SOCIOLOGICAL THOUGHT
From Comte to Sorokin

by Francis Abraham
& John H. Morgan

(§ Previously published by Macmillan India Limited.)

Francis Abraham (Ph.D., Michigan State University) is Professor of Sociology and Director of International Studies at Grambling State University.

John H. Morgan (Ph.D., Hartford Seminary Foundation; Sc.D., London College of Applied Science) is Director of the Rhodes-Fulbright International Library.

Library of Congress Catalog Card Number
89-040442

ISBN 1-55605-104-2 (paperback)

WYNDHAM HALL PRESS
Lima, Ohio 45806
www.wyndhamhallpress.com

Printed in The United States of America

For

SOWMYA
SUJATHA
KENDRA
BETHANY
KYNA

CONTENTS

INTRODUCING SOCIOLOGICAL THOUGHT

Within the range of human experience, a sense of time is one of the most conspicuous sensibilities uniquely characteristic of the species. An awareness of history, the passage of time and experience, becomes for the human community the mechanism where we define ourselves, looking to our past for a self-authenticating sense of purpose and direction and then, in turn, looking to our future with resolve and determination.

Within the range of time-consciousness is a sense of "timing," things come into being and pass out of being with a kind of logic. Nowhere is this sense of timing more in evidence than in the world of the human mind, the sphere of ideas operative within the human intellect. This "thinking" drive of the human experience is one with the emergence of our special consciousness. Wherever people have engaged in corporate activities, there has been one among them who has attempted to "explain" what and why about the effort. Wherever one dreams, one has explained; wherever one acts, one has given reasons why.

Thus, when entering the world of thought, of reflective self-awareness and explanation, we enter not a new realm but one primordial. The need to act has always been conjoined with the need to know and explain the action. From the earliest of human thinking about human activity, of theorizing about social life, the human community has sought to understand not merely the "what" of human endeavors but the "why" of these endeavors. What happens as we interact with each other and why does it happen. Such is our primordial concerns. From the earliest records of the Assyrians and Egyptians, the Chinese and the Greeks, there has been a noble effort to understand human action.

Sociology is a new science addressed to an ancient concern,

namely, how to explain human relationships. Though the "scientific" effort is most recent, the special curiosity is primordial. This book has been written as a general introduction to the thinkers and thoughts about their social behaviour since the beginning of a "scientific" address to the study of society. It is not intended as a definitive treatment but rather a serious invitation to enter into the world of social thinking scientifically controlled. The authors have chosen key representative thinkers covering more than a century of sociological thought. Others could have been added or substituted and arguments for these could be made and with the authors' concurrence. But, since the study aims at an enticing "invitation" to sociological thought rather than the comprehensive treatment of it, the thinkers chosen here well serve this purpose. What will be done here briefly falls into three categories: First, a restatement of the intellectual forces operative in the nineteenth century which constituted the "seedbed" for sociological thought; second, a general statement about the nature of sociological thought; and third, a recitation of the major components in the theorizing enterprise.

INTELLECTUAL FORCES

Thoughts must emerge within a social framework and at a given time. That is, thoughts come from people, people who live at a particular time, in a particular place, and under specific circumstances. Any effort to separate thought from person or theory from thinker is fallacious and bound to prove trivial. Since all social theories were thought by social thinkers, we need to understand the social and cultural environment within which they did their thinking to come to a greater appreciation for the thoughts themselves. To presume that general intellectual ferment within a society is irrelevant to the thinking person theorizing about social behavior would be foolish. Therefore, in the following discussions we have divided the chapters into three parts, the first being a summary of the "life and times" of the theorist, the second being a recitation of the major theoretical contributions to sociology made by the particular theorist, and third a review of the lasting contributions made by each sociologist during the time of his work and its continuing relevance.

The nineteenth century for the European community and the western world generally was volatile, exciting, and revolutionary. Several competing attitudes about the meaning and nature of social life were struggling for dominance and each in its own way had profound and long-lasting importance for the social well-being of society and long-term influence upon social policies of the newly emerging governments and political forces emerging at the time. An era of rapid urbanization fostered by catapulting industrialization, European and American cities were a study in contrasts, of poverty and wealth, ignorance and educational advancement, debauchery and social morality. Governments were toppling and new political forces were gaining in respectability and power, religion was being confronted with serious intellectual problems brought on by scientific discoveries, and community life was being threatened with overworked and underfed children and families while others were revelling in financial prosperity.

Four major intellectual forces were operative during the nineteenth century, not always in discord but with a specific emphasis competing for allegiance from government and people. The first was Rationalism, a firm belief that life is explainable, that through the use of the human mind, society could address itself insightfully to its own problems and with concerted effort could bring about a logical and reasonable way of life for all people. Rationalism held firmly to the belief that man is a reasonable animal able to think himself out of difficulty and into serenity. Rationalism was a friend of science and was skeptical of sentimentality and superstitious religion. Though many rationalists were members of the established Church, they held firmly to the belief that God gave man a mind to use for the resolution of his own social and personal problems. Explanations about the nature and meaning of life were scientifically identifiable and therefore the fundamental challenge to the human community was the exercise of Reason in its corporate life.

Aligned with Rationalism and in support of its general attitudes about the nature and meaning of reality was Empiricism, the belief that through the use of science, reality could be understood and human life could be made better. Empiricism places its confidence in the ability of the human mind to understand and explain the complexities of reality, the intricate workings of the world and the ability of the human mind to apply itself to a discovery of the logical processes of material entities and their workings. Empiricism is in many respects the superstructure for all science, for without confidence in the ability to discover the logical composition and operation of all materials, science would be impossible. In the nineteenth century, much of profound and lasting importance was being discovered and developed within the scientific community. One major example was the development of the theory of evolution by Darwin using material evidence gained by scientific discovery and observation. With a growing confidence within the intellectual community in scientific effort, Empiricism became increasingly a generally understood posture legitimately taken in the consideration of any problem or question. Under such circumstances, the appearance of the social thought of Comte and Spencer can be more fully understood and appreciated. How their theories could gain such wide allegiance is explained by the growing confidence the intellectual community had in human reason and scientific method, i.e., the power and influence of Rationalism and Empiricism.

Not at fundamental variance but extremely at variance in practical application was Humanitarianism, a growing sense within the sphere of social consciousness of the plight of the poor, of the afflicted, and of children and the aged. Humanitarianism entered the realm of social consciousness along with Rationalism and Empiricism as an expression of growing sensitivity to the diversity of human circumstances and the need for "something to be done." Never before had social consciousness assumed a general sense of duty or obligation to the disinherited as under the impetus of Humanitarianism. Social service organizations, orphanages, poor houses, child protective laws, and widespread concern within the literary and artistic, religious and political communities made itself felt. The sense that things were not right for all people led to a belief that things might be made better by a serious application of human thought and will. It was not sufficient to merely understand the nature of the plighted community, a call from all quarters went out to make life better, to set things right. Hospitals and sanitaria sprang up in many cities and well-meaning individuals turned to the intellectual and educational communities for help in understanding social problems. The need for more "social philosophizing" was called for.

A genuine application of a science of human understanding was needed. Upon such a scene things were right for the appearance of Karl Mark and Emile Durkheim, studying in turn economic determination and deviancy.

Not surprisingly the various intellectual forces operative in the nineteenth century were not held without some passion. Indeed, there came a time when those aligned with one school of thought labored for an increasingly large portion of attention and power for their own interests and aspirations. The Rationalists as well as Empiricists became ensconced in their own ideas and attitudes and the Humanitarians became equally convinced of the righteousnes of their causes and sensibilities. Consequently, these various forces at work within the thinking community gave rise to a passion of allegiance known as Idealism, a sense in which one's ideas are the dominant and often "right" ideas about a thing and therefore constitute eventually something of a dogma. Idealism has always been in evidence wherever individuals think and take their thoughts seriously. Idealism is not intrinsically right or wrong, good or bad. Rather, Idealism is fundamentally indicative of the emotional and intellectual commitment individuals and society gave to their thinking. An age without Idealism is an age without passion, without dreams, without aspirations for a better world. But all Idealists are not alike. Indeed, there are as strong allegiances to the various ideological options as there are thinking people. Yet, the primary options seem to be either conservative, liberal or revolutionary/radical. The conservative camp Idealists are more interested in "understanding" than they are in changing the circumstances of that which they understand. There is a great reluctance to "tamper" with social forces. The conservatives maintain a hands-off posture respecting social actions preferring rather to "understand" the components but not to alter them; thus, social improvement and advancement comes by virtue of the knowledge gained and a sense of protective maintenance by avoiding problems versus manipulating social circumstances. The liberal camp of Idealists take a different stance believing firmly that it is not only possible but imperative for the rational community to apply itself to the altering of faulty social situations and conditions and such altering is based upon confidence in the ability of the thinking community to understand the reasons why social problems exist. The liberal community asserts its confidence in their capacity to know the nature of the problem to and be able to alter it for the better.

NATURE OF THE SCIENCE

Unlike economics (the study of financial systems), political science (the study of governmental power), and psychology (the study of the human psyche), sociology is a generalized science rather than a specific science. Sociology is the comprehensive study of human relations of two, three, small groups, and large scale organizations. It focuses upon the comprehensive matrix of all social activities which are made up of individuals in relationships with each other. As a generalized science, there is no shared human activity which falls outside the dominion of the science's scrutiny. While avoiding the "specialized" interest of economics or psychology, sociology considers all human activity as its legitimate field for study. As a generalized science, it is necessarily numble in the face of specialized science, deferring to them and seeking from them specialized insights into focussed topics yet bold in its grasp and assault upon the human sphere.

In addition to being a general science, it is also an abstract science seeking to draw from the specific broad notions and ideas about the way human beings behave. As an abstract science, sociology avoids the particular as the focus of its attention choosing rather to compare and contrast sets and groups and categories of data or materials with which to develop explanations and draw conclusions. The abstracting process, i.e., teasing from a complex of information those logically construed conclusions and observations which enhance understanding, constitutes the mechanism whereby sociologists develop theory, grand and bold or meagre and mundane explanations of social behavior, explanations which prove themselves through consistent application and corroboration.

Finally, sociology is not only a general science and an abstract science, it is also an empirical science which more conspicuously than any other single factor separates it from the "speculative" endeavors of philosophers and social thinkers. Everyone knows that in barber shops and beauty parlors the world over, people sit and expostulate about the nature and meaning of life, and particularly about how "those people" are different and thus worse than "we are." Any individual reading a daily newspaper, watching a nightly news broadcast, or talking with a friend across the backyard fence feels at liberty to dwell upon the human verities of crime and evil and intrigue. This is not sociology! It is not sociological theory! It is merely what people do because they are people. That subject-matter which more quickly than any other gains and sustains our attention is the human experience, the human community, social life itself. And everyone, by virtue of being a person, exercises the right to "explain" why people are the way they are. This, nevertheless, is not sociology nor social theory. Sociological theory is based upon "facts" what sociologists call "data," i.e., verifiable information gathered under controlled situations and with precisely established rules and guidelines. The child of rationalism and empiricism, sociology is an empirical science, basing its work upon information (facts) gathered through established means (methodology).

THE THEORIZING ENTERPRISE

All science is based upon data, empirical facts and evidence open for all scientists to know and understand. Without this corroborative component, science is impossible, for an observation, bit of data, instance of fact must be reduplicatable in order for science to verify its "findings." The verification process simply means that any analysis of data must be available for other scientists and any instrument or mechanism for the gathering of facts, data, or evidence must be usable by other scientists in order for the analysis, findings, or conclusions to be taken seriously. The process is somewhat more complicated than is suggested here and deserves a brief discussion before we end this introduction to sociological theory.

  The aim of any science is, of course, explanation (short-range goal) and eventually prediction (long-range goal). If a science cannot explain then it isn't science; and if it cannot predict then it has no real value. Explanation implies the ability to identify the ingredients and how they act upon each other to produce a particular composition and prediction means the ability to anticipate a given result when situations, conditions, or circumstances are the same.

The process involves essentially four steps, viz., observation, description, explanation, and prediction. Without these there is no science and without them there is no sociological theory. Theory is based upon the empirical superstructure of verifiable facts called data. The arrangement of data is a major function of any science. Whereas biologists and chemists use laboratory equipment such as beakers, bunsen burners, etc., the sociologist uses what might be called "conceptual tools for classification" called concepts. The development and employment of concepts is a major dimension to sociological work and theory development. Concepts are words (cognitive tools) which are applied to specific categories of social behavior and constitute a general agreement within the science as to their meaning and composition. Concepts emerge in the development of theory, a process which begins with observation. For sociologists, "observation" is a specifically controlled task which involves much training and profound sensitivity to the nuances of human action. But observation is not enough, one must be able to "explain" what one has observed. Further, the sociologist must not only observe and describe what has been observed but most importantly must be able to "explain" to another what has been observed and described. The explanation is the heart of the theoretical endeavor for when sociologists are dealing with their data, they are dealing with the human experience. A biologist may study a plant and chemist may observe a chemical compound, but when sociologists observe their data they are observing the human experience in action. They are themselves part of what they are observing and explaining. Max Weber has dealt with this point extensively.

Finally, in order for any science to be of value to the human community, it must have the capacity to "predict" future events based on its understanding of past actions. Prediction relative to the non-thinking world of plants, animals, and the inanimate is somewhat more controlled than a science studying human behavior for with people there is the element of "personal freedom." Since people are not robots, they exercise their own wills more or less and therefore prediction becomes more challenging and likewise more problematical. Nevertheless, and in spite of the introduction of "freedom" into the data of sociology, the science has established a respectable record of success in prediction by virtue of its ability to identify those complex ingredients which converge upon any specific social action. Criminal behavior is not merely random; rather, sociologists can identify personality types and environmental situations under which most crimes are likely to occur. So with all social behaviour.

The Growth of Sociological Thought
Although in a more rigorous fashion sociological theory is defined as "logical deductive-inductive system of concepts, definitions, and propositions which states a relationship between two or more selected aspects of phenomena from which testable hypotheses can be derived," in the humanistic tradition theory also incorporates classical works and sociological criticism[1]. If in the name of scientific exactness sociological theory were to exclude classics and commentaries, sociology would be a poor social science indeed. Not only does sociology have its roots in the Enlightenment, it is also the product of a time which sought to understand itself better. It is against this background that Comte emerge as a social philosopher interested in designing a new moral social order. Inspite of his concern with social reform and his passion for a new religion, Comte was a true positivist who wanted to understand and explain the social pheonomena. His ideas on methodology, evolution and the primacy of the system continue to influence theorizing enterprise in contemporary sociology.

Spencer defined the subject matter of sociology more precisely than Comte and provided the most elaborate exposition of the areas of interest to the new discipline. And, whereas Spencer coined the term 'survival of the fittest' and laid the foundation of Social Darwinism which influenced the course of theory in early sociology, Karl Marx expounded the concepts of economic determinism and class struggle and laid the foundation of social conflict theory which continues to influence the discipline in myriad ways. But it was Durkheim who made sociology truly a concern of social 'scientists' rather than of social philosophers (although these roles are often combined) and substituted 'armchair therorizing' with empirical theory construction. Durkheim is also thought to be the leading initiator of structural functionalsim as a sociological perspective.

1. Thomas J. Ward, 'Definitions of Theory in Sociology', in R. Serge Denisoff et. al (eds.), Theories and Paradigms in Contemporary Sociology (Ithaca, P. E. Peacock Publishers, 1974), p. 39.

Max Weber is sometimes regarded as the greatest sociologist ever and there is practically no area within sociology on which he has not left his indelible imprint. His contributions, original and insightful, have profoundly influenced theorizing enterprise in almost every major field within the discipline. Max Weber's contemporary, Georg Simmel laid the foundation of formal sociology. Several of the works of Weber and Simmel have contributed to the emergence of the symbolic interactionist perspective which had its independent origins especially in the works of W.I. Thomas, Charles Cooley and George Hebert Mead. Serveral of Cooley's concepts such as the 'looking-glass self', primary group and sympathetic introspection have enriched the insights of sociology which are 'imaginative reconstructions of life'. George Herbert Mead's conceptualization marked a welcome departure from the conventional psychological behaviorism and formulated a social psychological framework of symbolic interactionism based on assumptions about man's distinct characteristics—his possession of self and his ability to use symbols. Not only did his notion of self provide an effective counter to Freudianism and individual psychologies but by viewing man as an active agent of, rather than a passive recipient of external stimuli, Mead emphasized the idea of emergence in social relations.

Vilfredo Pareto's theory of the circulation of elites and his conceptualization of society as a system in equilibrium have had profound impact on theory construction in sociology. Through his contributions to political sociology, Pareto delivered his indictment on the early twentieth century polity. In a similar vein, Karl Mannheim continued his tirade against the social, economic and political make-up of the twentieth century. Manheimm's contributions to the sociology of knowledge and his reflections on the emerging social order provide most valuable insights into the dynamics of social phenomena. In a sense Pitirim Sorokin continued the tradition of Pareto and Mannheim but on a far more elaborate scale. He codified sociological theory, analyzed the dynamics of socio-cultural change and wrote extensively on problems and issues of modern society.

The main currents of sociological thought advanced by the founding fathers and the later masters represent different times, various cultural contexts and the many intellectual crosscurrents. Rigorously defined (and not necessarily appropriately), these are ideas, not theories but they are the building blocks of theory. They provide insights into and perspectives on the structure and functioning of social systems and the conceptual frameworks for their systematic analysis. The history of sociology is the history of social thought. Without the streams of thought from Comte to Sorokin, and of course before and after, there is no meanigful theory building in sociology. This volume provides only a cursory glance into the world of social thought spanning almost two centuries; therefore, omissions are many, and some significant. It is hoped, however, that beginners in sociology would find this book a useful introduction to the thoughts and theories of the giants of sociology.

1

AUGUSTE COMTE

LIFE AND TIMES

Sociology is a science of human behavior which emerged in the minds of men living through an age of unprecedented social and political revolutions. And of those early social scientists, Auguste Comte (1798-1857) leads the list. Isidore Auguste Marie Francois Xavier Comte was born in Montpellier of southern France on January 1, 1798, in a religious and aristocratic home of tradition and social standing. A family both Royalist in politics and staunch Roman Catholic in piety, the Comtes epitomized domestic stability, continuity, and propriety. Comte's father was a minor government official with hopes for his son in politics. Comte entered the respected imperial lycee in his hometown at the age of nine, quickly gaining attention for both his intellect and mischievousness. Scrutinized and admonished by his teachers and admired and encouraged by his peers, Comte rose to leadership in school both in academic affairs and rebelliousness. Romantic yet pragmatic, idealistic while practically minded, Comte abandoned early in life—some say by age 13—the faith of his family and substituted an unrelenting and passionate republican faith in human liberty. A love for the human community—for the social politic—consumed all of his other concerns. Not the individual, but the social whole, must concern the intellectual, the politician, and above all the scientist. Liberty for mankind must come by way of a realistic science.

Having distinguished himself academically at the lycee, though disappointingly unruly as a student, Comte sat for and sustained the competitive entrance examination to the Ecole Polytechnique in Paris. Though the Ecole was the intellectual center of political liberalism and progressive thought of the day, its agenda of research and activities did not include human affairs and social studies. Rather, its distinguished reputation throughout Europe rested upon its mathematical and natural sciences, with only an occasional professor willing to openly espouse or patronize a scientific interest in social phenomena. Adept in abstract science and mathematics, Comte was more concerned about the liberation of society through a scientific development of human consciousness. Comte's primary preoccupation centered around the improvement of society, and such improvement, he reasoned, necessitated the development of a theoretical science of society. To this he gave his life's wcrk, seeking to formulate a system of laws governing society such that on the basis of these laws social ills could be cured—crime, unemployment, wars, etc. His system, resembling a "Catholicism minus Christianity," consisted of an all-embracing hierarchical plan to society based on secular values of a strongly humanitarian variety.

Not long after entering the Ecole in 1814, he became embroiled in controversial and even explosive activities regarding national politics as well as disputes over policy issues at the Ecole itself. Due to his rebelliousness and strong-headed determination not to compromise the issues nor his own ideals, he left the school, never to return. At age 19, and just before his unfortunate departure from the Ecole, young Comte stumbled upon an elder social idealist who was destined to make a profound and lasting impression upon Comte and his work. The man was Comte Henri de Saint-Simon (1760-1825), a full but marginal member of the French aristocracy such as it was during these tumultuous times, but uncharacteristic of such citizenry, Saint-Simon was a strong utopian socialist. Comte, who became quickly enamoured of the old man's beliefs that science was the new spiritual power of the age and that soon both morals and politics would become positive sciences—sciences established upon objective data and empirical facts—became Saint-Simon's secretary, assisting in the production of the progressive periodical, *Industrie*.

Comte came under the spell of Saint-Simon, then aged 60, and soon he had coupled his own ideas about human society with the elitism and liberalism of Saint-Simon. So much so, that it was difficult, when reading their papers, to distinguish the pair's individual contributions. It has been suggested, without much dispute, that Comte's major ideas which were later developed into complex theories actually emerged during these formative years with Saint-Simon (1760-1825), though later Comte was to deny the suggestion vehemently.

As frequently happens between master and disciple (if we can so characterize this relationship), a breach came in 1824 between Comte and Saint-Simon resulting in a parting of the ways with denunciations on both sides which were never retracted. If Comte thought of the relationship with Saint-Simon as junior-senior colleague collaboration and mutual enterprise, Saint-Simon saw Comte as an understudy such that their publications were not so much collaboration and co-authorship as youthful and productive assistance to the seasoned scholar. Saint-Simon, possibly thinking of his old age, began also to press for immediate action in social reforms while young Comte wished rather to dwell long and carefully upon the theoretical development of his grand system of "positive physic." The breach came when Saint-Simon published a co-authored manuscript under his own name entitled, *Catechisme des Industrie*, while Comte protested, demanding that it be published under his name and entitled, *System de Politique Positive*. Finally, one hundred copies were published Comte's way, while one thousand copies were published Saint-Simon's way. The men parted company, never to collaborate or even say anything good about the other again.

At twenty-six and now without a colleague and no income, Comte was professionally adrift. His work ignored, or too readily associated with Saint-Simon who was mostly overlooked or mocked by the academic establishment as being a quack, Comte sought stability and security as he had known it at home as a young lad. The family, for Comte in all his writings as well as personal experience, constituted the basic social unit—the fundamental ingredient in society. In February of 1825, he married Caroline Massin, who had been a Parisian streetwalker but not an industrial employee. The marriage was a miserable failure, suffering through a perpetual tempest of confusions, misunderstandings, and incompatibilities. They finally separated, with Comte still unnoticed by academe and anchorless both emotionally and socially.

Living perennially on the margin of poverty, yet burning with his passion for a science of human society, he did do some sporadic paid writing for the journal *Producteur*, ironically, a periodical established by the disciples of the now late Saint-Simon. His progressive journalism was hardly of career strength or quality, but he was kept from starving, nonetheless. By now desperation had overtaken Comte, both for money and recognition. Therefore, in an attempt to gain some of both, he proposed to offer a course or series of lectures on his "positive physic."

The series of lectures offered by Comte as a private course attracted several distinguished scholars from the nearby Ecole as well as several colleagues of Comte's journalistic efforts for the *Producteur* and the *Industrie*. Several students came from the Ecole, and numerous industrial workers from the nearby factories that had come under the influence of Comte's writing in blue-collar literature. The diverse array of subscribers to the course provided a challenge to Comte's capacities as a populist and scholar as well as his sought-for forum to expound the merits of his new science of society, now being dubbed "sociology."

If the response was gratifying to Comte's quest for recognition and acceptance, his ability to deliver was not. The course began in April 1826, but under the strain of economic destitution and the burden of explaining his system to scholar and worker in one forum, he fell ill. A mental break-down caused the suspension of the lectures during which time he had to stay in a sanatorium but left it, so the records say, uncured. After extended care in his mother's home, Comte regained his strength of health and emotional energy such that the course was resumed in 1829, with a dwindling of interest by the Ecole community but with a continued and sedate loyalty among the laborers in the neighborhood.

Even in the best of times, a really creative and genuinely unique idea has a difficult time catching on, but Comte's time was not the best. There was war, revolution, rebellion, and social and political chaos and turmoil at every juncture. Events occurred in rapid succession—the French Revolution, Napoleon's rise to power and downfall, and the Restoration of the Monarchy.

Amidst it all, Comte survived and thrived, working on his science of society whereby both order and progress could be eventually realized. He was a product of the Enlightenment, though later in life he would turn from reading other's works, for during his formative years he was profoundly influenced by the thought of the age. As epitomized at the Ecole, the intellectual climate of nineteenth century France prided itself in its achievements in mathematics and the natural sciences. And, given the mood of the day, much expectation centered around the eminent discovery of comparable social laws of human progress. As with most intellectuals, Comte felt the pressure of the tumultuous age to stress the importance of social order as well as progress—a positive science of society could demonstrate the truth of these natural processes within human community. The French intellectual and literary legacy rallied to the support of such belief. Pascal (1623-1662) had intimated the ever-advancing march of human growth and knowledge while Montesquieu (1755-1789) had pointed to the social laws of human advance. Turgot (1727-1781) had worked specifically on the ideas of social laws of progress and the Marquis de Condorcet (1743-1794) even entitled his master work, *Historical Essay on the Progress of Human Reason.*

The key dispute within this intellectual legacy in France was the relationship between the individual and society. Rousseau had argued persuasively that man was pure and naturally good individually but was spoiled and corrupted by society's demands for social contracts to ensure order. On the other hand, de Bonald spoke for an equally strong legacy that argued for the redeeming quality of society in the evil nature of man. Comte favored society's redemptive qualities, being suspicious of individuality. What he disliked and abjured among the traditionalists was their retrograde characteristics. Progress must accompany order—Comte argued, using the power of his positive science for empirical illustration. Order, hierarchy, spirituality, social supremacy over the individual—these Comte supported but always within the context of progress.

Between 1830 and 1842, he wrote his magnum opus *Cours de Philosophie Positive.* Yet, and despite the relentless efforts of friends and himself, he was unable to secure a faculty post at the Ecole Polytechnique, the French Academy of Science, or the College de France. The disappointment bore heavily upon Comte as he tried over and over again to gain recognition for his work, for this science he had tried to develop lifelong and see accepted in the universities of France. He failed, and failed again. Hardly a consolation, he was made "repetiteur d'analyse et de mecanique" in 1832 and a travelling external examiner with per diem stipend in 1837 at the Ecole, but these positions paid poorly and carried no prestige or recognition whatsoever for his work. Even with these appointments, Comte continued to live in near abject poverty. Some relief to Comte came from some noteworthy praise and reviews of his work in the scholarly journals of England, especially from that of John Stuart Mill, but even that waned towards the end of Comte's life.

At the age of forty and towards the end of the writing of his *Cours*, he began to practise what he called "cerebral hygiene," viz., he ceased reading anyone's works, choosing to keep his mind clear for his own work. Towards the end of his life, he did read incessantly Thomas A Kempis' *Imitation of Christ*. In 1844, he received his final and public refusal of a post of the Ecole Polytechnique—"my greatest public humiliation"—and yet, ironically enough, that same year brought a rebirth of Comte's spirit, for in that year, he fell passionately and helplessly in love with one Clothilde de Vaux, an upper-class woman in her mid-thirties who had been abandoned by her husband. Comte, in his late forties, became totally pre-occupied with their relationship which she kept at a Platonic though encouraging level always resisting his proddings for marriage. She died within the year of tuberculosis. Comte, now deprived of the one *raison d'etre* in his life, turned more energetically than ever to his work. He dedicated his life to the love of her memory and his *System de Politique Positive* carried a dedication to Clothilde de Vaux.

As a result of this experience of love and deep emotion, Comte became obsessed with the primacy of emotion over intellect, of feeling over mind, such that he began to write and speak openly of his conviction that "universal love" was the only real solvent for all difficulties of the age. He began to devise a "Religion of Humanity" with which he thought of himself as the high priest. In fact, he began signing all of his correspondence with "The Founder of Universal Religion, Great Priest of Humanity." Four years after the death of Ms. de Vaux, Comte founded the Societe Positiviste, an organization of his disciples which included membership fees (which Comte used to live on) and regular meetings under his guidance and leadership. Missions were eventually begun in Spain, England, Holland, and even in the United States of

America. Losing interest in the purely academic life of the Ecole within which he was never allowed to participate, he redirected the remainder of his life to religious humanism for the working and laboring classes until his death on September 5, 1857, at the age of fifty-nine.

MAJOR THEORIES

Theory of Evolution and Progress

Comte regarded division of labor and population growth as corollaries of intellectual evolution—the predominant principle of social development. He believed, as did many at that time, that the evolution of the human mind parallels that of the development of the individual's intellect—i.e., phylogeny (development of the species) recapitulates ontogeny (development of the individual). In other words, individual mind, human activity and society pass through successive stages of historical evolution leading to some final stage of perfection.

The Law of Three Stages

Being a true science, sociology is always in search of laws—social laws to be applied to society such that society's past can best be understood and its future predicted. Of those laws discovered in social physics, Comte considered his law of the Three Stages based upon belief in social evolution to be the most important. "Each of our leading conceptions," Comte said in *Politique Positive*, "each branch of our knowledge, passes successively through three different theoretical conditions; the theological or fictitious; the metaphysical or abstract; and the scientific or positive."[1] As individuals develop from childhood superstitions and fears of supernatural powers, to adolescent belief in great cosmic principles and to adulthood's practical positivism, so do societies from primitive religion to more advanced philosophical idealism to modern scientific mentalities.

(a) *The Theological or Fictitious Stage.* This stage, dominated by priests and the military, is the period in which man seeks the essential nature of all beings, first and final causes, origins and purposes of all effects, and the overriding belief that all things are caused by supernatural beings. In this state, "all theoretical conceptions, whether general or special, bear a supernatural impress." The mind invokes gods and goddesses and seeks to explain phenomena by ascribing them to *beings* comparable to man himself. The Theological stage went through the three phases of fetishism, polytheism and monotheism.

(b) *The Metaphysical or Abstract Stage.* This stage is dominated by churchmen and lawyers, a stage in which mind presupposes abstract *forces,* veritable entities and personified abstractions capable of producing all phenomena. "It forms a link and is mongrel and transitional." The Metaphysical stage started about 1300 A.D. and was short-lived.

(c) *The Positive or Scientific Stage.* The dawn of the nineteenth century marked the beginning of the positive stage in which "observation predominates over imagination" and all theoretical concepts have become positive. In this final stage, dominated by industrial administrators and scientists, the nature of human mind has given up its childish and vain search for Absolute notions, origins and destinations of the universe and its causes but seeks to establish scientific *principles* governing phenomena.

Corresponding to the three stages of mental progress, there are three states or epochs of society. The theological and metaphysical stages are dominated by military values; however, the former is characterized by Conquest and the latter by Defence. The positive stage heralds the advent of Industrial society. Thus, Comte identified two major types of societies: the Theological-Military society, which was dying, and the Scientific-Industrial society, which was being born during his lifetime. The former is characterized by the predominance of theological thinking and military activity. Priests were endowed with intellectual and spiritual power while the military exercised temporal authority. In the scientific industrial society, priests and theologians are replaced by scientists who represent the new moral and intellectual power. With the growth of scientific thinking and effective organization of production, military activity becomes obsolete and the captains of industry dominate the major activities of society.

Comte believed that the new scientific-industrial society will become the society of all mankind. This is the ultimate stage in a series of successive transformations the human race goes through and each stage is decidedly superior to the previous one. The new system is built upon the destruction of the old, and, with evolution, come progress and the emancipation of the human mind.

Thus Comte's theory of progress, often referred to as the unilinear theory of evolution, involved the development of the human race to a single design: the culmination of the individual mind, the human mind, and the human society in an ultimate state of positivism. Human history is the history of a single people, Comte reasons, because the progress of the human mind gives unity to the entire history of society.

Hierarchy of the Sciences

As with individuals and societies, so with the sciences themselves—they all pass through the same stages. As astronomy began in mystical speculation and advanced through philosophical musings to finally scientific method, so did sociology, but has now arrived at a point in which not some religious notion or metaphysical cause but scientific observation and analysis tell man who and what he is and the true nature of all human relationships in society. "As long as men believe that social events were always exposed to disturbances by the accidental intervention of the legislator," Comte argued in his *Positive Philosophy*, "human or divine, no scientific previsions of them would be possible."[2]

The abstract and theoretical sciences form a hierarchy in which the more concrete and complex sciences succeed the more general and abstract sciences. The hierarchy, determined by the natural law of mental progress, is based on the order in which positive method comes to be adopted in the disciplines. The base of the hierarchy, is mathematics, followed by astronomy, because these are the sciences in which the positive method comes to be adopted first. In time, they are followed by mechanics, physics, chemistry, much later biology, and finally sociology.

The social sciences are at the apex of the hierarchy for they enjoy "all the resources of the anterior sciences" and offer "the attributes of a completion of the positive method. All others are preparatory to it. Here alone can the general sense of natural law be decisively developed in the most difficult case of all."[3] And, the positive method which has triumphed in all abstract sciences must essentially prevail in history and politics and culminate in the founding of a positive science of society, namely sociology, which is, in a word, the roof of all sciences. Thus, sociology, which stood at the head of the long line of positive sciences, was the crowning glory of man's ability to analyze, describe, and prognosticate, and the most difficult in view of the complexity of the human phenomena which it focused upon.

In establishing the hierarchy of the sciences, Comte also distinguished the methodological characteristics of the various disciplines. Beginning with biology, the discipline that immediately precedes social sciences in the hierarchy, there is a decisive reversal in methodology—the sciences have become holistic in character. Sciences are no longer analytic but essentially and necessarily synthetic. Unlike physics and chemistry, which analyze elements of inorganic matter and proceed to establish laws among isolated phenomena, biology takes a holistic approach and proceeds from the study of organic wholes. "In the inorganic sciences, the elements are much better known to us than the whole which they constitute; so that in that case we must proceed from the simple to the compound. But the reverse method is necessary in the study of Man and Society; Man and Society as a whole being better known to us, and more accessible subjects of study, than the parts which constitute them."[4] Just as biology cannot explain an organ or a function apart from the organism as a whole, sociology cannot explain social phenomena without reference to the total social context. This idea of organic unity or the primacy of the system over element has important theoretical implications. Comte has repeatedly asserted that one element of social entity could be understood only in terms of the entity as a whole; similarly, any particular moment in the historical evolution of this entity is to be understood only in terms of the total process of historical evolution as a whole. In the words of Comte, "There can be no scientific study of society either in its conditions or its movements, if it is separated into portions, and its divisions are studied apart."[5]

The True Science of Humanity
In spite of Comte's strong intellectual affinities with the Enlightenment and the liberal genre of the Ecole, he differed from the mood at key pcints. He objected, for instance, to the characteristic optimism of the scientific community regarding the nature of human development with its emphasis upon the supremacy of man's rational capabilities. As opposed to reason being the pivotal factor in human behavior, Comte argued rather that man will never be prompted by anything stronger and more fundamental

than his own emotions. Feelings rather than reason rule the mind. The goal of man, therefore, if he is to better his society is to be governed more and more by unselfish feelings and less and less by egotistical instincts. It is the scientific mind that can govern the feelings most effectively. The scientist is not necessarily more rational than other men; he is more likely, however, to govern his emotions more constructively for the corporate good. Comte's famous formula sums up best his thoughts on the human qualities of emotions, activity, and intellect—"Man is to act by emotion and to think in order to act."

If Comte was skeptical about the rationality of the human animal, he was equally so about the age's optimistic propensities which, he thought, defied the evidence to the contrary. Man is not and cannot be by instinct a positivist—his emotions are more likely to be governed by superstition and fear than by cool analysis and logical description. Man is not by nature a positivist Comte never tired of saying—he is not naturally scientific. He becomes so gradually, through the evolution and progress of society and the human mind. To be a positivist (or later to be called scientist), is to discover the laws governing phenomena, and time is required to glean such understanding from observation and experimentation. History, Comte reasoned, is necessary so that human intelligence may attain its intrinsic end, may realize its peculiar vocation, which is human progress and societal evolution under the governance of sociology.

For Comte, there was a direct correlation between the progress of the human mind and the evolution of human society. As one develops, so does the other. It is no accident, so the intimation is, that those societies which are the most advanced in complexity of associations and refinements of interaction are likewise the same societies in which the greatest intellectual development amongst individuals has occurred. "I mean," Comte explained once, "the relational coordination of the fundamental sequence of the various events of human history according to a single design" constituted the key to conceptual sociology. Human history is fundamentally the history of the progress of mind and society. In fact, it has been suggested that the "true science of the human mind" as envisaged by Comte is what today is called the sociology of knowledge. This true science—"positive physic" or "sociology"—consists of the observation, analysis, and comprehension of the capabilities of the human mind as they are revealed to us through their progressions in the course of history. The mind is both a social and an historical entity, and in each age, the mind of the scientist functions in a social matrix. To understand Comte is to understand the creative interfacing of mind and society in historical process. His aim was to create a naturalistic science of society which could explain the past development of mankind as well as predict its future advancement.

Originally, in his *Positive Philosophy*, Comte implied that the new science of sociology was the study of the totality of human intellect and its resulting social actions through time. Mind, society, and history converged in the new discipline. Later, realizing the need to more adequately circumscribe the legitimate parameters of the science of society, Comte qualified his earlier definition by suggesting that sociology was not the study of the intellect as such but of the cumulative results of the activity of the human mind. This definition is very much reflected in contemporary theoretical and cultural anthropology as a definition of "culture".

Comte's greatest battle with the intellectual bastions of his day was over the nature and function of this new science, orginally and preferably called "social physics" by Comte but owing to an unfortunate coincidence of the term appearing in the title of a "mere" statistical study by a Belgian scientist by the name of Quetelet, Comte was forced, happily now in retrospect, to concoct a neologian term—"sociology," combining the Latin word *socius* (society) and Greek word *logos* (study of). To establish sociology as the abstract theoretical science of social phenomena was Comte's life-long mission. This science, for him, was to be the culmination of all sciences. "Thus," he explained in *System of Positive Policy*, "we already possess celestial physics (astronomy), terrestrial physics (geology and geography), mechanical and chemical (engineering and chemistry), vegetable physics (botany), animal physics (zoology). We still need one physical science—social physics (sociology)—in order to complete the natural sciences, (parenthesis added)".[6] Within these rather high-minded terms, Comte took in hand to define and circumscribe the parameters of the new science. "I understand Social Physics to mean that science which occupies itself with the study of social phenomena, considered in the same light as astronomical, physical, chemical and physiological phenomena, that is to say, as being subject to natural and invariable laws the discovery of which is the special object of its researchers."[7] And, as Comte suggested in his emphasis upon the operation of evolution upon mind and society, he was particularly insistent that the primary aim of sociology was to discover by what necessary chain of successive transformations the human race, starting from a condition barely superior to that of a society of great apes, has been gradually led up to the present stage of European civilization."[8] And within this hierarchy of sciences, wherein the analysis and description of systems become increasingly complex beginning with stellar and ending in social constellations, all sciences will converge upon the culmination of their mutual enterprises in the advancement of mankind, sociology in the lead. From the meagre society of primitive men up to the crown of western culture in France itself, social evolution was understood to be the continuation of the general progression of biological evolution of plant and animal life.

Social Statics and Social Dynamics

The study of progress—of mind and society through history— was greatly facilitated by the fact that the development of all societies is governed by the same laws, so that the development of general principles may begin with the study of the advances made by the vanguard of humanity, viz., French culture.

In this study of social progress and human development, Comte saw two components at work—what he called statics and dynamics. Social statics, he pointed out, is the study of the conditions of society's existence at any given moment which is analyzed by means of a *theory of social order.* "The statical study of sociology consists in the investigation of the laws of action and reaction of the different parts of the social system—apart, for the occasion, from the fundamental movement which is always gradually modifying them."[9] Social dynamics, on the other hand, is the study of continuous movements in social phenomena through time by means of a *theory of social progress.* Throughout his writings, Comte wrestled with the dialectical tension he saw in the socio-political activities of his time between order and progress within society. A true science of humanity, of social life, must discover those laws making both order and progress possible. In Vol. II of his *Positive Philosophy*, Comte wrote: "The distinction is between two aspects of theory. It corresponds with the double conception of order and progress: for order consists in a permanent harmony among the conditions of social existence, and progress consists in social development."[10] By studying order, sociologists come to a better understanding of those components necessary to the existence of society; by studying progress, a better understanding of social movements is made. Both are essential.

A basic fact of the social order which, according to Comte is established by the laws of nature, is that of *consensus universalis*, a universal agreement among all societies of the dialectically creative role of order and progress. Such a consensus exists in all realms of life but reaches its climax in human society. Between all social components of human life—science, art, politics, values, ideas—the *consensus universalis* is the foundation of solidarity in a society. Within this context of analysis, Comte eliminated the study of individuals, contending that sociology is the study of social systems consisting of homogeneous elements. He argued that the family is the basic social unit, though he never completely excluded his work from the constant plague of individual versus society issues. Social statics consisted of the analysis of society's structure at a given moment, on the one hand, and on the other, of the analysis of the element(s) which at any given moment determine the consensus, which makes the collection of individuals into a society, the plurality of institutions into a unity. Social statics, then, is particularly adept at contributing to an understanding of the nature of social order.

Social dynamics which must be subordinated to social statics, consist merely of the description of the successive and necessary stages in the development of mind and society—incorporating historical analysis. Furthermore, social dynamics is history devoid of individual names, history of a scientific character in search of an abstract order of social laws operative in mind and society through historical progression. Fully and quite articulately affirming that progressive development in the evolution of society does not advance in a straight line—contrary to the Comtean antagonists who have for decades falsely accused him of being a unilateralist in social evolution—Comte did believe that the study of social dynamics must rightfully begin with human development and social progress. For Comte, the two causal corollaries of progress were population increase and the growth of human mental abilities. He once argued persuasively to his readers that children of each society develop in quantity and speed commensurate with their society's corporate development. Progress, he reasoned, is observable in all aspects of society—physical, moral, intellectual, political. The intellect is fundamental and most conspicuous since history is dominated by the development of ideas. And, concomitantly, intellectual development stimulates material development. Among these lines, Comte suggested by way of explanation that the differential velocity of progress so blatantly evidenced in Europe and the world was traceable to such variables as race, geography, and political system.

The concept of statics can be logically divided into two parts: the study of the structure of human nature, on the one hand, and the study of the structure of social nature, on the other. The concept of dynamics involves the theory of progress, the law of three stages and the inevitable evolutionary development of order. "In short, social dynamics studies the laws of succession, while social statics enquires into those of coexistence; so that the use of the first is to furnish the true service in regard to order, and this suitability to the needs of modern society is a strong confirmation of the philosophical character of such a combination."[11]

Methodology
All along, we have seen Comte's emphasis upon historical analysis as an indispensable component in sociological methodology. Sociology for Comte was nothing if it was not informed by a sense of historical evolution—a cognizant demonstration of mind and society in dialectical creativity through time. In order to legitimize the utility of the new science of human society, Comte insisted that it be "positive," i.e., scientific in methods of analysis and prognosis. Sociology must use the "positive" method, which, for Comte, meant the subordination of concepts to facts and the acceptance of the idea that social phenomena are subject to general laws—social laws. Yet, as he consistently pointed out, owing to the complexity of human relationships, attitudes, and behaviors, these social laws are necessarily less rigid than biological laws. And most importantly, Comte wanted his disciples to understand that social science must not be simply identified with

mathematics and statistics, as helpful as they are in sociological analysis. "The idea of treating social science," Comte explained in *System of Positive Polity*, "as an application of mathematics in order to give it a positive character had its source in the metaphysical prejudice that outside of mathematics there can be no real certainty."[12] Comte identifies this bias with the times of prepositive science, and as being now pre-empted by the higher science of complex social life. "This prejudice," he continues, was natural at the period when all positive knowledge lay within the sphere of applied mathematics . . . But since the rise of the great positive sciences . . . such a prejudice is entirely inexcusable."

Positive knowledge is to be gained by sociology in employing a three-step methodology buttressed by historical analysis. *Observation*, which must be guided by a theory of social phenomena; *experimentation*, which in sociology means *controlled observation* and the careful scrutiny of what Comte called "pathological cases" as the true scientific equivalent in sociology of pure experimentation; and *comparison*, which included human to animal, society to society, like to unlike, etc. "Central to sociology," Comte once said, "is the comparison of the different coexisting states of human society on the various parts of the earth's surface . . . "By this method," he explained, "the different stages of evolution may all be observed at once. These conventional methods of science—observation, experimentation and comparison—must be used in combination with the *historical method*." "The historical comparison of the consecutive states of humanity is not only the chief scientific device of the new political philosophy . . . it constitutes the sub-stratum of the science, in whatever is essential to it."[13] The historical method involved the search for general laws governing the successive transformations of humanity through fixed, but limited number of stages. Comte insisted that we could not understand a particular social phenomenon unless we restore it to its social context. To understand the significance of a religion, one should understand the entire social and cultural context; and a particular moment in history is to be understood against the whole historical process. "The chief phenomenon in society—the gradual and continuous influence of generations upon each other—would be disguised or unnoticed for want of the necessary key, viz., historical analysis."[14] Mind and society in interaction must be studied in their histori-

cal setting, as processes of human development. Sociological
method for Comte assured the scientific quality of "social physics," and though the precision was quantitatively short of pure
mathematics, the quality of its analysis into the complexities of
social life catapulted the science of humanity to the top rung in
the scientific ladder. Comte argued in the first volume of his
Positive Philosophy for the indispensability of these natural laws
to be discovered by sociology—"We shall find that there is no
chance of order and agreement but in subjecting social phenomena, like all others, to invariable natural laws, which shall, as
a whole, prescribe for each period, with entire certainty, the
limits and character of social action."[15]

Scientific Theory of Morality
Convinced that the intellectual supremacy of positivism had been
successfully established in his earlier work, Comte devoted his
later writings to moral and religious considerations rather than
scientific and sociological inquiries. He wanted to create a new
social order based on moral unity and a new religion of humanity.
The supernatural religion based on revelation is to be replaced
by a demonstrated religion based on the scientific synthesis of
human intellect, action and feeling. With the ascendance of positivism and moral unity, will come the gradual elimination of
egoism and the triumph of altruism. All elements and processes
of society "will cooperate willingly in perfecting the order of the
world." To Comte, the final stage of evolution was the golden
age of positivism, a new civilization which was characterized by
the homogeneity of beliefs and emotions and which permitted the
fullest expression of individual talent and action but yet tempered by education and moral training.

Comte prepared an elaborate blueprint of the golden age of the
future. The new positive society, which Comte labelled as Sociocracy, will be an organic, hierarchic society based on the natural
talents of individuals. While personal ownership of property is
necessary and inevitable, it will be exercised only as a collective
function and a social duty. The goal of every individual will be,
to rise in the spiritual hierarchy of merit and moral worth, not
the temporal hierarchy of wealth and power. The industrial order
assigned each man a position commensurate with his merit; the
only hierarchy that counts in the positive sociocracy is the hier-

archy of merit and of the heart. The new society of peace and harmony will endure only because it is tempered and regulated by a moral and spiritual power. Now that the accumulation of wealth does not depend on the creation of large states through military conquest, wars have outlived their purpose, Comte reasoned; wealth depended on the scientific organization of labor in the industrial enterprise.

Comte assigned great prestige and responsibility to sociologists in his society of the future. The sociologists must constitute an academy of secular priests endowed with the spiritual power of the new positive religion. These scientific sociologist-priests would act as the moral guides and censors of the community and the directors of education. Having acquired positive knowledge of what is good and evil, they would be able to judge abilities of each member of society and hold men to their collective duty by means of education and moral training. In the religion of humanity, "Live for Others" will be the supreme commandment, Love its major principle, Order its basis and Progress its aim.

Summary and Appreciation
From the very earliest efforts at constructing a positive "social physics," young Comte perceived the function of the new science to be the essential understanding of the necessary, indispensable, and inevitable course of history in such a way as to promote the realization of the new order now dawning upon human society. The subject matter of the science Comte wanted to establish, viz., sociology, was the history of the human race regarded as a whole. His science was meant to resolve the crisis of the modern world, to provide a system of scientific ideas which will preside over the reorganization of society, the true emergence of social engineers, though Comte never used that now popular title. Comte's humanitarian preoccupation was reflected in his description of the function of the new science. Social science must ultimately be dedicated to concrete benefit of mankind—to the amelioration of the human condition. "From science comes Prevision," Comte wrote at the beginning of his *Positive Philosophy*, "and from Prevision comes Action."

Comte's humanism and the real meaning of his subjective synthesis is based on the fact that nature becomes conscious of itself in man so that, as Comte put it, "man sums up in himself

all the laws of the world." His main interest, as we have illustrated, was in the systematization of the social background of
human history into one body of knowledge, in preparation for
a practical approach to social reform based on a lasting order,
the theoretical and moral principles of which, he saw in the development of a new science, sociology. The universal sense of
human interdependence, said Comte, would provide the new
science a laboratory for analytical work. This sense of dependence, he suggested, consisted of three components—a common
language within a society, a common religion which is the root
of social order indispensable for making legitimate the demands
of government, and a common division of labor. Any body of
knowledge produced by the new science would have to focus its
attention here. To understand society, the sociologist must understand these components, and though language and religion are
indispensable ingredients for order and progress, the division of
labor fascinated Comte most. "Men are bound together," he said
in the second volume of *Positive Philosophy*, "by the very dis-
tributions of their occupations; and it is this distribution which
causes the extent and growing complexity of the social organism."[16] The importance of this bit of writing is realized later in
the study by Durkheim into this whole area which we will explore
in a subsequent chapter.

Comte believed that the division of labor was the fundamental
cause of the growing complexity of society. Solidarity and cooperation must, therefore, characterize the relationship of individuals to each other in society. Within this context, Comte coined the word "altruism." Later, Durkheim turned his attention to
the study of social solidarity as well as drew freely from Comte's
insights. In volume two of his *Positive Philosophy*, Comte had
said regarding the functional connection between statics (order)
and dynamics (progress), "there must always be a spontaneous
harmony between the parts and the whole of the social system."
This intimation of the importance of the function of social structures was eventually to emerge under the leadership of Weber
and Durkheim as a major theoretical school of sociology called
structural-functionalism, the dominant mode of sociological analysis today. He went on to say that "it is evident that not only
must political institutions and social manners, on the one hand,
and manners and ideas on the other hand, be always mutually

connected; but further that this consolidated whole must always be connected by its nature, with the corresponding state of the integral development of humanity."[17]

For too long, Comte was fashionably but most regrettably ignored as an eccentric with a few good ideas. Today, he has become the focus of attention as the history of sociology becomes an increasingly important enterprise of the discipline. More and more historians of social theory are discovering and acknowledging the tremendous impact his writings have had upon the masters of sociological thought. Admittedly, he was limited as any scholar might who sets out to create a new science. But his definitions and circumscriptions of the legitimate dominion of the new science were sound, and his methodology good—observation, comparison, experimentation, and historical analysis are still the cornerstones of sociological method. His emphasis upon sociology's role as an instrument of reform and its descriptive task are most valuable yet. He made naive and potentially serious errors—he was wrong about the demise of religion and philosophy. His opposition to scientific positivism's preoccupation with numbers and data is still of value today. And not least is his now evident influence upon the works of such later distinguished philosophers as John Stuart Mill, anthropologists as Levy-Bruhl, and sociologists as France's Durkheim and America's Lester Ward. A scholar must not be judged strictly by his accomplishments in scientific discovery alone, as important as that judgment might be; he must also be assessed in the social and historical context within which his thought took place. Comte, while making naive mistakes and wrong decisions, nevertheless, set the stage for the development of one of the most important scientific adventures of modern man, viz., the emergence of the social science of sociology.

2

KARL MARX

LIFE AND TIMES

In 1817, the year before Karl Marx (1818-1883) was born to Heinrich and Henrietta Marx, his father had joined the Lutheran Church of Prussia. Coming from a long line of rabbis, Heinrich Marx, a lawyer and head of the bar in Trier, in Germany, found it necessary to seek refuge in the liberal Protestant body. This was due to the increased pressure and persecution of the Jews under the newly established Prussian regime following the fall of the more lenient Napoleonic government. Henrietta, a rabbi's daughter from Holland, gave birth to Karl Marx on the 5th of May, 1818, and though she herself does not seem to have a great influence on him, his father Heinrich most definitely did. Born in a bourgeois household and brought up by a highly educated lawyer, a disciple of the Enlightenment and a student of Leibniz and Voltaire, Kant and Lessing, Marx naturally thought of pursuing an advanced university education upon completing his early studies at the Trier gymnasium. At age 17, in 1835, Karl Marx entered the university of Bonn to study law. The following year, unlike most German students who attend several universities before sitting for the university degree-examinations, he journeyed to Berlin to study on the university faculty. Though Hegel had died in 1831, the university was still very much under the spell of his theory of history. Quickly succumbing to Hegelianism, he joined a rather loosely knit band of young radicals marginally affiliated with the university, who called themselves unabashedly the Doktorklub.

Law was abandoned, and joining these Young Hegelians,

Marx took up the study of philosophy. Marx was inclined to frequent expensive taverns and restaurants, inevitably joining in an Hegelian-fest with kindred minds. Finally, in 1841 at the age of twenty-three, he received the doctorate degree from the University of Jena for his thesis, entitled, "On the Differences between the Natural Philosophy of Democritus and Epicurus." Having destroyed his chances at a university teaching career due to his radical and outspoken views, shortly after completing his studies, he began writing for a radical, left-wing paper in Cologne, *Rheinische Zeitung*, and became its editor in 1842. Following the forced closure of the paper by the government because of a series of radically controversial articles by Marx on social conditions, Marx travelled to Paris, the then gathering place for European political refugees and the politically left-wing emigre community. Feeling ideologically at home in Paris among socialists from all over Europe, and being himself technically a former "Young Hegelian," Marx continued to write extensively upon the Hegelian themes of "alienation," "estrangement" and "loss of being" confronting modern industrial man. These *Paris Manuscripts* were destined to become major papers in his posthumous legacy to western culture.

Before leaving for Paris, Marx had married Jenny von Westphalen, a childhood girlfriend of a higher social class, precipitating a barrage of criticism and hostility from her family and friends. The Paris years, 1843 to 1845, proved determinative in Marx's intellectual ferment comparable to his German years among the Hegelians. And most significantly, he met Friedrich Engels (1820-1895) there, and the friendship was immediate and eternal. The political atmosphere and the radical colleagues with whom Marx associated created just the right alchemy for creative productivity. Particularly the friendship with Engels affected Marx's political and economic theories. His movement away from Hegelian historicism towards a developing socialism accelerated in the Parisian milieu. But, as in Germany two years before, the governmental authorities, this time of Guizot in Paris, expelled Marx and many of his associates. Moving to Brussels, he re-established contact with like-minded German refugees there, especially a socialist organization called the German Workers' Educational Association. This organization interestingly had headquarters in London and was federated with the

Communist League of Europe. With a draft from Engels, and under commission from the G.W.E.A., Marx wrote *The Communist Manifesto* which was sent on to London headquarters in 1848.

Under what appeared to be favorable but later proved unfavorable circumstances, Marx and Engels returned to Paris following the outbreak of revolution in Germany, assuming the editorship of the radical paper, *Neue Rheinische Zeitung*. Failing to work out a working-class/bourgeoisie alliance against the feudal government, Marx was presented an ultimatum by the government in August, 1849, of retiring to the French hinterlands or leaving the country. Opting for the latter, Marx migrated to London where he established permanent residence. The first few years in London proved productive, intellectually and literally, producing such works as *The Class Struggles in France* (1850), *The 18th Brumaire of Louis Bonaparte* (1852), and *Contributions to a Critique of Political Economy* (1859). During these years, Marx also spent a great deal of time researching for his major work, the three-volume *Capital*. In 1867, the first volume appeared but the other two could not be published until after his death, Engels bringing them out in 1885 and 1894.

Arriving in London in 1849 at the age of thirty one, Marx's life was just half over—a refugee thrice, twice exiled as an editor of a radical political paper, and once as the author of *The Communist Manifesto*, it would appear he had much to live and hope for. But in London, he withdrew with Engels into a close-knit circle composed of his family and a select few devoted disciples. This self-enforced isolation continued throughout the remainder of his life. After securing an admission card to the British Museum's reading room, much of the remainder of his active life centered around the analysis and the criticism of the industrial capitalism of the day. During this period, he was desperately impoverished, and save for the loyal assistance of Engels, all might have been lost. Three children died in the Marx household owing to malnutrition and impoverishment during the time he was completing the first volume of *Das Kapital*. Except for the one pound sterling he received for each article he wrote for the *New York Daily Tribune*, he had nothing. For a brief time, Marx came out of seclusion and was saved from continued poverty due to the appearance of and subsequent leadership offered by him to *The*

International, an international federation of European and
English workers committed to altering the present economic
system. Marx produced the inaugural address at the London
Exhibition of Modern Industry and took over the world-wide
leadership until its final decline, and termination in Philadelphia
in 1876. Marx, now wrecked by illness and broken health due to
early poverty, and unfulfilled dreams, produced little during his
last remaining years. Though a little comfortable towards the
end of his life financially, and a distinct celebrity, for socialist
leaders from all over the world came to visit him in London, he
sustained two blows—the deaths of his eldest daughter and wife—
from which he never recovered. Marx died on March 14, 1883.

HEGEL AND HISTORY IN MARXIAN THOUGHT

No idea nor any intellectual can claim absolute uniqueness, for
all human thought is done within a social situation of human
ideas and thoughts. Marx's genius lay not so much in his absolute originality but rather in the constellation and configuration
of his ideas and insights gained from cross-fertilization. Hegel's
influence upon him, for instance, is illustrative of Marx's recepti-
vity and ability to modify a fundamental theory. Georg F.W. Hegel
(1770-1831) was a German philosopher who dominated the entire
intellectual horizon of his day. Marx's Berlin years made him a
Young Hegelian by virtue of the strength of Hegel's thought
upon the Berlin university community. Hegel "was a liberal,
after the German fashion," explain Collins and Makowski,
"which meant that he believed in the rule of law rather than the
arbitrary rule of men and hence supported the Prussian state.
Hegel's philosophy culminated the idealist tradition that began
with Kant; it held that the essence of reality is Reason, but that
the spirit of Reason manifests itself only gradually, revealing
more and more facets of itself during the course of time."[1] The
importance of historical interpretation, historiography, and
historicism greatly influenced not only the Marxist perception but
virtually every other system developed out of early nineteenth
century German philosophy. Hegel argued persuasively that
"History is the growth of Reason to consciousness of itself, and
the constitutional,legalistic state is the culmination of history."

But most important for the Marxist ideology was the adoption and adaptation of "dialectics" from Hegel by Marx. Though we will discuss the relationship of dialectics to Marxian methodology later in this study, it is important that we make a few descriptive comments here. "According to Hegel," Timasheff explains, "each statement of truth, or thesis, has its opposite statement, or antithesis, which is also true. The thesis and antithesis may be reconciled on a higher level of synthesis, but this is not the end for the dialectical process then continues as the synthesis becomes a new thesis with its antithesis, and so on."[2] Unlike the Hegelian idealism which perceived truths in ideas, Marx claimed the contrary, namely, that ideas were not the realm of truth but rather matter is. Whereas Hegel's system could be called "dialectical idealism," Marx gave himself over to the development of what came to be called, not by him but his followers, "dialectical materialism." Marx, too, was interested in the analysis of the nature and meaning as well as the truth of history, but unlike Hegel, he believed that a "materialistic" analysis and not an idealistic approach to history would render the truth. The popular image of "turning Hegel upside down" or "standing Hegel on his head" is illustrative of the Marxian corrective to Hegelian idealism. According to Marx:

> In direct contrast to German philosophy which descends from heaven to earth, here we ascend from earth to heaven. That is to say, we do not set out from what men say, imagine, conceive, nor from men as narrated, thought of, imagined, conceived, in order to arrive at men in the flesh. We set out from real, active men, and on the basis of their real life-process we demonstrate the development of the ideological reflexes and echoes of this life-process—Morality, religion, metaphysics, all the rest of ideology and their corresponding forms of consciousness, thus no longer retain the semblance of independence…Life is not determined by conciousness, but consciousness by life.[3]

This materialistic emphasis appears to be a passionate reaction of Marx to Hegel's idealistic interpretation of history which attributed a major determining role to the progressive evolution of ideas. Marx would not ascribe an independent, determinate role to ideas or philosophical conception, for they, he believed, reflected, rather than caused, changes in social and material life. Two points must be stressed in this context. First, Marx had no quarrel with Hegel's dialectical logic; what he rejected was the "idealistic trammel" of Hegel's philosophy. Second, although Marx emphasized the importance of material conditions in opposition to Hegelian idealism, he did not deny the reality of subjective consciousness or its significance in social change. Marx also came under the influence of Ludwig Feuerbach. Feuerbach particularly and the Young Hegelians generally were at odds about the interpretation of religious ideas and behavior, the latter thinking of religious ideas as only reflection (s) of social reality while the former thought of religious ideas as "substitutes" for truth and reality. Feuerbach, and later Marx, turned "from a spirit-centred or God-centred world (as found in Hegelianism) to the analysis of those unhappy social conditions which had led men to find consolation in a world of religious entities of their own creation..."[4] Marx, Feuerbach and others, were led "to anchor (their) views in an examination of the social system—of the social relationships in which men were enmeshed—rather than the world of disembodied ideas and the Spirit." The shift is reflected in Marx's adoption of French radicalism and the economic pragmatism of the British theorist Adam Smith.

This adaptation of Hegelian idealism to historical materialism coupled with his acceptance of British economic theory led Marx to believe that the motivating factor in human existence was not ideas about religion and society but a materialistic realism having to do with survival. This survival, the necessity to produce the means of subsistence, was fundamental to human life and human action in community and society. It was a staple fact underlying all human interaction. "The first historical act," wrote Marx, "is the production of material life itself. This is indeed a historical act, a fundamental condition of all history."[5] Having accepted the evolutionary perspective on human development popular in the nineteenth century European thought, Marx thought of society as an arena within which the struggle and strife between groups of people, competing forces for survival and improved livelihood, generated social change. Instead of the Rousseauian notion of peaceful harmony and movement forward within a cooperating and helpful community of likeminded citizens bound together with an agreed-upon social contract, Marx thought of struggle and contention, strife and competition as the mechanism for social advancement in community. The utopian philosophers of the eighteenth century with their peace and harmony in an advancing community had given way to a nineteenth century pessimism about man's ability to make and keep pledges of peace and cooperation, presuming that human society best survives within the arena of struggle and competition, violence and revolution. History, for Hegel and Marx and for most European intellectuals, was the focus of their theories of human existence. For Marx, human history was the record of human struggle amongst men and human efforts to dominate and control the environment, physical and social. Also, and constituting a major source of human frustration, was the inevitable emergence of "alienation" between groups of persons, between individuals, and between man and his natural environment, a theme to which we will return later.

The changing of society was the fundamental focus of Marx's intellectual work, for men must be liberated from the shackles which they unwittingly have produced for themselves. And in changing society, men must come to realize that they themselves not only can bring about legitimate and positive change but that they are personally responsible for the way things are, for "men make their own history." Thus, when men come to realize and accept the fact that "human history is the process through which men change themselves even as they pit themselves against nature to dominate it," they are on their way to self-liberation. "Men begin," says Marx, "to distinguish themselves from animals as soon as they begin to produce their means of subsistence ... In producing their means of subsistence men indirectly produce their actual material life."[6] This remaking of their own lives as Marx understands the true meaning of human work is to occur within the framework of a progressive historical evolution.

Just as Comte distinguished three phases of human evolution, on the basis of ways of thinking, Marx identified four stages of human history on the basis of modes of production: primitive communism, ancient slave production, feudalism, and capitalism. The relationship which men have with one another varies with the mode of production. Primitive communism signified communal ownership whereas ancient mode of production was characterized by slavery, the feudal mode of production by serfdom, and the capitalist system by the bourgeois exploitation of wage earners. Each of these stages, except primitive communism, constituted a distinct mode of man's exploitation by man and his struggle for freedom. Marx was committed not only to the analysis of this scenario but more particularly to its final culmination in the classless society of socialism. Thus, even though men are destined to fight for the establishment and maintenance of their material existence, they will not forever engage in war and revolution. Marx believed that the process of dialectical materialism in which men struggle for survival in competition would come to end when the working people of the world (the proletariat) came to be sufficiently strong and politically conscious that capitalism would be finally overthrown and socialism would be installed. This fifth and final state would constitute a classless society with no private property, and no distinctions between controllers and the controlled. War and rebellion would vanish. "Therein," Timasheff comments, ."may be seen the inherent notion of historical progress and utopianism in Marx's thought, for human history is treated as an inevitable succession of stages culminating in the best possible social order."[7]

DIALECTICS AND METHODOLOGY

Dialecticas Materialism
As we have already indicated earlier, Marx was not satisfied with Hegelian idealism but Hegel's use of the dialectical methodology did grab Marx's imagination. By turning from idealism to materialism (i.e., inverting Hegel), Marx was able to make good use of the dialectic in what came to be called "dialectical materialism" or "historical materialism." Marx drew heavily from Hegel in terms of his "manner of approach" to social phenomena and his analysis of it. However, Hegel was an idealist who asserted the primacy of "mind," whereas Marx was a "materialist" who asserted the primacy of "matter." "To Marx," explains Larson, "matter is not a product of mind; on the contrary mind is simply the most advanced product of matter. Though Marx rejected Hegel's content orientation, he retained his dialectical structure."[8] Marx was quick to give Hegel the credit for what he owed him, but became very hostile when accused of merely taking over the Hegelian methodology without significantly modifying or improving it. "My dialectic method," Marx burst out in his early writ-

ings in defence of his system, "is not only different from the Hegelian, but is its direct opposite. To Hegel, the life-process of the human brain, i.e., the process of thinking, which, under the name of 'the idea', he even transforms into an independent subject, is the demi-urge of the real world, and the real world is only the external, phenomenal form of 'the idea'. With me, on the contrary, the ideal is nothing else than the material world reflected by the human mind, and translated into forms of thought."[9] Hegel's passion was for the Absolute Idea and his system concentrated its developmental tasks there; Marx's singularity of concern was the creation of an interpretative and analytical methodology which would account for the dynamics of human social activity, thinking and action.

Larson has very nicely outlined the basic postulates of Marxian dialectical method as follows. "(1) all the phenomena of nature are part of an integrated whole; (2) nature is in a continuous state of movement and change; (3) the developmental process is a product of quantitative advances which culminate in abrupt qualitative changes; and (4) contradictions are inherent in all realms of nature—but particularly human society."[10] This methodology perceived history as a series of stages based on a particular mode of production and characterized by a particular type of economic organization. Because of the inherent contradictions, each stage contained the seeds of its own destruction. And in the words of Stalin, "the dialectical method holds that the process of development should be understood not as movement in a circle, not as a simple repetition of what has already occurred, but as an onward and upward movement, as transition from an old qualitative state to a new qualitative state, from the lower to the higher."[11]

Marx believed that no matter how well a society functions in terms of its own order and structure, it was destined to turmoil and revolution until the final breakdown of all class divisions. Even when a society exemplifies the best that mankind can establish in terms of harmony and cooperation, "in time", Timasheff explains, "the established order becomes an obstacle to progress, and a new order (the antithesis) begins to arise. A struggle ensues between the class representing the old order and the class representing the new order. The emerging class is eventually victorious, creating a new order of production that is a synthesis of the old and the new. This new order, however, contains the seeds of its eventual destruction and the dialectical process continues."[21] The inevitability of the continuing struggle is related to the emergence of the division of labor within society, for it is this phenomenon of labour differentiation which forms antagonistic classes that in turn become the centre of competition and struggle against nature as well as against other elements within society.

The use of the dialectic in the analysis of society and history became a major characteristic of Marxism. It was Lenin who was to appropriate the Marxist view of the world and turn it to practical consequences. He has said or Marx's methodology that "materialism in general recognizes objectively real being (matter) as independent of consciousness, sensation, experience ... Consciousness is only the reflection of being, at best, an approximately true (adequate, ideal) reflection of it."[13] And if this statement isn't sufficiently anti-idealistic and positively materialistic, then we find a further clarification from Stalin again on materialism. "Marx's philosophical materialism," Stalin explains, "holds the world is by its very nature material, that the multifold phenomena of the world constitute different forms of matter in motion, that interconnection and interdependence of phenomena, as established by the dialectical method, are a law of the development of moving matter, and that the world develops in accordance with the laws of movement in matter and stands in no need of a 'universal spirit'.[14] The dialectic is found within the interaction of society under the influence of matter, materialistic phenomena, and the methodology is to employ the primacy of matter as an interpretative mechanism to grasp the essence of human activity, especially the realm of economic activity.

Economic Infrastructure and Socio-Economic Superstructure

Although Marx did not consistently argue for a crude economic determinism, he left no doubt that he considered the economy to be the foundation of the whole socio-cultural system. Throughout their study, Marx and Engles emphasized the primacy of economics in human relationship and the centrality of the economic dimension in political structures. The economic system of production and distribution, or the means and relations of production in the Marxian sense, constitute the basic structure of society on which are built all other social institutions, particularly the state and legal system. According to Engels, ". . . the production of immediate material means of subsistence, and consequently, the degree of economic development attained by a given people or during a given epoch, form the foundation upon which the state institutions, the legal conceptions, the ideas on art, and even on religion, of the people concerned have been evolved."[15]

The following passage which appears in the *Preface to A Contribution to the Critique of Political Economy* contains all the essential ideas of Marx's economic interpretation of history and social change.

> The general conclusion at which I arrived and which, once obtained, served to guide me in my studies, may be summarized as follows. In the social production which men carry on they enter into definite relations that are indispensable and independent of their will; these relations of production correspond to a definite stage of development of their material powers of production. The sum total of these relations of production constitutes the economic structure of society-the real foundation on which rise legal and political superstructures and to which correspond definite forms of social consciousness. The mode of production in material life determines the general character of the social, political and spiritual processes of life. It is not the consciousness of men that determines their existence, but, on the contrary, their social existence determines their consciousness. At a certain stage of their development, the material forces of production in society come into conflict with the existing relations of production, or—what is but a legal expression for the same thing—with the property relations within which they had been at work. From forms of development of the forces of production, these relations turn into their fetters. Then comes the period of social revolution. With the change of the economic foundation the entire immense superstructure is more or less rapidly transformed. In considering such transformation the distinction should always be made between the material transformation of the economic conditions of production which can be determined with the precision of natural science, and the legal, political, religious, aesthetic or philosophic—in short ideological-forms in which men become conscious of this conflict and fight it out. Just as our opinion of an individual is not based on what he thinks of himself, so we cannot judge such a period of transformation by its own consciousness; on the contrary, this consciousness must rather be explained from the

contradictions of material life, from the existing conflict between the social forces of production and the relations of
production."[16]

Under the influence of the forces and relations of production,
men spend their lives struggling with and against one another
for survival and power. Having adopted the evolutionary perspective on the emergence of human society, Marx believed that
the materialistic conditions within which mankind finds itself are
reflective of that which most nearly established man's humanity,
i.e., his ability to create for himself that which he needs for
survival. "Legal relations", he wrote, "as well as the form of
state are to be grasped neither from themselves nor from the so-
called general development of the human mind, but rather have
their roots in the material conditions of life, the sum total of
which Hegel . . . combines under the name of 'civil society' . . .
The anatomy of civil society is to be sought in political economy."[17]
In other words, understand economics, and you can potentially
control the cause and source of human competition. As Freud
was dominated by the sexual metaphor in his analysis of all
forms of mental illness, Marx was dominated by the economic
metaphor in his attempt to understand and control all forms of
human activity in competition, cooperation, and revolution. Like
Freud, Marx was unwilling to allow any other variable in the
human arena of thought and action to share the spotlight with
his one overriding premise: sex for Freud, and economics for
Marx were paramount. All other factors in the human experience
of social relations were subservient and dependent upon the economic factor in the Marxian theory of social relationships. "The
political, legal, philosophical, literary, and artistic development,"
Marx wrote, "rests on the economic. But they all react upon one
another and upon the economic base. It is not that the economic
situation is the sole active cause and that everything else is
merely a passive effect, there is, rather a reciprocity within a field
of economic necessity which in the last instance always asserts
itself".[18] He would argue, even, that human thought, human
awareness, and human consciousness, were not self-originating
but were derivatives of the economic principle. And it is in the
arena of political economy that governments and religions must
be controlled and human consciousness brought under dominance;

particularly when it comes to the governance of the material
world, men must realize that the social environment is dependent
upon the economics of the situation and that classes, if they are
to cease their competitiveness and potential destruction of society,
must be abolished by the removal of structures which nurture
class divisions. As Doyle Johnson reminds us, Marx may have
overstated his case to establish his point against competing viewpoints but Marx's economic interpretation of history "provides
a note of hard realism that is sometimes lacking in more idealistic theories of society."[19]

Social Location of Ideas
Consistent with his economic interpretation of history, Marx
developed a variant of the sociology of knowledge which stressed
the primacy of the economic principle in the evolution of ideologies, philosophical systems, politics, ethics and religion. The
central thesis of Marx is this: "It is not the unfolding of ideas
that explains the historical development of society (as Hegel and
Comte would have argued), but the development of the social
structure in response to changing material conditions that explains
the emergence of new ideas."[20] According to Marx, ideas belong
to the realm of the superstructure and are determined by the
economic infrastructure. He believed that the ideologies prevail-
ing at any particular point in time reflect the worldview of the
dominant class. In other words, ideas depend on the social positions—particularly on the class positions of their proponents.
These views, moreover, tend either to enhance or undermine the
power and control of whatever class happens to be dominant at
the time. If generated from the dominant class, they tend to be
supportive and reinforce the predominance of the social structures. "The ideas of the ruling class", Marx pointed out "are, in
every age, the ruling ideas: i.e., the class which is the dominant
material force in society is at the same time its dominant *intellectual* force. The class which has the means of material production
at its disposal, has control at the same time over the means of
mental production."[21]

Marx warned that we will fail to understand the historical
process "if... we detach the ideas of the ruling class from the
ruling class itself and attribute to them an independent existence,
if we confine ourselves to saying that in a particular age these or

those ideas were dominant, without paying attention to the conditions of production and the producers of these ideas, and if we thus ignore the individuals and the world conditions which are the source of these ideas."[22] Thus Marx sought to trace the evolution of ideas to the life conditions in general, and the forces and relations of production in particular. As it is with conservative ideas, so it is with revolutionary ideas: the former originate in the worldview of the ruling class and the latter in the material conditions of the revolutionary class.

Theory of Class and Class Conflict

"A social class in Marx's terms is any aggregate of persons who perform the same function in the organization of production."[23] It is determined not by occupation or income but by the position an individual occupies and the function he performs in the process of production. For example, two carpenters, of whom one is the shop owner and the other his paid worker, belong to two different classes even though their occupation is the same. Bendix and Lipset have identified five variables that determine a class in the Marxian sense:

"(1) Conflicts over the distribution of economic rewards between the classes;

(2) Easy communication between the individuals in the same class positions so that ideas and action programs are readily disseminated;

(3) Growth of class consciousness in the sense that the members of the class have a feeling of solidarity and understanding of their historic role;

(4) Profound dissatisfaction of the lower class over its inability to control the economic structure of which it feels itself to be the exploited victim;

(5) Establishment of a political organization resulting from the economic structure, the historical situation and maturation of class-consciousness."[24]

According to Marx, the organization of production is not a sufficient condition for the development of social classes. There must also be a physical concentration of masses of people, easy communication among them, repeated conflicts over economic rewards and the growth of class consciousness. The small peasants

form a vast mass and live in similar conditions but they are isolated from one another and are not conscious of their common
interests and predicament; hence they do not constitute a class.
"In so far as millions of families live under economic conditions
of existence that divide their mode of life, their interests and
their culture from those of other classes, and put them into hostile
contrast to the latter, they form a class. In so far as there is
merely a local interconnection among these small peasants, and
the identity of their interests begets no unity, no national union,
and no political organization, they do not form a class."[25]

From the beginning of human existence in community, society
has been divided into classes because of its absolute dependence
on the division of labor which precipitated dominance among the
ruling class and subordination among the subjugated class. Marx's
classic statement clearly establishes the most fundamental premise
of all his theoretical work on the question of class:

> The history of all hitherto existing society is the history of
> class struggles. Free men and slave, patrician and plebian,
> lord and serf, guildmaster and journeyman, in a word, oppr-
> essor and oppressed, stood in constant opposition to one
> another, carried on an uninterrupted, now hidden, now open
> fight, a fight that each time ended either in a revolutionary
> reconstitution of society at large or in the common ruin of the
> contending classes."[26]

Although the class war has always been between the oppressor
and the oppressed, the leading contenders in the social drama of
conflict differed markedly in different historical periods. "The
fact that modern workers are formally 'free' to sell their labor
while being existentially constrained to do so makes their condition historically specific and functionally distinct from that of
earlier exploited classes".[27]

In addition to a recognition of the origin of class, Marx was
even more interested in the future of class, especially as that future
relates to the emergence of class-consciousness, an awareness of
shared interests and the necessity of mutual support to other
struggling classes against the ruling class. Marx made a distinction between "class in itself" and "class for itself" to reflect the
movement from a class's potential self-awareness to actual self-
awareness. Only when the "common struggle" as a point of consciousness appears within a class does that class actually emerge

as a potential power force. "Self-conscious classes", Coser explains, "arise only if and when there exists a convergence of what Max Weber later called 'ideal' and 'material' interests, that is the combination of economic and political demands with moral and ideological quests."[28]

The assault upon the class structure of western society was almost an obsession with Marx. And the changing of social class was not to be thought of as manageable in terms of "social mobility," for which Marx gave virtually no room in his methodology or analysis. Social class was bigger than the individual and the individual was dominated by it. It fell upon the responsibility of the class system itself, of the state, to take in hand steps to alter the situation.

In his *Capital* Marx said that "here individuals are dealt with only in so far as they are personifications of economic categories, embodiments of particular class-relations and class-interests." To deal with the predicament of modern man, alienated, dominated, and estranged from himself, his neighbours, and his world, the analyst must not begin with the individual but with the social structures within which the individual is essentially caught up and lost as a person.

This emphasis on the objective determinants of man's class-bound behavior does not mean that Marx reified society and class at the expense of the individual; rather his primary interest lay in the identification of the source of the problem of modern man and his entrapment in the complexities of social relations that control and constrain him. "The individual is a *social being*", Marx insisted. "The manifestation of his life—even when it does not appear directly in the form of social manifestation, accomplished in association with other men—is therefore a manifestation and affirmation of social life."[29]

Marx developed his theory of class conflict in his analysis and critique of the capitalist society. The main ingredients of the theory may be summarized as follows:

1. *The development of the proletariat.* Marx described the process of development of the proletariat as follows:

> The first attempts of the workers to *associate* among themselves always take place in the form of combinations (unions). Large-scale industry concentrates in one place a crowd of people unknown to one another. Competition divides their

interest. But the maintenance of wages, this common interest which they have against their boss, unites them in a common thought of resistance—combination. Thus combination always has a double aim, that of stopping the competition among themselves, in order to bring about a general competition with the capitalist.[30]

The capitalist economic system transformed the masses of people into workers, created for them a common situation and inculcated in them an awareness of common interest. Through the development of class consciousness, the economic conditions of capitalism united the masses and constituted them into a class for itself.

2. *The importance of property.* To Marx, the most distinguishing characteristic of any society is its form of property, and the crucial determinant of an individual's behavior is his relation to property. Classes are determined on the basis of individual's relation to the means of production. It is not a man's occupation but his position relative to the instruments of production that determines his class. Property divisions are the crucial breaking lines in the class structure. Development of class consciousness and conflict over the distribution of economic rewards fortified the class barriers. Since work was the basic form of man's self-realization, economic conditions of the particular historic era determined the social, political and legal arrangements and set in motion the processes of evolution and societal transformation.

3. *The identification of economic and political power and authority.* Although classes are founded on the forces and relations of production, they become socially significant only in the political sphere. Since the capitalist society is based on the concentration of the means of production and distribution in the hands of a few, political power becomes the means by which the ruling class perpetuates its domination and exploitation of the masses. The capitalists who hold the monopoly of effective private property take control of the political machinery, and their interests converge in the political and ideological spheres. "Political power, properly so called, is merely the organized power of one class for oppressing another."[31] The bourgeoisie use the State as an instrument of economic exploitation and consolidation of self interests.

"The State is the form in which the individuals of a ruling class assert their common interest."[32] The economic power of the bourgeoisie is transformed into political power, and the entire political processes and institutions including the courts, the police and the military and the ruling elites become subservient to the interests of the capitalists.

4. *Polarization of classes.* Inherent in capitalist society is a tendency toward radical polarization of classes. "The whole society breaks up more and more into two great hostile camps, two great, directly antagonistic classes: bourgeoisie and proletariat."[33] The capitalists who own the means of production and distribution, and the working classes who own nothing but their own labor. This is not to deny the existence of other classes; indeed, Marx repeatedly referred to the small capitalists, the *petit bourgeoisie*, and the *lumpenproletariat*. But on maturation of class consciousness and at the height of the conflict, the *petit bourgeoisie* and small capitalists will be deprived of their property and drawn into the ranks of the proletariat. This is what Aron calls the process of proletarianization which "means that, along with the development of the capitalist regime, the intermediate strata between capitalists and proletarians will be worn thin and that an increasing number of the representatives of these intermediate strata will be absorbed by the proletariat."[34] Marx is emphatic that only two classes—capitalist and proletariat—represent a possibility for a political regime and that on the day of the decisive conflict, every man will be forced to join either of the two contending classes.

5. *The theory of surplus value.* Capitalists accumulate profit through the exploitation of labor. The value of any commodity is determined by the amount of labor it takes to produce it. "The labor time necessary for the worker to produce a value equal to the one he receives in the form of wages is less than the actual duration of his work. Let us say that the worker produces in five hours a value equal to the one contained in his wage, and that he works ten hours. Thus he works half of his time for himself and the other half for the entrepreneur. Let us use the term "surplus value" to refer to the quantity of value produced by the worker beyond the necessary labor time, meaning by the latter the working time required to produce a value -equal to the one he has

received in the form of wages."[35] Since employers have the monopoly of the instruments of production, they can force workers to do extra hours of work, and profits tend to accumulate with increasing exploitation of labor.

6. *Pauperization.* Poverty of the proletariat grows with increasing exploitation of labor. One capitalist kills many others and the wealth of the bourgeoisie is swelled by large profits with corresponding increase in "the mass of poverty, of pressure, of slavery, of exploitation," of the proletariat. "It follows that in every mode of production which involves the exploitation of man by man, the social product is so distributed that the majority of people, the people who labor, are condemned to toil for no more than the barest necessities of life. Sometimes favorable circumstances arise when they can win more, but more often they get the barest minimum—and at times not even that. On the other hand, a minority, the owners of means of production, the property owners, enjoy leisure and luxury. Society is divided into rich and poor."[36] Thus, to Marx poverty is the result of exploitation, not of scarcity.

7. *Alienation.* The economic exploitation and inhuman working conditions lead to increasing alienation of man, a theme about which we will have more to say later. Here we will only reproduce an extended passage from Marx:

> ...Within the capitalist system all methods for raising the social productiveness of labor are brought about at the cost of the individual laborer; all means for the development of production transform themselves into means of domination over, and exploitation of, the producers; they mutilate the laborer into a fragment of a man, degrade him to the level of an appendage of a machine, destroy every remnant of charm in his work and turn it into hated toil; they estrange from him the intellectual potentialities of the labor-process in the same proportion as science is incorporated in it as an independent power; they distort the conditions under which he works, subject him during the labor-process to a despotism the more hateful for its meanness; they transform his life time into working-time and drag his wife and child under the wheels of the Juggernaut of capital. But all methods for the accumulation of surplus value are at the same time methods of accumulation; and every extension of accumulation becomes again a means for the development of those methods. It follows

therefore that in proportion as capital accumulates, the lot of the laborer, be his payments high or low, must grow worse."[37] Work is no longer an expression of man himself, only a degraded instrument of livelihood. It is external to the worker and imposed upon him; there is no fulfillment in work. The product of work becomes an instrument of alien purpose. The worker becomes estranged from himself, from the process as well as the product of his labor, from his fellow men and from the human community itself.

8. *Class solidarity and antagonism.* With the growth of class consciousness, the crystallization of social relations into two groups becomes streamlined and the classes tend to become internally homogeneous, and the class struggle more intensified. In the words of Marx:

"... with the development of industry, the proletariat not only increases in number; it becomes concentrated in greater masses, its strength grows, and it feels that strength more. The various interests and conditions of life within the ranks of the proletariat are more and more equalized, in proportion as machinery obliterates all distinctions of labor and nearly everywhere reduces wages to the same low level. The growing competition among the bourgeoisie and the resulting commercial crises make the wages of the workers ever more fluctuated. The increasing improvement of machinery, ever more rapidly developing, makes their livelihood more and more precarious; the collisions between individual workmen and individual bourgeoisie take more and more the character of collisions between two classes. Thereupon the workers begin to form combination (trade unions) against the bourgeoisie; they club together in order to keep up the rate of wages; they found permanent associations in order to make provisions beforehand for these occasional revolts. Here and there the contest breaks out into riots."[38]

9. *Revolution.* At the height of the class war a violent revolution breaks out which destroys the structure of capitalist society. This revolution is most likely to occur at the peak of an economic crisis which is part of the recurring booms and repressions characteristic of capitalism. To quote Marx: "Finally, in times when the class struggle nears the decisive hour, the process of dissolution going on within the ruling class, in fact within the whole range of old society, assumes such a violent, glaring character, that a small section of the ruling class cuts itself adrift and

joins the revolutionary class, the class that holds the future in its hands. Just as therefore, at an earlier period, a section of the nobility went over to the bourgeoisie, so now a portion of the bourgeois ideologists who have raised themselves to the level of comprehending theoretically the historical movement as a whole."[39]

10. *The dictatorship of the proletariat.* The bloody revolution terminates capitalist society and leads to the social dictatorship of the proletariat. The revolution is violent but does not necessarily involve mass killings of the bourgeoisie; since property is wrested from them, the bourgeoisie will cease to have power and will be transformed into the ranks of the proletariat. Thus the inevitable historical process destroys the bourgeoisie and the proletariat establishes a social dictatorship, merely a transitional phase, to consolidate the gains of the revolution. The political expression of the social dictatorship was conceived as a form of worker's democracy which later became "a fateful bone of contention" among Marxists. Irving Howe observes: "By now, almost all socialists have abandoned the treacherous phrase 'dictatorship of the proletariat', both because it is open to obvious misconstruction and because it has acquired, in the Stalinist and post-Stalinist dictatorships, abhorrent connotations. Marx himself had written that he differentiated himself from 'those communists who were out to destroy personal liberty and who wish to turn the world into one large barrack or into a gigantic warehouse".'[40]

11. *Inauguration of the communist society.* Socialization of effective private property will eliminate class and thereby the causes of social conflict. The state will eventually wither away as it becomes obsolete in a classless society in which nobody owns anything but everybody owns everything and each individual contributes according to his ability and receives according to his need.

This, in a nutshell, is Karl Marx's theory of class conflict.

Alienation
In order to fulfill their human needs men must engage in productive activity which involves an expenditure of human energy and creative ability. But the forces and social relations of production determine man's relations to other men, to nature and to elements of superstructure. The material conditions of life generate alienation, and no institution, whether religious, political or

economic, is exempt from the condition of alienation. "Objectification", Marx wrote, "is the practice of alienation. Just as man,
so long as he is engrossed in religion, can only objectify his
essence by an Alien and fantastic being, so under the sway of
egoistic need, he can only affirm himself and produce objects in
practice by subordinating his products and his own activity to
the domination of an alien entity, and by attributing to them the
significance of an alien entity, namely money."[41] Marx was convinced that systems of political economy had some control over
the level and intensity of this alienation, and he sought to analyze
the cause and consequences of alienation. Particularly, he was dis-
traught over the nature and function of money in society, for
"money", he believed, "is the alienated essence of man's work
and existence; the essence dominates him and he worships it."[42]
Though religion and educational systems foster intellectual alienation, it is economic alienation, particularly as nurtured under
capitalism, which touches every aspect of people's lives and not
just their minds. "Religious alienation as such occurs only in the
sphere of consciousness, in the inner life of man", Marx writes,
"but economic alienation is that of *real life* . . . It therefore affects
both aspects (mind and action)."[43]

However, Marx was particularly interested in the process of
alienation in capitalist society. Owing to his close association
with Engels, Marx became personally aware of the anguish and
alienation of the urban industrial workers. While alienation is
commonplace in capitalist society and dominates every institutional sphere such as religion, economy, and polity, its predominance in workplace assumes an overriding importance for Marx.
Estranged or alienated labor involves four aspects: workers'
alienation from the object he produces, from the process of production and himself, and from the community of his fellowmen.
According to Marx, "alienation appears not merely in the result
but also in the *process of production*, within *productive activity*
itself. . . If the product of labor is alienation, production itself
must be active alienation…The alienation of the object of labor
merely summarizes the alienation in the work activity itself."[44]

The worker is a victim of exploitation at the hands of the
bourgeoisie. The more wealth the worker produces, the poorer
he becomes. Just as labor produces the world of things, it also
creates the devaluation of the world of men. This devaluation in-

creases in direct proportion to the increase in the production of commodities. The worker sinks to the level of a commodity and becomes indeed the most wretched of commodities. "This fact expresses merely that the object which labor produces—labor's product—confronts it as *something alien*, as a power independent of the producer. The product of labor which has been congealed in an object, which has become material: it is the *objectification* of labor. Labor's realization is its objectification. In the conditions dealt with by political economy this realization of labor appears as *loss of reality* for the workers; objectification as *loss of the object* and *object-bondage*, appropriation as *estrangement*, as *alienation*."[45]

The more the worker spends himself, the less he has of himself. The worker puts his life into the object he creates but the very object becomes an instrument of alien purpose and strengthens the hands of his exploiters. The worker becomes a slave of his object. "The *alienation* of the worker in his product means not only that his labor becomes an object, an *external* existence, but that it exists *outside him*, independently, as something alien to him, and that it becomes a power on its own confronting him; it means that the life which he has conferred on the object confronts him as something hostile and alien."[46] In short, the worker spends his life and produces everything not for himself but for the powers that manipulate him. While labor may produce beauty, luxury and intelligence, for the worker it produces only the opposite— deformity, misery and idiocy. Marx summarizes the alienation of labor in the following inimitable words:

First, the fact that labor is *external* to the worker, i.e., it does not belong to his essential being; that in his work, therefore, he does not affirm himself but denies himself, does not feel content but unhappy, does not develop freely his physical and mental energy but mortifies his body and ruins his mind. The worker therefore only feels himself outside his work, and in his work feels outside himself. He is at home when he is not working, and when he is working he is not at home. His labor is therefore not voluntary, but coerced; it is *forced labor*. It is therefore not the satisfaction of a need; it is merely a *means* to satisfy needs external to it. Its alien character emerges clearly in the fact that as soon as no physical or other compulsion exists, labour is shunned like the plague. External labor, labor in which man alienates himself, is a labor of self-sacrifice, of mortification. Lastly,

the external character of labor for the worker appears in the
fact that it is not his own, but someone else's, that it does not
belong to him that in it he belongs, not to himself, but to
another. Just as in religion the spontaneous activity of the
human imagination, of the human brain and the human heart,
operates independently of the individual—that is, operates
on him as an alien, divine or diabolical activity—in the same
way the worker's activity is not his spontaneous activity. It
belongs to another; it is the loss of his self.[47]

Thus Marx has identified two 'hostile powers' which render labor
and its product alien. One is the 'other man', the capitalist, who
commands production. The other is the economic system, the
market situation which governs the behavior of capital and the
process of production. The former is a human power and the latter
an "inhuman power."[48] As a worker, I am at the mercy of the
'other man' who decides what I should make and how I should
make it. My product bears no relation to my personality and
interest; it ceases to be an expression of my creative powers. Indeed, it never is my product at all; it is an alien object produced at my expense, at the cost of my self-realization and
physical well-being, and against my will but at the bidding of
"another alien, hostile, powerful and independent man."[49] Once
the object is finished, it belongs to the other man who is free to use
it in whatever manner he chooses. As it becomes an instrument
of his will, he becomes all the more powerful. And my product
becomes an "alien, hostile, powerful and independent object,"
an instrument of my own oppression at the hands of the other
man who is "lord of this object."[50] To Marx, "Alienation is
apparent not only in the fact that *my* means of life belong to
someone else..., but also that...an *inhuman power* rules over everything".[51] The impersonal forces of the market economy are alien
to the worker; they make him "dependent upon all the fluctuations in market price and in the movement of capital." They
have no regard for his welfare, are independent of his will, and,
ultimately produce his "beggary or starvation."

Schacht in his detailed evaluation of Marxian thought suggests
that Marx's concept of alienation implies two meanings: alienation
from other men, and self-alienation. The first meaning is reflected
in Marx's treatment of estranged labor, alienation of the worker
from the process of production and its product, and alienation
in relation to the two "hostile powers" discussed above. Schacht

writes: "A man is self-alienated for Marx if his true 'human' nature is something alien to him—if his life fails to manifest the characteristics of a truly human life. There are three such characteristics of Marx: individuality, sociality, and cultivated sensibility. Self-alienation thus takes the form of dehumanization in the spheres of life which correspond to them: production, social life, and sensuous life. It may best be understood in terms of dehumanization in each of these areas."[52]

Since the worker's own activity does not belong to him because it is a coerced activity, the entire process of production, of estranged labor, is performed in the service, and under the yoke of, a powerful and hostile force. The man who regards himself as a species being and a free being feels doubly deprived. Moreover, the condition of subservience to another man engenders his relation to other men.

"Through *estranged, alienated* labor then, the worker produces the relationship to this labor of a man alien to labor and standing outside it. The relationship of the worker to labor engenders the relation to it of the capitalist, or whatever, one chooses to call the master of labor. *Private property* is thus the product, the result, the necessary consequence, of alienated labor, of the external relation of the worker to nature and to himself."[53] And, the alien being to whom labor and the product of labor belong continue to dominate the life of the worker. He manipulates the political structure, lends legitimacy to the system of production and distribution, and seeks to solidify his privileged position. And the cycle of exploitation continues.

Thus, in summary, several elements are involved in the Marxian concept of alienation: estrangement or man's alienation from himself and from nature, powerlessness or political alienation, religious alienation and the workers' alienation in relation to the process of production and the object they produce. And estranged labor constitutes the most recurrent theme in the Marxian conception of alienation.

Marx: An Assessment

Marx had almost no influence on the development of early sociology which was dominated by evolutionists, particularly social Darwinists. The mid-twentieth century witnessed the rebirth of Marxist sociology which remains today at the centre of dialectic and conflict analysis. The ideas of Marx constitute the gospel of revolution, and the *Communist Manifesto* is the handbook of revolutionaries around the world. Marxism has become the state dogma and the creed of political orthodoxy in many countries. However, the theory of Marx is plagued by several methodological and conceptual problems. His theory about capitalist society's inevitable tendency towards radical polarization and self-destruction is too simplistic and in error. The most distinct characteristic of modern capitalism has been the emergence of a large, "contented and conservative" middle-class consisting of managerial, professional, supervisory, and technical personnel. Modern corporations entail a separation between ownership and control; the capitalists who own the instruments of production are not necessarily the "effective" decision-makers. Also the widespread ownership of the means of production through investment in stocks, and the great expansion of government role in the regulation of big business, redistribution of wealth and general social welfare functions were not anticipated by Marx. Today's capitalism does not justify Marx's belief that class conflict is essentially revolutionary in character and that structure changes are always the product of violent upheavals; organized labor has been able to sway the balance of power and effect profound structure changes without violent revolution. Marx's theory of labor and the deductive reasoning which flows directly from it, namely the pauperization of the masses, are wrong. If the value of surplus labor is the only basis of profit, there is no way to eliminate exploitation and profit accumulation. In fact, most socialist countries have a higher percentage of accumulation than do capitalist countries.

Marx misjudged the extent of alienation in the average worker. The great depth of alienation and frustration which Marx "witnessed" among the workers of his day is not "typical" of today's capitalism or its worker who tends to indentify increasingly with a number of "meaningful" groups—religious, ethnic, occupational and local. This is not to deny the existence of alienation but to point out that alienation results more from the structure of bureaucracy and of mass society than from economic exploitation. Marx also over emphasized the economic base of political power and ignored other important sources of power. Moreover, Marx's predictions about the downfall of capitalism

have not come true. Contrary to his belief, socialism has triumphed in predominantly peasant societies whereas capitalist societies show no signs of destructive class war. And Marx's classless
and stateless society is an utopia; there can be no society without an authority structure or a regulatory mechanism which
inevitably leads to a crystallization of social relations between
the rulers and the ruled, with inherent poissbilities of internal
contradiction and conflict.

Today's Marxists, however, are striking back. They blame
imperialism for the failure of Marx's prophecy. They argue that
advanced industrialized nations have been able to fortify their
capitalist economy by exploiting the rest of the world through
colonialism and the "sovereign" multi-national corporations.
Conflict sociologists make effective use of Marxian theoretical
schema to explain the processes of class conflict and revolutionary
movements around the world: conflicts between landless peasantry
and landed aristocracy, between political and military elite, between incongruent status groups in newly emerging industrial
societies, populist movements and conservative counter-revolu-
tions, colonialism and imperialism, international conspiracies and
ideological warfares, and between socialism and democracy.
Contemporary Marxist sociology has accumulated a considerable
amount of "evidence" to substantiate the Marxian postulates
that economic position is the major determinant of one's life-
style, attitudes, and behaviour, and that strategic position in the
economic structure along with access to effective means of production and distribution hold the key to political power. The
modern theory of power elite is only a variation of the Marxian
theme of economic determinism.

Above all, Marx's theory of class is not a theory of stratification but a comprehensive theory of social change—a tool for the
explanation of change in total societies. This, T.B. Bottomore, a
leading expert on Marxist sociology, considers to be a major
contribution of Marx to sociological analysis: ". . . the view of
societies as inherently mutable systems, in which changes are
produced largely by internal contradictions and conflicts, and the
assumption that such changes, if observed in a large number of
instances, will show a sufficient degree of regularity to allow the
formulation of general statements about their causes and consequences."[54]

Bottomore accounts for the recent growth of Marxist sociology as follows:

One important reason for the present revival of interest is the fact that Marx's theory stands in direct opposition on every major point to the functionalist theory which has dominated sociology and anthropology for the past twenty or thirty years, but which has been found increasingly unsatisfactory. Where functionalism emphasizes social harmony, Marxism emphasizes social conflict; where functionalism directs attention to the stability and persistence of social forms, Marxism is radically historical in its outlook and emphasizes the changing structure of society; where functionalism concentrates upon the regulation of social life by general values and norms, Marxism stresses the divergence of interests and values within each society and the role of force in maintaining over a longer or shorter period of time, a given social order. The contrast between "equilibrium" and "conflict" models of society, which was stated forcefully by Dahrendorf in 1958, has now become commonplace; and Marx's theories are regularly invoked in opposition to those of Durkheim, Pareto and Malinowski, the principal architects of the functionalist theory".[55]

Herbert Marcuse's *Re-examination of the Concept of Revolution* is a significant contribution to Marxist sociology. According to him, "the *Marxian concept of a revolution* carried by the majority of the exploited masses, culminating in the 'seizure of power' and in the setting up of a proletarian dictatorship which initiates socialization, is *'over-taken' by the historical development*: it pertains to a stage of capitalist productivity and organization which has been overtaken; it does not project the higher stage of capitalist productivity, including the productivity of destruction, and the terrifying concentration of the instruments of annihilation and of indoctrination in the hands of the powers that be."[56] Although the Marxian prophecy of the downfall of capitalism has not come true, Marx's concept of revolution which is at once a historical concept and a dialectical concept is relevant in two different contexts:

(a) In the capitalist countries, there is a standing opposition whose members are drawn from the ghetto population and the middle-class intelligentsia, especially among students.

These groups are vocal; they reject the "system" form counter-cultures and profess adherence to radical political beliefs and new lifestyles. Yet, they cannot become agents of revolutionary change unless actively supported by a politically articulate working class freed from the shackles of bureaucratic trade unions and establishment-oriented party machinery.

(b) In the predominantly agrarian countries of the Third World, there are peasant revolutions and national liberation movements. Marcuse also perceives a "fateful link" between the two revolutionary movements. In the first place, the national liberation movements in the developing countries '"are expressive of the *internal contradictions* of the global capitalist system"—the colonialism and economic exploitation perpetrated by the corporate capitalism. This position is actively endorsed by Andre Gunder Frank[52] whose extensive research in Latin America has led him to conclude that the underdevelopment of the Third World countries is initiated and aggravated by the capitalist system of the developed countries which have satellized and exploited developing countries. Marcuse identifies specifically the following objective factors which "announce themselves in the strains and stresses of the corporate economy":

1. The necessity of competition, and the threat of progressive automation, with the ensuing unemployment, demand over enlarged absorption of labor by non-productive, parasitarian jobs and services.
2. The costs of neo-colonial wars, or controls over corrupt dictatorships, increase more and more.
3. As a result of the increasing reduction of human labor power in the process of production, the margin of profit declines.
4. Society requires the creation of needs, the satisfaction of which tends to conflict with the morale and discipline necessary for work under capitalism. The realm of necessity is invaded by the non-necessary gadgets and luxury devices that exist side by side with continuing poverty and misery, "luxuries" become necessities in the competitive struggle for existence."[53]

Thus the radical protest in capitalist countries and the revolutionary tendencies in the developing nations are closely related— in their opposition to multinational corporate capitalism and their orientation to the imperatives of a global revolution. "The

Marxian concept of revolution must comprehend the changes in the scope and social structure of advanced capitalism and the new forms of the contradictions characteristic of the latest stage of capitalism in its global framework. The modifications of the Marxian concept then appear, not as extraneous additions or adjustments, but rather as the elaboration of Marxian theory itself."

In summary, to evaluate the contributions and influences of Karl Marx is a task both for the disciple and the antagonist of contemporary Marxism. That he has profoundly influenced Western thought, sociological, economic, and political, cannot be denied. Although many of his predictions have not come true, the fact that those who have read his work have changed the world also cannot be denied. Even the worst critics agree that Marxian theory provides an excellent framework for the analysis of conflict and change in modern society. And Marx's influence on contemporary sociological theory is growing and Marxist sociology has already become an established branch of the discipline.

3

HERBERT SPENCER

LIFE AND TIMES

The oldest and only surviving child in the George Spencer family of Derby, England, Herbert was born on April 27, 1820, into a staunchly non-conformist family of dissenting individualists. His father was a school teacher, a bit of an eccentric who combined sympathies about religious liberty and dissent with Benthamite radicalism in politics. The entire Spencer family, including a clerical uncle of Protestant persuasion, were rabidly anti-clergy. Spencer's mother, by no means an intellectual and seemingly devoid of either strong ideas about religion or politics, made a home for Herbert amidst an unending round of political diatribes and anti-Anglicanisms flowing freely from the Spencer patriarchs.

Herbert was not untouched by these strongly radical and often powerfully liberal feelings about government and organized religion. In early nineteenth century England, Dissenters—those Englishmen not of the Church of England—were not only discriminated against and made to suffer for religious reasons, they were also treated as social inferiors. A proud and noble family, the Spencers, found such treatment abhorrent and debilitating. Herbert, because of his non-conformist religious views as were all other Dissenters, was forbidden an education at Oxford and Cambridge. The many ways the established society of the English had of both reminding Dissenters of their lower class status and the response of the oppressed to such treatment adversely affected both the family in general and Herbert in particular. Later in life, he reflected upon this dimension of his upbringing in the

second volume of his *Autobiography:* "In families brought up
from generation to generation ascetically, and acting up to the
belief that the pursuit of pleasure is wrong, it happens that while
there is a frequent witnessing of suffering there is a relatively
infrequent witnessing of pleasure and consequently a relative
inability to sympathize with pleasure... the temptation to give
pleasure must be less than usual."[1]

As a child, Spencer was weak and sickly. He never attended a
regular school, being instructed in an irregular fashion by mother
or father. At thirteen years of age, he went to stay with his uncle,
the Dissenting clergyman, who, though, gifted in philosophical
radicalism and the natural science and thus taught these things
well to his pupil, was not trained at all in the classics, philosophy,
history, or the good literature of traditional studies, thus producing a pupil of a pronounced one-sidedness. Spencer never made
up the deficiencies in his domestic education but used well what
he knew. By the age of sixteen, Spencer was well-trained in
mathematics and the natural sciences. While being gifted in these,
his passion lay in ethics and politics. But, necessity taking reasonable precedence over preference, the following year Spencer took
a position as an engineer with the London and Birmingham
Railroad and the following year, 1838, with the Birmingham and
Gloucester Railroad. The contract having been completed by the
B & G Railroad in 1841 and his job terminated, Spencer returned home to mother and Derby.

At first after publishing several articles on engineering in
professional journals, soon Spencer directed his attention to his
life's real interest—social and political qcestions. He began to publish a series of articles on various topics in the radical press dealing
with social and political issues. During this period, he wrote a
provocative and well received article entitled, "The Proper Sphere
of Government", which appeared in *The Nonconformist,* in which
he argued that the whole field of human activity, excepting for
policing and national defence, should be left to private enterprise.
Though writing an occasionally well-received article in radical
politics, Spencer remained for several years on the fringe of radical journalism and radical politics until, in 1848, he accepted a
rather plum position and assured income as sub-editor of one of
London's finest journals, the *Economist.*

Within two years, Spencer published his first book, *Social Sta-*

tics, a study in political philosophy. It was an immediate and overwhelming success within the radical intelligentsia. Two years later, in 1852, he published an article in the *Leader*, entitled, "The Development Hypothesis", in which he openly rejected special creation and espoused organic evolution, and this some seven years before Darwin's *Origin of Species* appeared. "Progress" was the popular word with Comte and most radicals but Spencer substituted "evolution" because, as he put it, "the word 'progress' has an anthropocentric meaning, and there is needed a word free from that." Having already struck favor among the radicals with his laissez-faire politics in *The Nonconformist* article, he now further ingratiated himself with his views on progress and social evolution, first intimated in his 1850 book. He had argued persuasively that man does best when not artificially interfered with, thus government is best that governs least. Progress, he reasoned, was development from conditions in which like parts perform like functions to conditions in which unlike parts perform unlike functions—i.e., from the uniform to the multi-form. The year before his second book appeared, he became acquainted with biological theory of evolution. He learned that organisms change from homogeneity or uniformity of structure to heterogeneity or multi-formity. During the next three years of the mid-1850s, Spencer had what in his autobiography he referred to as an "inspiration". He perceived that the advance from homogeneity to heterogeneity was the universal law of progress, whether inorganic, organic, or super-organic (social). The causal factor of this universal tendency, he learned, was the perpetual instability of the homogeneous. His whole theory of social evolution and its concomitant laissez-faire politics was, thus, adopted without significant modification from the physical sciences.

In 1853, his rich uncle under whom he had learned mathematics and radical philosophy died, leaving Spencer a sizeable sum as an endowment. Desiring the life of a private scholar and living frugally and even parsimoniously as a life-long bachelor, Spencer was able to give up his sub-editorship at the *Economist* and live the life he wanted most. The following year, his second book was published, *The Principles of Psychology*, and to his dismay was not well received and, even worse, was by and large ignored. He fell seriously ill, suffering from a nervous disorder causing acute insomnia to combat which he took heavy doses of opium for many years. He never fully recovered but his productivity accelerated all the while. An introverted personality, Spencer's childhood seems to have so conditioned him as to preclude closeness with others, which he himself confessed and somewhat bemoaned in his autobiography. He had intellectual friends, people with whom he spent time, sharing ideas and being nurtured by their breadth of experience while sharing his depth of knowledge. But the friends were excluded from his inner world, even George Eliot who for a time looked to be his wife, but nothing beyond regal platonic love developed.

In 1859, Charles Darwin's *The Origin of Species*, appeared and was received with acclamation in most intellectual circles, save the Church, and Spencer himself adopted the work openly and with praise; though he pointed out that such a view had already been expounded by himself in the *Westminister Review* as early as 1852. "Some division of the species", he had said, "will become slightly more heterogeneous. In the absence of the species change in conditions, natural selection would affect comparatively little." But later, he freely used the concept of "survival of the fittest", asserting that the conquest of one people over another has been the conquest of the social over the anti-social, the more adapted over the less adapted. All of this, of course, was grist to the mill of laissez-faire politics.

About 1860, with concepts, theories, and all-encompassing universal laws rather well developed, Spencer undertook an intellectually demanding writing schema which would baffle most scholars' minds. He set out to write a comprehensive philosophical system based upon his discovery of the universal law of social evolution. The magnum opus was called *Synthetic Philosophy* in which he believed he could include all sciences relevant to a thorough understanding of man and his world in evolutionary terms. In 1862, *First Principles* appeared, followed in 1867 by a multi-volume work called *Principles of Biology*; then by a multi-volume work in 1872, *Principles of Psychology*, followed by a multi-volume set entitled, *Principles of Sociology*, in 1896. He also concurrently, had written an eight-volume study on Descriptive Sociology (1873-1894) as well as his highly acclaimed *The Study of Sociology* (1873). One of his most noteworthy statements about the emergence of the scientific study of society appeared in this work—"There can be no complete acceptance of sociology so long as the belief in a social order not conforming to natural law survives." (p. 360).

By the 1870s, Spencer enjoyed the esteem of the entire intellectual and academic communities of England, America, and Europe, though not the acceptance of his total scheme. He was constantly seen in the company of such scholars and persons of renown as John Stuart Mill, Thomas Huxley, Tyndall, and George Eliot. He had become a very successful author, with books selling in hundreds of thousands in England and America as well as translations in German, Spanish, Italian, and even Russian. At Oxford University, his *Principles of Biology* was a standard text in the science syllabus; at Harvard University, William James required his students to read *First Principles* and *Principles of Psychology*; while at Yale University, William Graham Sumner taught Spencerian doctrines. But, by the end of the century, times had changed radically in the social and political arena—with England economy booming in the 1860s and 1870s but also grinding down the poorer classes necessitating relief programmes. Also, science had made major leaps in the theory of evolution, antiquating beyond salvage many of Spencer's writings. Only in America, which was trailing England in the proliferation of social ills, was his work still acclaimed.

Spencer's early background among the nonconformists probably accounts for his later psychic breakdown and invalidism—or so some historians of sociology and biographers seem to think. For Spencer, there was not even the alternative of rebelling against the social order. He could permit himself only those minor gestures of disdain for official society, such as the refusal of all its honors, which was in tune with his Nonconformist upbringing. As a result, the repressed furies turned inward, so it seems and he became ill. His eccentricities and illness provided a means of withdrawal and isolation from a society in which he felt a stranger and sorely alone. Coser has said—"The self-denying atmosphere of his youth left its permanent mark on Spencer... inner-directed, conscience-driven, ascetic, lonely." When he died in Derby, December 8, 1903, he was a lonely embittered old man. Ignored for fifty years, his work is now being re-evaluated by contemporary scholars in social and political thought. Without doubt, Herbert Spencer was the second founding father of sociology, preceded only by Auguste Comte himself.

MAJOR THEORIES

Science and Society

Like Comte, Spencer believed in and worked for a science of society which they both argued to be possible because there is, as they assessed the characteristics of society, an order of coexistence and progress. And, where there is order, the components of that order may form the subject of a science. This social science-sociology-is the science of what Spencer preferred to call the super-organic, i.e., social evolution. Spencer had divided all phenomena in the universe into three categories—inorganic, organic, and super-organic (social)—and had placed them all upon an evolutionary continum. And, in a rather popularistic fashion, Spencer had characterized society as the science concerned exclusively with the phenomena resulting from the cooperation of citizens.

Social laws, he insisted, are like all other natural laws—"sure, inflexible, ever active, and having no expectations". Unlike his French counterpart Comte, who stressed that men should aim at discovering the laws of society in order to act collectively in the social world, Spencer argued with equal conviction that we should study them in order that society does not violate such laws. Spencer, under exaggerated accusations of plagiarism, had taken pains in his *Autobiography* to articulate and accentuate the distinction between him and Comte, not over what the scientific character of sociology is, but what the function of that science should be in society. "What is Comte's professed aim?", inquired Spencer rhetorically, answering, "to give a coherent account of the progress of *human conceptions*". Whereas on the other hand, Spencer saw his aim as giving "a coherent account of the external world." He goes on by way of clarification: "I propose to describe the necessary and the actual, filiation of things. Comte professes to interpret the genesis of our knowledge of nature. My aim is to interpret. . . the genesis of the phenomena which constitute nature. The one is subjective. The other is objective."

The science of society was for both Comte and Spencer a positive science of natural phenomena—sociology is true science. But, a serious breach existed between their perceptions of the new science's function in a modern state. Whereas Comte wanted

sociology to guide men in building a better society in which to
live, Spencer countered that the new science should demonstrate
to the modern state that mankind should not interfere or tamper
with the natural processes occurring within society—a pure
laissez-faire social policy serves society's interests best and
sociology demonstrates how and why that is true.

There is a tendency within all natural phenomena to improve
itself, and society, being a natural phenomenon, is no exception.
Within the context of this argument, Spencer, like Comte, had
called upon history's service to the new science. But Spencer would
specify and circumscribe the precise nature and legitimate parameters of history. "That which it really concerns us to know is the
natural history of society", having stated his notions about what
an authentic history should be. "The only history that is of practical history, "is what may be called Descriptive Sociology. And
the highest office which the historian can discharge, is that of so
narrating the lives of nations, as to furnish materials for a Comparative Sociology; and for the subsequent determination of the
Ultimate laws to which social phenomena conform." History,
then, according to Spencer's system, if done well, is essentially
sociology, a careful description of social phenomena in evolution.
And so, the historian and the sociologist, working together, assess
the origins, present structure, and future prognoses of social evolution—evolution is the universal character of all things. And as
all phenomena, whether inorganic, organic, or super-organic,
have a tendency to improve and advance, so historians and sociologists observe, describe, and compare the nature of social phenomena in evolutionary change. "The seeds of civilization existing
in the aboriginal man and distributed over the earth were certain
in the lapse of time to fall here and there into circumstances fit
for their development." Spencer believed, as we have pointed
out, that man by his nature was predestined to progress through
what he thought of as social evolution—a key concept in his total
system.

Organic Analogy

Though a confirmed individualist, Spencer took great pains to
elaborate in great detail the organic analogy which is the identification of society with a biological organism. Indeed, he regarded
the recognition of the similarity between society and organism

as the first step toward a general theory of evolution. In his *Principles of Sociology*, Spencer expounded more thoroughly the evolutionary underpinnings of his sociological theory. "So completely is society organized on the same system as an individual", he argued, "that we may perceive something more than an analogy between them, the same definition of life applies to both (biological and social organism). Only when one sees that the transformation passed through during the growth, maturity, and decay of a society, conforms to the same principles as do the transformations passed through by aggregates of all orders, inorganic and organic, is there reached the concept of sociology as a science."[2]

The organic analogy, which is a staple of ancient and medieval social thought, was reformulated by Spencer as follows: "It is also a character of social bodies, as of living bodies, that while they increase in size they increase in structure. Like a low animal, the embryo of a high one has few distinguishable parts; but while it is acquiring greater mass, its parts multiply and differentiate. It is thus with a society. At first the unlikenesses among its groups of units are inconspicuous in number and degree; but as population augments, divisions and sub-divisions become more numerous and more decided. Further, in the social organism as in the individual organism, differentiation ceases only with that completion of the type which marks maturity and precedes decay".[3] Society is thus viewed as being essentially analogous to an organism, with its interdependent parts or organs making up the body of society. Both society and organism undergo growth. Their parts are inter-related and their functions reciprocal. As they grow in size, they increase in complexity of structure and their parts become more differentiated. As a living organism is a nation of units, so is the society.

Having carried the analogy this far, Spencer attempted to overcome the basic incompatibility between individualism and organism. Just as he emphasized the similarities between society and organism, he also spelled out the differences between them. "The parts of an animal form a concrete whole, but the parts of society form a whole which is discrete. While the living units composing the one are bound together in close contact, the living units composing the other are free, are not in contact, and are more or less widely dispersed."[4] In other words, the organism is a concrete, integrated whole whereas society is a whole composed of discrete and dispersed elements. "In the (biological organism) consciousness is concentrated in a small part of the aggregate. In the (social organism) it is diffused throughout the aggregate: all the units possess the capacity for happiness and misery, if not in equal degree, still in degrees that approximate. As, then, there is no social sensorium, the welfare of the aggregate, considered apart from that of the units, is not an end to be sought. The society exists for the benefit of its members; not its members for the benefit of society."[5]

In spite of such elaborate attempts to establish the similarities and differences between organism and society, in his later writings Spencer claimed that he used the organic analogy "only as a scaffolding to help in building up a coherent body of sociological induction". The fact remains, however, that he continued to use the analogy as a scientific premise to build his theory of evolution.

The Theory of Evolution

Spencer's first and foremost concern was with evolutionary change in social structures and social institutions. 'The average opinion in every age and country", observed Spencer, "is a function of the social structure in that age and country." He had argued persuasively that the evolution of human societies, far from being different from other evolutionary phenomena, is but a special case of a universally applicable natural law. Profoundly influenced by the scientific advances in biological researches, Spencer concentrated his efforts upon the parallelisms between organic and social evolution. Ultimately, all universal phenomena—inorganic, organic, supra-organic—are subject to the natural law of evolution.

By combining belief in the evolutionary character of all phenomena with the analogy of organism and society, Spencer produced a dual theory of progress applicable at all stages of human history. And human progress intrigued him throughout his studies—"The advance from the simple to the complex", he explained, "through a process of successive differentiations, is seen alike in the earliest changes of the Universe. . . It is seen in the geologic and climatic evolution of the Earth; it is seen in the unfolding of every single organism on its surface. . . it is seen in the evolution of Humanity, whether contemplated in the civilized individual, or in the aggregate of races; it is seen in the evolution of Society in respect alike of its political, its religious, and its economic organizations; and it is seen in the evolution of all those endless concrete and abstract products of human activity . . ." [6]

Though too frequently ignored or overlooked by his critics, Spencer never supported the naive unilinear or deterministic view of evolution. Spencer called in his *First Principles* "erroneous" any evolutionary doctrine which implied some "intrinsic proclivity" in every species towards a "higher form". Progress in evolution is not inevitable, only possible. Early in the *First Principles* Spencer attempts a rather cumbersome definition of evolution such that it covers all bases. The result was rather problematical. "Evolution", he wrote, "is an integration of matter and concomitant dissipation of notion; during which the matter passes from an indefinite, incoherent homogeneity to a definite, coherent heterogeneity; and during which the retained notion undergoes a parallel transformation." Within this framework of universal evolution, Spencer developed his "three basic laws" and his "four secondary propositions"—each building upon each and all upon the doctrine of evolution. The Three Basic Laws are: (1) the law of persistence of force (some ultimate cause that transcends knowledge); (2) the law of the indestructibility of matter (disproven by modern physics); and (3) the Law of the continuity of motion (energy passes from one form to another but always persists). And the Four Secondary Propositions are: (1) persistence of the relationship between the force (uniformity of law), (2) transformation and equivalence of forces, (3) tendency of everything to move along the line of least resistance and greatest attraction, and (4) the principle of the alternation or rhythm of motion.

Spencer's philosophy acknowledged only two fundamental categories:

a. The Unknowable (or the Absolute or unconditioned)
b. The Knowable (or the Finite or conditioned)

The unknowable is the legitimate domain of religion and the knowable of science.

The knowable universe consists of material aggregates (concentration of matter). These material aggregates are in a condition of incessant change, that is, evolution. To explain this process, Spencer formulated the *law of the continuous redistribution of matter and motion* which states that every object undergoes from instant to instant some alteration of state. The evolution is *simple* when material aggregates are unaffected or slightly affected by external, disturbing influences; it is *compound* when the concentration of matter is considerably affected so as to change the rate and course of its progress. Spencer emphasized the universal tendency of material aggregates to move from a condition of unstable to a condition of stable equilibrium. In this context, he expounded the *law of the instability of the homogeneous* which states that the homogeneous is inherently unstable and bound to change.

Spencer's theory of evolution involves two discernible but inter-related strains of thought.

1. The movement from simple societies to various levels of compound societies.

Spencer identified four types of societies in terms of their evolutionary stage—simple, compound, doubly compound and trebly compound—each being distinguishable on the basis of the more or less complexity of their social structures and functions. There is an inherent tendency for the homogeneous to become heterogeneous and for the uniform to become multiform. The aggregation of simple societies which consist of families gave rise to compound societies. Through further aggregation of compound societies which consist of families unified into clans, doubly compound societies develop. The aggregation of doubly compound societies which consist of clans unified into tribes led to trebly compound societies where tribes are organized into nation-states. The master trend in this process of universal evolution is the increased differentiation of social structures into specialized functional systems which lead, inevitably, to better integration and adaptation to environment.

2. Change from military (or militant) to industrial society.

This classification system, based on the type of internal regulation within societies, is rooted in a theory of society which states that "types of social structure depend on the relation of a society to other societies in its significant environment." This system ran the whole gamut of universal evolution from military to industrial societies, the former characterized by "compulsory cooperation", while the latter is based on "voluntary cooperation." The military society is also characterized by a centralized government,

62 SOCIOLOGICAL THOUGHT

a rigid system of stratification, economic autonomy and state domination of all social organizations. Free trade, loss of economic autonomy, independent voluntary organization, a relatively open system of stratification and a decentralized government characterize industrial society. In the military society individuals exist for the benefit of the state whereas in industrial society, state exists for the sake of individuals.

At this point, Spencer's proto-structural-functionalist tendencies emerge in which he theorizes that an increase in the size of social units invariably accompanies an increase in the complexity of structure. Social aggregates, as do organic ones, grow from relatively undifferentiated states in which the parts resemble one another into differentiated states in which these parts have become dissimilar. By so arguing, having pointed out that the more unlike individual roles become and social differentiation accelerated, Spencer illustrates why complex societies are necessarily more vulnerable and more fragile in structure and function than their earlier and simpler predecessors.

> Like evolving aggregates in general, societies show *integration*, both by simple increase of mass and by coalescence and recoalescence of masses. The change from *homogeneity* to *heterogeneity* is multitudinously exemplified: up from the simple tribe, alike in all its parts, to the civilized nation, full of structural and functional unlikenesses. With progressing integration and heterogeneity goes increasing *coherence*. We see the wandering group dispersing, dividing, held together by no bonds; the tribe with parts made more coherent by subordination to a dominant man; the cluster of tribes united in a political plexus under a chief with sub-chiefs; and so on up to the civilized nation, consolidated enough to hold together for a thousand years or more. Simultaneously come increasing *definiteness*. Social organization is at first vague; advance brings settled arrangements which grow slowly more precise: customs pass into laws which, while gaining fixity, also become more specific in their applications to varieties of actions; and all institutions, at first confusedly intermingled, slowly separate, at the same time that each within itself marks off more distinctly its component structures. Thus in all respects is fulfilled the formula of evolution. There is progress towards greater size, coherence, multiformity, and definiteness.[7]

As mentioned in passing earlier, Spencer has been consistently but erroneously accused of supporting belief in "rectilinear evolution"—the view that cultural evolution proceeds in a straight line, without interruptions or regressions. That he did not, can be illustrated by two quotes from his *Principles of Sociology:* "Though, taking the entire assemblage of societies, evolution may be held inevitable, yet it cannot be held inevitable in each particular society, or even probable." Again, "Like other kinds of progress, social progress is not linear but divergent and redivergent. Each differentiated product gives origin to a new set of differentiated products".[8] Unfortunately, most critics have pounced on some isolated statements from his early writings, such as his first edition (1855) of *Principles of Evolution*, and failed to take account of the refinement of his theory in later works as reflected in the previous quotes. A standard excerpt for indictment is in Vol. I of the 1855 work: "Life under all its forms has arisen by a progressive, unbroken evolution; and through the immediate instrumentality of what we call natural causes."[9] In isolation, the statement is incriminating; in context and historical development of Spencer's ideas, it is quite defensible.

Spencer believed that societies do not develop irreversibly through predetermined stages but in direct response to their social and natural environment. He goes on to mention the importance of geography as well as social history as determining factors. "While spreading over the earth mankind found environments of various characters, and in each case the social life fallen into, partly determined by the social life previously led, has been partly determined by the influences of the new environment; so that the multiplying groups have tended ever to acquire differences, now major and now minor; there have arisen genera and species of societies."[10] Rather than argue for the simplistic determinism of Social Darwinism, Spencer argued that "differences between societies are determined by disturbances", e.g., (1) difference of endowments of the races, (2) effect of immediately preceding stage, (3) peculiarities of habit, (4) society's proximity to other societies, and (5) impact of the mixture of races. Spencer recognized that particular societies may retrograde as well as progress, and regularly employed the notions of social stagnation and retrogression. "While the current degradation theory is untenable, the theory of progression, in its ordinary form, seems to be untenable also—It is possible and, I believe, probably, that retrogression has been as frequent as progression."[11]

Social Darwinism

The attempt to apply Darwin's theory of evolution dealing with
the development of plants and animals to social phenomena is a
short-lived explanatory model of social interaction which exercised
considerable influence on the growth of early sociology. Herbert
Spencer and William Graham Sumner were two of the most
outspoken advocates of social Darwinism in sociology.

Spencer's social Darwinism centered around two fundamental
principles:

1. *The Principle of the Survival of the Fittest*

Spencer whole-heartedly endorsed the conception of a natural
process of conflict and survival which operates as a kind of
biologically purifying process. According to him, nature is endowed with a providential tendency to get rid of the unfit and to
make room for the better; it is the law of nature that the weak
should be eliminated for the sake of the strong. He deducted from
his system the conviction that the rapid elimination of unfit individuals from society through natural selection (not violent execu-
tions) would benefit the race biologically and that the state should
therefore do nothing to relieve the conditions of the poor, whom
he assumed to be less fit. By less fit, however, Spencer, did not
mean morally inferior but less healthy and less intelligent than
the social norm. In this context, Spencer lumped together stupi-
dity, vice, and, idleness with victims of sickness and deformity.
Spencer wrote: "It seems hard that widows and orphans should
be left to struggle for life or death. Nevertheless, when regarded
not separately but in connection with the interests of universal
humanity, these harsh fatalities are seen to be full of beneficence—the same beneficence which brings to early graves the
children of diseased parents, and singles out the intemperate and
the debilitated as the victims of an epidemic."[12]

Although he opposed governmental assistance to the less fit,
he did not oppose individual philanthropy. Individuals, he allowed, must combine philanthropic energy and philosophical calm
when treating such matter. Spencer also maintained that the economic system works best if each individual is allowed to seek his
own private interests and that consequently the state should not
intervene in the economy.

2. The Principle of Non-interference

As a logical corollary to his championing the ideology of social Darwinism, Spencer was an untiring advocate of individualism and laissez-faire politics. He opposed almost any form of state interference with private activity. He insisted that the state had no business in education, health and sanitation, postal service, money and banking, regulation of housing conditions or the elimination of poverty. Money used for such activities could be better spent "to support laborers employed in new reproductive works—land-drainage, machine building etc". For Spencer, the state was a sort of joint stock company whose only role was the protection of the rights of the individual and the defence of its citizens against external aggression.

Whereas Comte exhorted the scientist-priests to be actively involved in the social world—to reform and to change it—Spencer, on the other hand, argued that sociologists should convince the state and the citizen not to intervene in the natural process of selection operative in society. Nature is more intelligent than Man, he argued, and "once you begin to interfere with the order of nature there is no knowing where the result will end". The good society is based resolutely upon contracts between individuals pursuing their respective interests.

Scientific Method

When Comte and Spencer began to develop the idea of a science of society, a social physics or positive philosophy, nothing had been done before them by way of development of a scientific methodology for the study of society. Comte began to write of the importance of observation, experimentation, comparison, and historical analysis, and though he did not employ the proto-methodology often or consistently, it was a start in the development of the fledgling science. Spencer was aware of the special problems of objectivity that arise in the investigation of a social work in which the investigator is a part. The social scientist, Spencer had suggested, must make a deliberate effort to free himself from biases and sentiments. Evidence of his depth of insight into the methodological difficulties of a social science is his spending half of his *The Study of Sociology* closely analyzing the sources of bias and of the "intellectual and emotional difficulties" that face the sociologist. Spencer developed a rudimentary sociology of knowledge in which he showed how the defender of ideal or material interest tends to shape and distort perceptions of social reality. By having developed the parameters of such an investigation for social science, Spencer has earned his place among the early founders of the sociology of knowledge.

Spencer's heavy emphasis upon the comparative analysis of societies—past with present, like with unlike, etc.,—set the stage for the eventual emergence of ethnology (cultural and social anthropology) whose distinguishing mark is its major emphasis upon comparative approaches to the study of culture and sociology. "We must learn", wrote Spencer in *Principles of Sociology*, "by inspection, the relations of co-existence and sequence in which they (social phenomena) stand to one another". He goes on to point out that by "comparing societies of different kinds, and societies of different stages, we must ascertain what traits of size, structure, function, etc., are associated." The accuracy and utility of a science of social phenomena, for Spencer, was assured because of his thoroughgoing determinism—social as well as all other natural phenomena are determined in the activity and progress. Individual components, whether atoms or people, are not freely moving agents but deterministically directed parts of an evolving whole. Spencer maintained early and later that causation operates in human behavior just as it does in other spheres of nature and, therefore, Spencer regarded free will as an illusion. He, thus, defined sociology as a science dealing with genuine facts of social activity not unlike the precision and predictability of biology and physics. "Sociology", Spencer wrote in 1860, "deals with general facts, structural and functional, as gathered from a survey of societies and their changes: in other words, the empirical generalizations that are arrived at by comparing the different societies, and successive phases of the same society"

Functionalism and Individualism

As was earlier mentioned, Spencer was a thoroughgoing functionalist as well as an evolutionist. Before structural-functionalism became the reigning theoretical school in sociology, Spencer had already opened up the frontier for development in Volume III of his *The Principles of Sociology*. "There can be no true conception of a structure without a true conception of its function", he wrote in 1876. Function occurs within a social structure, and all social structures must have functions. "To understand how an organization originated and developed", he explained, "it is requisite to understand the need subserved at the outset and afterwards"[13]. Though the language is somewhat crude by later functionalist standards, the concept of the interplay between structure and function is most evident. Social institutions, Spencer believed, are not the result of deliberate intentions and motivations of actors but arise from the exigencies of social structures and functions. "Condition", Spencer had said, "and not intentions determine." For Spencer, any serious sociological analysis of social institutions must necessarily employ both the concepts of social evolution and social function. He had consistently emphasized the belief that changes in structure cannot occur without changes in functions and that increases in size of social units necessarily bring in their wake progressive differentiations in social activities. As reflected in the following quote, Spencer, who spoke most often of social institutions in functionalist terms, normally took as his point of departure the search for the functions subserved by a particular component. "To understand how an organization originated and developed, it is requisite to understand the need subserved at the outset and afterwards".

Not only a functionalist, Spencer was also a radical individualist, believing that the real or essential characteristic of the component parts of a society completely determine the characteristics of the whole of society, and that fundamental characteristic is the individual. If society is to evolve into higher and more advanced social structures and functions, it must move from the simple to the complex activities of a society which is moving from the lesser military to the more industrial activities. Whereas Comte was radically "social" in his theory, Spencer is equally radically "individualistic." Spencer conceived of society's origins in individualistic and utilitarian terms—society as a vehicle for the enhancement of individual's purposes. He said it best in his popular volume, *The Study of Sociology*: "There is no way of coming at a true theory of society, but by inquiring into the nature of its component individuals—Every phenomenon exhibited by an aggregation of men originates in some quality of man himself."[14] The best society, therefore, is a society that least controls the individual. Yet, as Spencer knew, the problem of the relationship between the individual and society was a difficult one. He dealt with the problem in terms of his extreme individualism—"the person is paramount and society should not interfere, for individuals acting in self-interest automatically act in the interest of society".

SIGNIFICANCE OF HIS WORK

Unlike his French counterpart Comte, Spencer enjoyed enormous acceptance and universal recognition during his lifetime. His books sold widely and sometimes even wildly in the intellectual centres of England, the United States of America, Europe, and especially in Russia. Without doubt, his were the dominant intellectual ideas about man and society at the time, particularly from the mid-1860's to the early years of the 1900's. His appeal, so it seems, was strong because his system was able to creatively respond to the urgent needs of those rather volatile times, viz., the desire for the unification of knowledge which was expanding by leaps and bounds bringing confusion, division, and directionlessness in its wake, and, second, a solid, rational, and respectable justification for the social, political, and economic laissez-faire in vogue in England and beginning in the United States. In 1882, when Spencer was at the peak of his international popularity, he visited America.

From his earliest essays, again unlike Comte, Spencer became the topic of discussion and the focus of attention amongst political liberals and laissez-faire intellectuals. This level of attention indicates that at the time there was a serious demand for what Spencer had to say. His evolutionary theory provided the solution for many of the dilemmas faced by the intellectuals at the time. In the late forties and early fifties, many among the middle-class educated had sensed a loss of moral direction. Educated people were increasingly deprived of the kind of certainties that used to be provided by the Church. Now, evolution had introduced a new cosmology and put mankind and human societies in a different light. If the new evolutionary perceptions of the world brought relativity to heretofore established ways of seeing and understanding the world and one's place in it, evolutionary theory of social life found a ready audience precisely because it seemed to address the most pressing questions of the day. It made it possible, for instance, to maintain the belief in the psychic unity of mankind within the matrix of human variability and cultural diversity. Differences in behavior were accounted for within the evolutionary schema. Man, as a natural organism, was subject to the laws of evolutionary progress as are all natural phenomena. Similarly, Spencer's theory satisfied the quest for an explanation in terms of the new-found theories of natural law—of evolution, especially vindicating the belief in moral superiority in Western civilization. "Progress", wrote Spencer, "is not an accident but a necessity. Surely must evil and immorality disappear; surely must man become perfect". By employing the scientific medium of evolutionary processes, it could be shown that more developed modes of behavior, such as those of contemporary Englishmen, represented a distillation of the moral excellence toward which mankind had unconsciously been striving for many generations.

Eventually, Spencer became more highly acclaimed and for a longer period of time in the United States than even in his homeland of England. Spencer's *The Study of Sociology* (1873) made a very strong impact in the United States, where Charles Horton Cooley, doyen of American sociology, said it "probably did more to arouse interest in the subject (of sociology) than any other publication before or since." Also, another distinguished sociologist, William Graham Sumner, said of Spencer's work—"It solved the old difficulty about the relation of social science to history, rescued social science from the dominion of cranks, and offered a definite and magnificent field for study". Sumner actually used the book at Yale University as the textbook in the first sociology course offered in America.

By and large, Spencer's influence remained strong and visible until about the first World War, lasting somewhat longer in America than in England. Following the war, his works became less and less important in sociological circles until by the mid-1930's they were hardly considered worthy of attention, save for their historical relevance. Given the turmoil in Europe and America caused by war, inflation, unemployment, etc., there was a growing feeling that society and politics need some rational control. Spencer's works remained on the shelves of ignored works until about 1960 when, especially in America, his works experienced something of a renaissance. Three themes in his opus were picked up again as timely addresses, albeit somewhat dated, to the

situations of the day—functionalism, his study of social engineering's difficulties in coping with individual unpredictability, and
his poignant criticism of governmental interference with individual freedom. His shortcomings, of course, are all too visible
today. For example, Spencer should have realized that societies
at the same stage of evolution, according to the principle of the
differentiation of social structure, do not necessarily possess similarities in politics, religion, morals, art, etc., and that contrari-
wise, similar types of government and forms of religion are found
among different structural types of societies.

Nevertheless, in spite of his errors, Spencer was among the
first of the social scientists of the nineteenth century to argue that
culture change is better explained in terms of socio-cultural forces
than as the result of actions of important men. The "great men
make history" idea was obnoxious to Spencer. By and large,
much of his thought even by today's standards was sound, e.g.,
he did not believe the incest taboo was innate, nor that sexual
promiscuity was the earliest stage of marriage, nor that polygamy
preceded monogamy, arguing the reverse, as well as arguing
against the notion that primitive communism was man's first form
of community life. His direct and visible long-term influence upon
the development of sociology is somewhat negligible, but his indirect influence is profound. Among the giants he influenced,
Durkheim looms largest, having influenced Durkheim to favor
the comparative approach to social analysis, as well as impressing
him with Spencer's typologies of human society, his essays on
the division of labor, and most importantly his early work on
structural-functionalism. The flow of ideas from Spencer to Durkheim is traced further to Radcliffe-Brown and the British school
of functionalist anthropology and finally to structural-functional
sociology in America. Spencer's treatment of evolution has
strongly influenced modern anthropology in America and ethnology in Britain.

The major fallacies of Spencer's thought have been fairly well
overcome today. His fallacies included (1) his belief that organisms form concrete wholes, whereas today sociology emphasizes
their free character, (2) that organisms are consciously concentrated, whereas today we speak of societal dispersal, and (3) his
belief that social parts exist for the social whole, but today we
are well aware of society's focus upon the benefits of individuals.

Today, in place of the cumbersome and problematic concept of "evolution", sociology employs the term "system" to describe that which is scientifically analyzable within social phenomena. System designates anything that may be conceived as a whole, consisting of interdependent and semi-autonomous parts. Spencer's work in this area has been corrected and significantly utilized in the work of the Italian sociologist Vilfredo Pareto in the area of social systems.

No one after Spencer ever matched either the sheer volume of sociological writing nor made more significant contributions to the science of human society. A lonely, troubled, intellectual who favored individualism and laissez-faire politics, Spencer spoke in his writings to the needs of his time. Times have changed, but once again his work seems to commend itself to our age as it searches for answers to age-old questions about how to live in community while maintaining individuality.

4

VILFREDO PARETO

Life and Times

Ennobled in the eighteenth century, the Pareto family of Genovese ancestry had remained rooted in and were staunch supporters of Italian politics and high culture until the second quarter of the nineteenth century. Because of political dangers and fears, the Marquis Raphael Pareto had fled to France, there marrying Marie Metenier, a Parisian. Two daughters and one son, the Marquis Vilfredo Frederico Damaso Pareto (1848-1923), were born in France but in 1855, seven years after the birth of Vilfredo on July 15, 1848, the Pareto family returned to a more peaceful and politically safe and stable Italy than earlier. The happy result of this repatriation for Vilfredo Pareto was his bilinguality in French and Italian. His youthful education in Italy was grounded well in traditional classical studies as was most prevalent at the time. Following his secondary education, Pareto entered the prestigious Polytechnic-Institute in Turin where his five-year course provided serious studies in mathematics, natural and physical sciences, and engineering, the latter being his chosen career. His graduate thesis for degree completion at the Institute, entitled "The Fundamental Principles of Equilibrium in Solid Bodies," proved determinative later in his study of society. Upon graduating in 1870, he took a position as director of the Rome Railroad Company for a while, later taking a managerial post as superintendent of the iron mines production company at Florence. In keeping with his breeding and pedigree, Pareto spent time amongst the aristocratic families in the high society salons of Rome. While rubbing shoulders with the high bourgeoisie of Italy, he espoused a passionate allegiance to ideals of democracy, republicanism, and pacifism; his father's well-known position was the same on all points.

However, by the time Pareto reached the age of thirty, he had denounced these family ideals in exchange for a pessimistic and sometimes even nihilistic view of human society and politics. In 1876, the rightist party which supported free trade policies dear to Pareto fell from power being replaced by a moderate leftist group who were in policy and practice opposed to free trade and leaned toward socialism and even communism. To this, Pareto was vehemently and outspokenly opposed. Six years later, in an attempt to assist in turning the government around, Pareto ran for public office but was roundly defeated by the opposition he despised so much. That same year, his father died and not long after his mother as well. Pareto's whole life-style underwent a radical transformation so that in 1889, he gave up the directorship of the iron production company in Florence, married Alessandrina Bakunin, a young impoverished Russian girl living in Venice, and moved to semi-retirement in a villa at Fiesole. Owing to the rich legacy and inheritance left him by his parents, Pareto was able to live a private life as a gentleman scholar without financial worry. He spent his early years at the villa in Fiesole translating the great classics, revelling in his ability to read seven languages fluently, and more importantly turning his attention to a serious study of economics.

After his open rejection of his father's ideals, Pareto turned his violent criticism pointedly upon the new government's socialistic tendencies, especially launching a fierce crusade against the government's restrictions upon free trade in foreign and domestic policies. Italy's willingness to vote into power such a government shattered Pareto's early confidence in the virtues of humanity, cultivating now a cynical contempt for humanitarianism, republicanism, and progress. Owing to the publication of some of his brilliant essays in mathematical and theoretical economics, Pareto was called to the University at Lausanne in April, 1893, as "extraordinary professor" of political economy. The following year, he was made a full and permanent professor of the university at the age of forty-six. His establishment as an international scholar of high repute came two years later with the publication of his two-volume study, entitled, *Cours d'Economie Politique*. By this work alone, Pareto established himself as a major figure in economic theory for all time. Until 1898 and obviously under the weighty influence of the intellectual milieu of the university, Pareto was a casual supporter of liberal policies. But following the infamous May Riots at Milan, Pareto's politics changed radically, and he completely abandoned his hope for a liberal restructuring of Italian politics and government. He redirected his articulate furore now against all expressions of democratic ideals while nurturing a rather all-encompassing hatred for liberalism generally. On one occasion, Pareto wrote: "I gave up the combat in defence of liberal economic theories in Italy. My friends and I get nowhere and lose our time; this time is much more fruitfully directed to scientific study." He despaired over debate, anguished over recalcitrance in government, and became, in the process a cynical, rancorous, utterly disillusioned loner, at variance with all the dominant tendencies of the age, despising them with a pathological fervor without discrimination.

Adding insult to injury, Pareto was dealt another serious blow besides a breach with family and friends over politics. The insult, which naturally would have confirmed Pareto's hostile feelings about man, came when one evening Pareto returned from a business trip to Paris to find that Alessandrina, his wife, had absconded with thirty cases of his villa treasures as well as with the chef, her lover. The blow was severe and determinative in the extreme—he never recovered but became even more psychopathological with increasing age. His lack of optimism about humanity evolved into an aggressive religious denunciation of human efforts at self-help.

When Pareto went up to the University of Lausanne as a social economist, he found himself quite alone, being at the faculty of law where he alone taught social and economic theory. Nevertheless and in spite of loneliness and intellectual isolation, he moved quickly from extraordinary to full professor and in 1896 he was elected dean of the faculty of law. All the while and aside from professional promotions, he was stifled in his efforts to reform and restructure the social studies curriculum at the university because of resistance and lack of cooperation from colleagues. Not only was his attempt to strengthen sociology thwarted, his inability to realize success in teaching was evident to all, despising as he did the lecturing to beginning students. On one occasion he expressed his revulsion for such teaching by writing that such teaching of the same materials over and over again made him feel like a parrot. "There may have been a parrot among my Darwinian ancestors," he wrote with sardonic bitterness, "this would explain my usage of automatic language."

Intellectual genius and pedagogical effectiveness are seldom complements of the same scholar and certainly with Pareto, if the former was true of him the latter most definitely was not. His lack of skill in such lecturing, being known by student and colleague alike, led Pareto to reduce his teaching responsibility, eventually reducing his lecture time to one hour per week yet retaining the chair of sociology. His instructional fields continued for several years to be political sociology and the history of economic and social doctrines. Finally, in 1907, he relinquished the chair in political economy completely and became full professor of political and social science, teaching actually only three months a year. In 1909, after sixteen years of teaching at the university, he gave up his teaching altogether visiting the university campus and the city of Lausanne only rarely. To his villa in Celigny, he retired "like a snail in its shell," he was heard to lament, to live out his sad and embittered life.

A few years before, as noted earlier, Pareto had acquired a very considerable legacy in 1898 with the death of his father, and due to his now financial independence and coupled with his increasingly unhappy relations at the university, Pareto built himself a villa near Celigny not far from Lausanne. Taking only the finest wines and culinary delights, his life of an independent scholar and man of means served well his scientific work. Continuing to write and study, he published in 1902 his now famous *Les Systemes Socialistes*. Prior to publishing this work, Pareto had become convinced that the better part of human behavior is not guided by rationality but rather by what he thought of as sentiments and feelings, superstitions and similar non-rational factors. Attributing, for example, his failure to convince friends and family to favor economic liberalism and rational rather than non-rational factors of resistance, he became convinced that rational argument as such would continually fail to move the uneducated and recalcitrant masses of people since they were by and large governed not by reason but by non-rational beliefs, sentiments, fears, and the like.

This position, which Pareto first revealed in an essay published in 1900 came to full developmental fruition in 1906 under the title, *Manual of Political Economy*, followed ten years later by a more thorough treatment of this theory in his *magnum opus* of one million words, entitled, *Treatise on General Sociology*, translated in English as *The Mind and Society*. It became his best known work in the English speaking world.

Owing to his rejection of democracy and its concomitant belief in humanity's ability to improve and advance by goodwill and self-determination, Pareto welcomed Italian Fascism in its early and benign form under the banner of Mussolini. Mussolini is purported to have held Pareto as a political genius saying even that the great sociologist's conceptualization of the circulation and theory of elites was "probably the most extraordinary sociological conception of modern times." To the early Fascists, Pareto's political sociology provided a readymade system for defense and propagation of their plans for Italy's control. And at first Pareto seemed pleased with the attention but, true to his integrity as a scholar and free intellectual, when Mussolini dared to subdue dissent by stifling the universities in Italy, and restricting free speech, Pareto wailed loudly. Fortunately, Pareto lived only long enough to see Mussolini's Fascism in its fledgling form. Early in 1923, as he knew death was approaching, Pareto was finally able to marry Jane Regis, his longtime mistress and companion, by becoming a citizen of the city-state of Fiume where his divorce of Alessandrina was recognized. At the age of seventy-five, Pareto died on August 19, 1923, following a brief illness. He is interred on his Celigny villa grounds simply and without epitaph save his name and dates. Born in the year of Italy's embracing of liberal politics and economic policy, Pareto died just a year before the debilitating ascent of Mussolini's Fascism, and infamous March on Rome.

MAJOR THEORIES

Sociology: Its Nature and Method

As has already been noted, Pareto's fervent desire in his scientific researches was to discover a means of rationally explaining the pervasiveness of irrationality and non-rationality in human behavior. Wishing not to dispose of the importance of economic theory in explaining human activity as did Thorstein Veblen and others, Pareto rather sought to supplement economic theory with sociological conceptualizations which would more correctly interpret those characteristics of human behavior which economic analysis and abstract theory were ill-equipped to do.

Pareto, ever the scientist, was anxious to construct a system of sociological theory and method comparable to the precision and refinement of physiology and chemistry. He was particularly interested in expanding his abilities as a social scientist in explaining human activity beyond the scope of economic theory which he came to believe was insufficiently broad to grasp the total subject matter. Within this framework, the development of sociology's theoretical task was essentially a logical extension of economics. Pareto characterized sociology as that social science which dealt with non-logical action of people, leaving the analysis of logical actions to economics, technology, and military science. Because of his concern with the motivational factors and non-logical and irrational actions of individuals as a means of explaining social life—its structures and changes—Pareto's sociology has been called a type of psychological sociology by some contemporary writers, a characterization which Pareto most likely would have objected to.

Unlike Herbert Spencer, Pareto was a well-educated and well-rounded scholar in all of the then appropriate humanistic fields of study as well as trained scientifically. Thanks to the classical system of Italian education, Pareto was steeped in the history and literature of the ancient world and the Renaissance, competent in Latin and several modern languages, as well as trained in the physical sciences and engineering, taking his degree in mechanical engineering from the Polytechnic Institute. This background nurtured a strong commitment to scientific work—its strengths and reasonable limitations. He insisted upon limiting the scope of science—it must be allowed to function exclusively within the logico-experimental method. Furthermore, science is precluded by this circumscription from passing judgements upon or participating in the construction of the ultimate values and goals of society, since the nature of values is established upon non-logical evaluations and not upon the logico-experimental method. Therefore and in contradistinction to Durkheim's presumptions, science cannot be a secular substitute for religion nor for traditional morality. This argument, today held firmly by a dominant school of thought, was not looked upon favourably by the Comtean and Durkheimian intellectuals of the nineteenth and early twentieth centuries.

Observation, experiment and reasoning constitute the most fundamental methods of Pareto's science. The logico-experimental science must dismiss all extra- or meta-empirical notions. All concepts must be defined in terms of observed or observable facts; they must correspond to realities which we can either perceive directly or create by experimentation. All other notions, of a religious kind or of a philosophical order, must be rigorously excluded from science. Nothing that transcends experience has a place in logico-experimental science, and scientific discussion must always pertain to reality, not to the meanings we assign words.

Pareto recognizes only one scientific procedure: the logico-experimental method. *Logic* implies that, in terms of definitions laid down or relations observed, it is legitimate to deduce conclusions which result from the premises; the term, *experimental*, covers both observation and experimentation. Science is experimental because it refers to the real as the origin and criterion of all propositions; a proposition that cannot be substantiated or regulated by means of experiment is not scientific. And the aim of logico-experimental science is to discover what Pareto calls experimental uniformities, that is, regular relations between phenomena. Pareto's procedure is as follows: "Science always begins with simplifications. It observes certain aspects of certain phenomena; it designates what aspects of phenomena are to be retained by rigorous concepts; it establishes relations between the phenomena covered by the concepts, and it endeavors to combine simplified approaches gradually in order to recreate the complex reality."[1] Pareto also warns that science by nature is partial and incomplete and can never account for reality in all its complexity. Science is only a group of propositions, of fact or of causality, that correspond to some segment of reality. It can never be normative and therefore never provide the equivalent of what religion offers. Therefore sociologists (like Comte and Durkheim) who imagine that sociology can establish a scientific theory or foundation of morality are laboring under an illusion.

Pareto was most anxious to address the non-rational qualities of human action, but approached such phenomena by way of a careful analysis of phenomena which were of the experimental world, such as ideas, abstractions, opinions, beliefs and sentiments. He, therefore, considered his main task to be the transformation of these phenomena into empirical data, into observable facts of the world of reality. All the while, he warned against verbal procedures—he wrote in his *Treatise* the most provocative and comprehensive analysis of this approach, arguing against the dangers in sociological theory of the merely verbal exercise in abstract logic: "Natural sciences were never built up by studying and classifying the terms of ordinary language, but by studying and classifying facts. Let us try to do the same for sociology."[2] Pareto's approach to sociology comprised a major thrust toward scientific precision in empirical analysis. In his *Treatise on General Sociology* (1916), he scathingly criticizes both Comte and Spencer for what he called their "pseudoscientism," also accosting the superficiality of the secular religions of progress, humanity, and democracy. His call for the centrality of the logico-experimental method based upon observation and logical inference reflected Pareto's heavy reliance upon the philosophical method of John Stuart Mill.

In his methodology, Pareto drew from Mill a philosophical support for the concept of "logical action" used in his assessment of the scientific character of the act of observing. Observation is done by an observer, whether scientist or layman, and the observer is simultaneously observed object and observing subject. A perpetual dialectic, therefore, evolves for the researcher. The "good scientist," Pareto argued, took cognizance of the dialectic and turned it to advantage in careful analysis, and the good scientist will bring about the desired results. The objective and the subjective ends will coincide in any particular instance so that the theory guiding the action can be said to subscribe to the logico-experimental standard of true science. Two paradigms were developed by Pareto as a framework for the analysis of social actions: First, the "subject" in social action was conceived by Pareto not only as "knower" but also as actor; and second, this actor-knower becomes the "object" of observation by the social scientist himself. These two paradigms served to differentiate while holding together the action of observed objects and that of the action of the observer in his relations to these objects.

Pareto was not immune to British positivism and Spencerian evolutionism or to social Darwinism in general. These thoughts were in the air in the European universities and Pareto breathed that air. In his *Cours* (1896), he reflected a rather typically liberal bent in social and political thought in keeping with the moods of the day in vogue about the intelligentsia, not only opposing, for instance, state interference and battling for free trade and individual liberty but also exemplifying a rather pronounced amenability, to the notion of social progress. Throughout the *Cours*, for example, he utilizes extensively Spencerian concepts such as "differentiation," arguing in support of the concept that societies have moved from an undifferentiated homogeneity to heterogeneity. He went so far as to suggest that there has been a cumulative increase in the degree of social differentiation from the days of the Romans down to the present.

However and in spite of the cogency with which he argued his case within the positivistic and evolutionary camps, when Pareto wrote his most notable *Treatise*, he scrapped social progress in exchange for Machiavellian cynicism with respect to social history, arguing now for a relative constancy of essential human characteristics. Turning his venom upon his old position, he accosted and denigrated social Darwinism and especially Herbert Spencer's work. Subsequently restricting his reference to their works, Pareto became highly critical of Spencer and Comte and the dual concepts of social evolution and progress. He especially assailed the popular notion that environmental changes could explain changes in social institutions. Nonetheless, his debt to Darwinian and Spencerian notions such as mutual interdependence of all social phenomena is well evident. As with Cooley and Mead in America, Pareto gleaned from the study of Darwin and Spencer a view of the interrelatedness of the various components of the social whole.

Though disparaging the works of Spencer and Comte and belittling his reliance upon their thought, Pareto did openly and frequently acknowledge reliance upon the work of Karl Marx. Especially, Pareto was grateful to Marx for accentuating the importance of the disharmony between the social classes. Pareto wrote of this in his *Cours:* "The socialists are entirely right in emphasizing the great importance of the class struggle, and in stating that it is the great dominant fact in history. In this respect, the works of Marx and Loria deserve the greatest attention."[3] Demeaning social evolution and progress, Pareto extolled the virtues of Marx, even going so far as to suggest that the notion of class struggle had made a significant impact upon his own view of social history. Though highly critical of Marx's utopianism as so much poppy-cock, Pareto admired the careful analysis of the class struggle undertaken by Marx even suggesting in his dialectical scrutiny of dominance and power a kinship with himself and Machiavelli.

Society as a System in Equilibrium
Pareto's conceptualization of society as a system in equilibrium is thought by many to be his greatest contribution to sociological theory. Systems analysis was, of course, derived from his engineering training days at the Institute where he studied analytical mechanics and where he first applied that technique to economic analysis. And the resulting concept of equilibrium was central to that type of systems analysis. Equilibrium is defined as a state X or normal state which, if disturbed by temporary disruptions, will automatically restore balance (or normalcy). Society, Pareto explained, is a system in equilibrium composed of individuals who are exposed to numerous forces which determine the condition of the social system. The two most important forces which Pareto analyzed exhaustively are sentiments and residues. And, he contended, the basic unit for sociological analysis is a simple, single manifestation of these persistent underlying forces.

Pareto's emphasis upon the "system" concept in sociological analysis was ingenous and served well his work and subsequent sociology. Society, he explained, is a system in which all components are interdependent, forming a whole. From physics he had learned this, and thus by analogy he applied to society the fact that change in any particle of the whole necessarily affects the entire composite of society. The "material points of molecules" of the system of society, he explained, are individuals who are affected by social forces with the constant or common properties. By applying this concept of society as a system in equilibrium, Pareto freed sociological theory from the anachronistic shackles of the organistic worldview so troubling to Comte and early sociology, while allowing for the maintenance of the strong points of early theory.

Having established firmly the concept of a social system in equilibrium, Pareto tried to demonstrate its analytical capabilities by calling attention to its ability to assess the overall condition of a society by a tripartite analysis, viz., first, an analysis of the extra-human environment; second, an investigation of those other elements exterior to the society at the time, including other societies and the given society's previous states of well-being or ill-being; and thirdly, scrutiny of the inner elements of the system, such as interests, knowledge, and most importantly, "residues" and "derivations" that are manifestations of "sentiments." All of the implications and ramifications of this rather complex of concepts Pareto naturally could not explore. He did, however, engage in a rather careful and in retrospect in admirable fashion, the classification of residues which at least in part was based upon his knowledge of classical literature and history. Pareto believed and argued persuasively that a great literature roughly reflects actual life experiences at any given time in a rather comprehensive manner. Furthermore, he believed that such classical literature, if it forms the concentrated focus of the investigative scientist, will necessarily preclude his biases from the material being scrutinized. Finally, since the residues present in the literature remain relatively constant, he felt that universal propositions could be derived from a careful analysis of such classical literature. This procedure, it might be mentioned, is the nearest thing to the inductive method in Pareto's work.

In Pareto's treatment of equilibrium, he allowed no place for such cultural phenomena as law, politics, religion, or art. Though he would concede that these elements do play a part in maintaining the social system, he believed they did so only in so far as they manifested basic sentiments intrinsic in society. The role of sentiments is for Pareto essential in the maintenance of social equilibrium. We have already mentioned the fact that, for Pareto, there exist forces that maintain the form or configuration of society through change and stability. In cases of social change, equilibrium in society functions as a dynamic quality. Pareto suggested that in cases where the social system is subjected to controlled or modulated forces exterior to society, forces within that society would push toward the re-establishment of equilibrium bringing the social system back to a functional stability. These inner forces, Pareto believed, consist primarily of the sentiment of revulsion against anything that disturbs society's internal equilibrium. Without this particular sentiment, he believed, every little alteration of the social system would face little obstacle in potentially developing into a force of destruction or decay.

It has been suggested that Pareto's theorem of the "restoration of equilibrium" within social systems has been confirmed by the study of social reactions to crime, the outcome of political and cultural revolutions, and the impact of war on societies. For example, abnormal states of crime or violent political upheavals that disrupt the social order also bring about corresponding changes such as strong counter forces, stern punitive measures or modification of the political system that tend to restore social equilibrium. In each of these cases there is a confirmation of Pareto's intimation about the generally temporary nature of social upheavals and the overall persistence of the quality of social stability in structures and functions.

Behavior and Ideas: A Complex Relationship

Pareto remained fascinated throughout his career with the relational complexity between behavior and ideas. To analyse this complexity was a major preoccupation in his research and even though he considered the task among the most difficult in the science, the rewards merited the venture. For Pareto, a direct causal relationship between theory and action does not exist. Rather, both idea and behavior are caused by a more fundamental psychic element, viz., what Pareto chose to label "sentiment." Though sentiments appear as constants in all human activity, they are evident but vary randomly in ideational processes such as theory-construction and self-justifications. Every mode of behavior, Pareto believed, is justified or vindicated by some theory. But, what is most crucial in analysis is the recognition that in every particular instance the "theoretical justification" is determined more or less by an accident of inventiveness. This random and chance character of justification reduces its value considerably in efforts to analyze behavior.

On the other hand, Pareto was resolutely convinced that value in understanding would come from a sustained concentration of his attention upon the actual theories and belief-systems that regularly function to justify or rationalize non-logical and irrational behavior. One of his overriding concerns was with an

exhaustive critique of non-scientific theories associated with behavior, especially as used to defend a particular human act. No
ideational elements of culture escape his scrutiny, submitting
metaphysical, religious, and moral systems alike to his destructive analysis. He attempts to demonstrate, and succeeds to his
own satisfaction at least, that none of these theory-constructs
have any qualities whatsoever resembling scientific precision in
spite of their respective claims to ultimate truth. Such notions or
ideas as liberty, equality, progress, or the general will are as
devoid of substantive and demonstrative meaning as the sham
rituals and priestly incantations of tribal peoples. Pareto believed
all to be unverifiable because they all are fictitious concoctions
attempting to rationalize and justify behavior which emanate
from the sentiments of social life. The justifications and rationalizations are, in essence, *ex post facto* vindications of sentiment-
ally motivated behavior. The exposing of such social deception
Pareto sees as the fundamental task of sociological analysis. "We
have to see," he wrote in his *Treatise*, "to what extent reality is
disfigured in the theories and descriptions of it that one finds in
the literature of thought. We have an image in a curved mirror;
our problem is to discover the form of the object so altered by
refraction."[4] Action and its motivating theory or idea was what
Pareto most desired to understand.

Logical and Non-logical Action
Behavior, Pareto believed, that is logical is so, both subjectively
and objectively. An action is logical if the end is objectively
attainable and if the means employed are objectively united with
the end within the framework of the best knowledge available.
For an action to be logical, the logical connection between the
means and the end must exist both in the mind of the actor who
performs the act and in objective reality, that is, "from the standpoint of other persons who have a more extensive knowledge."
Non-logical action means simply all human action not falling
within the scope of the logical (which does not mean that they
are necessarily illogical); it is for Pareto a residual category.
Pareto is convinced that truly logical action is very rare indeed.
    Though suggesting that civil law represents a theoretical form
of logical action, Pareto even dubs the behavior of trial judges
as being often non-logical. He argues so because, says he, even

the role of the judge necessarily involves more than the mere logical application of abstract legal rules to specific objective cases. He contends that judicial decisions to a great extent manifest the judge's sentiments and, Pareto points out, any reference to written law is an *ex post facto* explanation of a decision gained in another way. "Court decisions", he wrote in his *Treatise*, "depend largely upon the interests and sentiments operative in a society at a given moment; and also upon individual whims and chance events; and but slightly, and sometimes not at all, upon codes or written law."[5] The analysis of these inner forces operative in the decision-making process is based upon the critical distinction between logical and non-logical action.

Generally speaking, logical actions are those motivated by reasoning while non-logical actions are those that involve to some degree a motivation by sentiment. Since according to Pareto's rigorous definition of logical-experimental method, science covers only a narrow domain of reality, logical behavior can cover only a limited part of the whole range of human behavior. In most cases science cannot help us determine our goals or foresee the consequences of our acts; therefore, the greater part of the human behavior will be non-logical. However, all men want to give an appearance of logic to behavior. Thus by following an inductive procedure in developing his conceptual framework for the analysis of the non-logical element in human behavior, he is able to argue that although individuals most often fail to demonstrate logical action they do have a rather powerful urge to "logicalize" their behavior. In other words, Pareto believed that individuals wish to make their behavior appear logically to follow from a legitimate set of ideas both to themselves (self-deception) and to others (public deceit).

Aron presents Pareto's central thesis in the following diagram:[6]

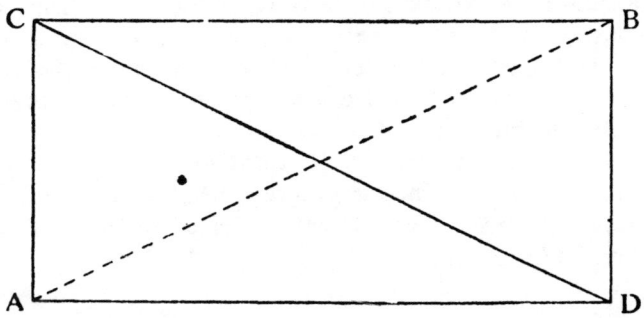

A—The actor's state of mind which we do not know;
B—Creed or a combination of rationalizations, ideologies and
    doctrines;
C—The various expressions of the actors, especially their words;
D—Act or the behavior of the actors.

Reciprocal relations exist between expressions, creed, and acts.
Creed may exercise an influence upon theories by reinforcing
the convictions of those who practise it, as I have remarked.
Creed may also exercise an influence upon acts . . . Non-
logical actions are presented to us in a three-fold form: acts;
theories which justify acts; and, in the case of certain beliefs,
in the form of creeds, which both entertain and express
theories—the whole of these three terms being determined by
a state of mind or a sentiment, the two words being inter-
changeable and designating a reality which we do not know
directly but which we know by observation to be the chief
cause of the manifestation, i.e., theories, creed, or acts.[7]

Residues and Derivations
Although most of human behavior is non-logical, man is a born
reasoner who prefers to believe that his behavior is logical and
determined by his theories; he does not like to think that it is
determined by emotions. So he invents all sorts of "logical" explanations to rationalize his actions. Pareto studied a large number of customs, curious practices, theories, belief-systems, forms
of religious worship, practices of magic or sorcery, doctrines and
dogmas that are found in both archaic and advanced societies.
A careful analysis of such customs, practices and doctrines reveals
a certain element of consistency. Pareto believed for example,
throughout the most diverse civilizations men have assigned a
beneficent or maleficent value to certain objects, places, numbers
or certain days. References to "lucky number," "auspicious
hour," "bad omen," etc., are examples. Men seek to offer pseudo-
logical reasons to logicalize such patterns of behavior. Thus the
phenomenon under observation involves two fundamental elements: (1) the *constant element* (or element *a*) of the concrete
phenomenon under consideration, that is man's tendency to establish relations between things or to attribute meanings and omens
to numbers, places, hours, etc.; (2) those numerous and ingenious theories by which men seek to rationalize their actions. The
former, to use Pareto's terminology, is called *residues* and the
latter *derivations*.

Pareto writes:

> The element a corresponds perhaps to certain instincts of
> man, or rather of men, because a has no objective existence
> and differs in different men, and it is probably because it
> corresponds to these instincts that it is almost constant in
> phenomena. The element b corresponds to the work accom-
> plished by the mind to account for element a; this is why it
> is much more variable, since it reflects the work of the imagi-
> nation. If part a corresponds to certain instincts, it is very far
> from including all of them. This is clear from the manner in
> which it was determined: we analyzed rationalizations and
> looked for the constant element. Therefore, we can only have
> found those instincts which give rise to rationalizations; we
> cannot have encountered those which are not concealed by
> rationalizations. There remain then all the simple appetites,
> tastes, and inclinations and in the social realm that very im-
> portant category known as self-interest.[8]

Pareto continued to emphasize the difference between human
behavior as such and rationalistic explanations of that behavior.
Rationalistic explanation of human action assumes that human
beings first think and formulate their ideas and theories and only
after this intellectual function is accomplished do they act in com-
pliance with such formulations. According to Pareto, quite the
opposite is actually what occurs, viz., behavior does not follow
but precedes theory, or in other words, "commission precedes
rationalization." Pareto's growing cynicism about mankind ema-
nated from his rather bold indictment of man's integrity, his
honor, his ability and willingness to think before acting. Most
human activity, Pareto argued, follows this non-logical scenario. In
summary, *derivations* are those changing elements which account
for the development of non-scientific theories or rationalizations
of human behavior while *residues* are those relatively unchanging and generally permanent elements. Residues, about which
Pareto wrote much, were conceived of as manifestations of sentiments or at least as corresponding to them and not as equivalents
of sentiments. Pareto believed that residues, those permanent elements in man's rationalization of his behavior, are intermediary
between sentiments which are beyond our direct knowledge in
analysis and belief systems, and concomitant behavior which are
readily susceptible to scrutiny and analysis. And, whereas residues
are related to what Pareto thought of as human instincts though
not synonymous with them, derivations on the other hand only

appear when there is reasoning, argumentation, and ideological justification of human action. For example, if you like Chinese food, it is only a matter of taste, but if you are to develop ingenious theories regarding the superiority of Chinese cooking, then it is a matter of derivations.

More can be said on this point of non-logical action's relationship to residues and derivations. Residues, Pareto explained, are motivating forces stemming directly from sentiments. As manifestations of sentiments, they are less deeply buried in the individual, they are more on the surface and thus discernible for analysis of the relationship between ideas and behavior of an individual, of what he "does" and "says." Residues Pareto considers as a fundamental analytical concept of sociology, whereas the analysis of sentiments belongs to the field of pure psychology. Derivations, then, are in effect rationalizations or attempts to give a logical explanation for non-logical behavior.

In his *Treatise*, Pareto reiterates over and over again what he thinks to be the most important fact in the sociological analysis of the complex relationship between behavior and theory, between action and idea. Pareto cautions the serious minded person never to take ideas at their face value, that is, instead of just listening to what people say about their actions, look rather in a deeply probing fashion for the well-springs of those actions below the level of verbal explanation. And for this, Pareto explains, we must look to residues, which he has classified into six groupings which correspond more or less to certain instincts or emotional propensities of mankind. They are: (1) the instinct of combinations, or the faculty of associating things; (2) the residue of the persistence of aggregates or what might be called the conservative tendency; (3) the residue of the manifestation of sentiments through exterior acts such as self-expression; (4) the residue of sociability, or the drive to compose societies and to impose uniform conduct; (5) the residue of personal integrity leading to actions that restore lost integrity such as those forming the source of criminal law; and finally, (6) the sexual residue. Such a classification, Aron feels, "proves dramatically that human behavior is structured, that residues are not a random affair, that motivation for behavior is not anarchic, that there is an internal order to human nature, and that one can discover a kind of logic in the non-logico-experimental behavior of men in society."

Though Pareto was careful in his explorations of residues, his analysis of derivations is much less detailed. Derivations, for Pareto, are conceived of as surface manifestations ostensibly as explanations of underlying forces in social life. Examples are numerous. The child is told that he must obey because daddy wants him to. We are asked to accept a theory or doctrine because Aristotle or the Church expounded it. The ruling elites justify their positions of power in the name of the General Will, Divine Right, social solidarity, freedom, democracy or national integration. There are essentially four categories of derivations in Pareto's system: (1) derivations of assertion, including affirmations of facts and sentiments; (2) derivations of authority whether of individuals, groups, customs, or divinities; (3) derivations that are in accord with and therefore serve to maintain common sentiments and principles; and finally, (4) derivations of verbal proof, such as in the form of metaphors and analogies.

As already noted, Pareto's overarching analytical interest was non-logical action defended as rational by the actor, or more formally put, Pareto focused on behavior which is conceived of as logical by the actor but appears objectively non-logical to the observer. In other words, the observer perceives the so-called logical action culminating in consequences other than those being pursued by the actor. Pareto addressed the issue in this manner: "The experimental truth of a theory and its social utility are different things. A theory that is experimentally true may now be advantageous, now detrimental to society; and the same applies to a theory that is experimentally false."[9] And in his *The Mind and Society*, he puts it this way: "A theory may be in accord with experience and yet be harmful to society, or in discord with experience and yet be beneficial to society."[10] Therefore, Pareto was the first to point out the dangers of his probing analysis of behavior and ideas, particularly as residues tend to surface with sentiments in such research.

Pareto was anxious to illustrate the utility and effectiveness of his analytical use of his theory. He demonstrated, for example, how the same residue can produce a wide spectrum of belief systems or derivations, thereby driving home his contention that individuals deceive themselves when they believe that they take a given course of action on the basis of a particular theory. They do not, says Pareto, in spite of their quick rationalizations to the contrary. He uses an illustration to corroborate his point: "A Chinese, a Muslim, a Calvinist, a Catholic, a Kantian, a Hegelian, a Materialist, all refrain from stealing; but each gives a different explanation for his conduct." Since, says Pareto, each of these good fellows behaves alike—at least in this particular instance—yet gives radically different explanations for their actions, we must conclude that the true cause of such behavior actually lies out of the sight of the actor and below his explanation. The real cause of the similar behavior must be found, not in the verbal explanation of the actor himself, but rather in the constancy of a residue underlying the different derivations. Pareto concluded that all these adherents of different belief systems have a common need to maintain the integrity of their personality and to preserve their self-regard. Therefore, says Pareto, residue from the fifth classification, viz., personal integrity, best explains the true reasons for his behavior while the religious explanation is mere *ex post facto* rationalization.

Yet, Pareto, while taking on the whole world as it were in his attack upon the integrity and authenticity of rational explanation of behavior would not argue with a believer. He contended that to discuss the truth of a doctrine was useless with a believer in that doctrine. Only a scientific strategy that allows us to trace the multiplicity of ideologies and theories to their common source in basic residues can contribute to a building up of the science and produce in men an insight into themselves and others.

Theory of Social Utility
Pareto's most notable observations about the inter-relationship of logical and non-logical behavior and about their relation to the social system as such are to be found in his consideration of the theory of social utility. This theory, one of the first and most important formulations of the concept of the limitations of welfare economics, began with an economic foundation, viz., his doctrine of maximum satisfaction, and then built upon it the social dimensions of utility in social action. Moving away from classical liberal economics which assumed that total benefits for a community simply involved a sum total of the benefits derived by each individual member, Pareto made a crucial distinction between the maximum utility *of* and the maximum utility *for*, the collectivity. The maximum utility for a collectivity means the maximum

possible private satisfaction for each individual member. This refers to the point beyond which it is impossible to increase the utility of an individual member without decreasing that of another. This is the type of utility considered by the economist. Since the economist can consider only the wants of individuals who are dissimilar and whose private satisfactions cannot be added up to yield a measure of the maximum utility for the collectivity as a whole, Pareto argued that in economics a community cannot be regarded as a person. On the other hand in sociology a collectivity is considered as the equivalent of a person or at least as a unity. Therefore, the concept of the maximum utility *of* the group or society as a whole makes sense.

The maximum utility *for* a community is not necessarily the same as maximum utility *of* a community; indeed, they may not coincide too often. As Aron points out, "There is a radical discrepancy between the notion of maximum satisfaction for the greatest possible number of individuals and the notion of the power or glory of the collectivity: the most prosperous society is not necessarily the most powerful or the most glorious."[11] For example, while Japan was a great military power in 1937, the situation hardly represented maximum utility *for* the collectivity because the standard of living of the Japanese population was relatively low and the political regime authoritarian. But today's Japan has the highest rate of growth in gross national product of any nation in the world, a stable democracy, greater degree of individual freedom and a very high standard of living but Japan is no longer a military power. Similarly the richest nation on earth with the highest per capita income, which represents the maximum utility *of* the collectivity as a whole may contain great inequalities in income distribution and major pockets of poverty, thus demonstrating serious divergencies between utilities accruing to a total social system and maximum satisfactions of individuals and sub-groups.

Pareto cautions that the governing elites often obfuscate the distinction between the maximum utility *of* and the maximum utility *for* a community in order to make it appear as if subject individuals would benefit from certain measures initiated by the elite when this is in fact seldom the case. Ruling elites manipulate the masses and exhort them to make sacrifices for the common good so that they can justify their actions which, in fact, are designed to further their own interests.

Pareto observed:

> The ruling classes often times show a confusion of a problem
> of maximum utility *of* the community and a problem of maxi-
> mum utility *for* the community. They (try) to make the "sub-
> ject" classes believe that there is an indirect utility which,
> when properly taken into account, turns the sacrifice required
> of them into a gain . . . In reality, in cases such as these, non-
> logical impulse can serve to induce the subject classes to for-
> get the maximum utility of the community, or merely of the
> ruling classes.[12]

Both Durkheim and Pareto rejected utilitarian and individualistic notions and stressed the need to consider the requirements of the social system as a whole. But they differed on
methodological ground. Durkheim believed that the needs of the
system could be determined objectively and scientifically. For
Pareto, however, the maximum utility *of* a collectivity is not and
cannot be the object of logico-experimental determination. Since
a collectivity is not a person and the values and preferences of
individual members are not all the same, the maximum utility *of*
a collectivity can only be determined by an arbitrary decision
that chooses a particular criterion such as power, glory and prosperity, a decision that cannot be reached scientifically.

Elites: Foxes and Lions in Circulation

Not reticent and being somewhat liberated from the liberal
humanism of democratic egalitarianism, Pareto was quick to
point out that people are no more equal intellectually and morally
than they are physically. And, he chose to call "elites" those who
are the most capable in any particular group. "Elites" as a concept is devoid of any moral or honorific connotations in Pareto's
writings. The term simply denotes "a class of the people who
have the highest indices in their branch of activity." The successful businessman, the successful artist, the successful writer and
the successful professor are all elites. Owing to already identified
predispositions, Pareto had little confidence that the elite positions would actually coincide with superior capacity in only perfectly open societies which have perfect social mobility, and of
these none actually exist in the real world. In view of the inevitable
divergencies between the correctly ascribed position and the
actual achievement and capacity of elites, Pareto strongly defends
maximum social mobility and careers open to all risers. The

danger he saw was where the elite positions which were once occupied by individuals of real talent would in the course of time be pre-empted by individuals devoid of such talents.

Pareto further divided the elite class into two categories: "a governing elite, comprising individuals who, directly or indirectly play some considerable part in government, and a non-governing elite comprising the rest". A very unequal distribution of power and prestige enables the few to govern the many. Following the Machiavellian formula, Pareto states that the elites are able to manipulate and control the masses by resorting to two methods: force or fraud which corresponds to Machiavelli's famous antithesis between the "Lions" and the "Foxes."

The foxes are elites abundantly endowed with residues of the first class which includes the propensities in social groups to adapt flexibly to environmental or situational exigencies. They are capable of innovation and experiment, prefer materialistic to idealistic goals, but lack fidelity to principles and use strategies that vary from emotional appeal to unadulterated fraud. They maintain their power by cunning propaganda and by multiplying politico-financial combinations. The lions, on the other hand, are conservative elites in whom the second class of residues (persistence of aggregates) predominate. They have faith and ideology; they display group loyalty and class solidarity; they gain and retain power by the use of force.

In every society there are potential and dissatisfied leaders who must be either absorbed into the ranks of the governing elites or eliminated by them. Further, every society is disturbed by fluctuations in the frequency of residues of the first and second classes. When an elite has been in power for a long time, one of two things is bound to happen. Either it develops a tendency to close ranks against potential elites. Or, it becomes dominated by the residues of the first class and increasingly reluctant to employ force. They concern themselves with intellectual combinations and sometimes higher pleasures of civilization and art. They become more tolerant and moderate and lose the propensity toward forceful action required by the social order. When this happens, the family of the lions will mobilize the masses against the elite foxes. History is, to use Pareto's celebrated expression, "a graveyard of aristocracies." Ruling elites emerge, dominate, fall into decadence and will be replaced by new, non-decadent elites.

Pareto further cautioned that when governing elites attempt to close themselves to the inflow of new and capable elements from the social strata below, that is to say, when the circulation of elites is inhibited, the social equilibrium is altered and the social order experiences decay. An imbalance results from this situation, and unless the governing elite "finds ways to assimilate the exceptional individuals who come to the front in the subject classes," either by rapid social change or violent revolution the old elite is replaced by a new one capable of governing. At this point, Pareto was quick to point out that owing to the power for social change concentrated in the elites of society, the distribution of residues is much more important for social stability and progress than among the rest of society.

Pareto believed that in the European societies of his day the foxes were in the ascendancy. Political wheelers and dealers and unscrupulous lawyers seek to maintain themselves in positions of domination by the use of fraud and tend to lose their capacity for violence. But he also saw a new kind of elite emerging, the family of lions, men of conservatism and persistence who are capable of forceful action and who would sweep the reign of foxes aside and establish a new order of stability and equilibrium.

Corresponding to the lions and the foxes among the political elites, there are "rentiers" and "speculators" in the economic realm. Pareto writes:

> In the speculator group Class I residues predominate, in the rentier group, Class II residues . . . The two groups perform functions of differing utility in society. The (speculator) group is primarily responsible for change, for economic and social progress. The (rentier) group, instead, is a powerful element in stability, and in many cases counteracts the dangers attending the adventurous capers of the (speculators). A society in which (the speculators) predominate lacks stability, lives in a state of shaky equilibrium that may be upset by a slight accident from within or from without.[13]

Pareto has consistently maintained that a stable social order requires a judicious mixture in top elites of men with Class I and Class II residues. That is, judicious combinations of lions and foxes in the political realm, and of speculators and rentiers in the economic realm would maintain the social system in equilibrium by providing the necessary checks and balances.

On the strictly scientific level, Pareto's theoretical procedures were conservative in a positive sense—viz., he employed simple analytical categories and proceeded step by step toward an inductively based generalization. For Pareto, of course, belief in social evolution or progress was utter nonsense. Human society, he believed, was bound to eternally repeat the cycle from rule by lions to rule by foxes. Equilibrium is always being sought for and realized more or less in the process. Nothing new exists under the sun; all human effort is vanity; utopian dreams are so much nothingness.

Summary and Appreciation

Pareto brought to sociology an impressive array of skills and interests, and as he constructed his methodological orientation and its concomitant theoretical formulations, he drew from his whole repertoire of knowledge. Standing firmly within the matrix of the classical literature and history of his traditional Italian education, Pareto quickly and creatively grasped abstract mathematics, applying its functions to mechanical engineering and social system analysis with equal ease and grace. But of equal importance was his rather conscious effort to link Italian Machiavellian social and political theory in its traditional form with the Positivism of Comte, Spencer, and the social Darwinists of the nineteenth century. The effort, requiring a genius in synthetic thought and intellectual gymnastics resulted in Pareto's rather impressive legacy of good work and sound theory.

The Machiavellian tradition of Italian social thought was ever in the foreground of Pareto's work. For this tradition, the initial step in social thought did not begin with man as a social being woven about with self-spun entrapments of human relations but rather with the philosophical question of the nature of man himself. According to the Italian school of philosophical anthropology, mankind possesses certain unchanging characteristics, and the social philosopher and theorist should concern himself primarily with accentuating and analyzing this human nature with an eye on understanding and perceiving how such a universal nature affects a particular mode of activity in a variety of situations. For example, one should be keen to learn how the power of some individual is exercised over others and to understand the ability of the few to impose their will upon the many. These questions or problems constitute the fundamental focus of theoretical work

within Italian social thought from Machiavelli to at least the
days of Pareto and later.

Obviously, Pareto is by proud admission a true disciple of
Machiavelli and a strong proponent of Machiavellian social
theory albeit modified and refined by Pareto's reading of the
British and French positivists and early sociologists. With Machiavelli, Pareto wanted to construct a science of power—a science
which would ferret out the roots of human action grounded in
man's nature. For Pareto, this science would explain how the
few in society are able to govern the many. As with Machiavelli,
so with Pareto: the answer to this question constitutes the driving
force in their researches and the *raison d'etre* of their social
thought.

Pareto heaps sarcasm upon the humanitarians who are eager
to defend the rights of criminals and forget the sufferings of their
victims. Exaggeration of humanitarianism precedes collective
violence and great massacres which will lead to the establishment
of a strong authority that is indifferent to the sufferings of others.
Of course, Pareto is not advocating violence but he remained
convinced that both excessive humanitarianism and extreme
brutality are dangerous to social equilibrium. He is merciless
toward those moralists who try to improve the morals of their
fellow citizens or recommend an "acceptable" code of conduct.
Pareto is equally critical of the "decadent" bourgeoisie, the elite
that has lost the sense of its own interests, that is wedded to
blind pity and excessive humanism, that has lost its proclivity
toward violence and forceful action necessitated by the exigencies
of social order but seeks to maintain itself in power by ruse and
propaganda. When the aristocracy of foxes degenerates like this,
a new family of lions who have vision, courage, idealism and
above all the readiness to use force when necessary will emerge
and form an oligarchical government. Pareto maintains that in all
societies the masses were always governed by a privileged minority.
Such a minority must consist of people who are capable of performing the functions effectively and forcefully, and the tender-
hearted who want to eschew all forms of violence must step aside.

Such were the pronouncements of Pareto that led many to
characterize him as a doctrinaire of authoritarian regimes or a
theoretician of Italian fascism. Indeed, many Italian Fascist intellectuals called themselves followers of Pareto and presented them-

selves as the non-decadent bourgeoisie, the generations of lions, destined to take over the reins of power from the decadent aristocracy of foxes. They defended an oligarchical form of government and defended violence. However, as Raymond Aron points out, it is unfair to treat Pareto as a doctrinaire for any particular type of regime. If Pareto can be interpreted as a Fascist, he can also be interpreted as a liberal democrat. He provides arguments for many regimes, and his writings can be interpreted in many ways. Just as those who are in power can legitimize their position with reference to Pareto's analysis, those who are outside of it can readily find justification in it. Aron has ably demonstrated that in terms of his economic doctrine Pareto is a liberal and on the political level he is at once authoritarian and moderate. "The regime most desirable for all, at least according to his conception of the good of all, is a regime in which those who govern have the ability to make decisions but do not seek to control everything, and above all do not seek to impose upon the citizens ... what they must think and believe. In other words, Pareto would have favored a strong and liberal government, from the economic as well as the scientific point of view."[14] Aron summarizes his assessment of Pareto in the following words:

> ... by comparing his experience as an engineer and economist with his observation of the political scene, Pareto conceives what is the fundamental theme of his work, the antimony between logical and non-logical actions, and in so doing he discovers that the worst illusion is that of the liberals and democrats who imagined that the advance of reason was about to lead humanity to a phase without precedent. Pareto thinks against the erroneous convictions of the previous generation. Observing what actual democracy has become and how representative institutions function, he concludes with a sort of ironic pleasure that nothing has changed: it is still the privileged minorities who run the show. They constantly change their derivations, i.e., their justifying theory, but the essentials are unchanged. Every political regime is oligarchial and every political man is either selfish or naive. Which of the two is preferable? It all depends on circumstances, but very often the less naive, that is, the less honest, is the more useful to society.[15]

Throughout his productive but tragic career, Pareto held confidently to the belief that his theory of residues and derivations was his greatest contribution to the development and furtherance of the discipline of sociology. In spite of that belief, the scholar community disagrees almost as a consensus, pointing to several other achievements as having greater and longer lasting effect upon the science. For example, he developed the first really precise statement of the idea of a social system that can be analyzed in terms of the inter-relationships and reciprocal dependencies between components. His theory of elitism and the circulation of elites has continued to inspire careful and critical investigations of the functional nature of the upper strata of government and industrial classes. These contributions are real and important, and though much of what he wrote during his last years were the embittered cyñicisms of a lonely old man, many of his ideas are still significant for our own time.

Pareto insisted that a logico-experimental study of non-logical behavior should be morally and politically neutral, free of value judgments and sentiments. But this is a maxim that Pareto himself did not follow, for his own major work, *Treatise*, is full of sentiments, value judgments and stinging sarcasm.

Pareto's main contributions are his insistence that sociology must be governed strictly by scientific canons and the concept of society as a system in imperfect equilibrium. He also, of course, contributed to the furtherance of sociological theory by distinguishing between truth and utility—i.e., a belief widely held by society may not be true while serving a useful social purpose. Talcott Parsons has said that most of the neglect of Pareto has not been the irrelevance of his work but rather the nastiness of his personality. He has written that "it seems fair to suggest that his (Pareto's) reputation and influence have not been as great as they intrinsically deserve." Possibly, Parsons suggests, Pareto should be ranked in importance just under Durkheim and Weber in his own time. Ever since the publication of C. Wright Mills' *Power Elite* (1959), there has been a revival of interest in Pareto's work in America. Testimony for such a claim is seen in the appearance of such recent works as Suzanne Keller's *Beyond the Ruling Class* (1963) and T.B. Bottomore's *Elites and Society* (1964). Bitter, cynical, and sad, Pareto wrote in solitude about elites and social equilibrium, and his genius for analysis lives on in modern sociological theory and research. His thought transcended his personality.

5

EMILE DURKHEIM

LIFE AND TIMES

Emile Durkheim (1858-1917) was not only the first real practitioner of the new science of society emerging during the last quarter of the nineteenth century, he was the first professor of sociology as well. Whereas Comte had come from amongst the French radical aristocracy and never gained legitimate entry into academia, Durkheim forged such a path into the halls of the Sorbonne that the French intelligentsia stepped aside while throwing garlands in his path of entry. And, whereas Spencer had spurned academic opportunities in deference to his chosen life of the private scholar, Durkheim created for himself the first course and first chair in sociology to be recognized anywhere in the world. Indeed, if Comte and even Spencer can be rightfully called fathers of the discipline, Durkheim must assuredly be called the grandfather. A man who devoted his entire life to the great moral questions of his time, Durkheim wanted to make a contribution to the moral and political consolidation of his country's new and struggling but promising government, the Third Republic of France. And he determined to do this by a solid scientific training and study of the science of society. It was for him, said Durkheim, "imperative to construct a scientific sociological system, not as an end in itself, but as a means for the moral direction of society."

In the village of Epinal in the Vosges near Strasbourg, France, Emile Durkheim was born in 1858, the son of a rabbi and in a family which boasted a long line of rabbis in this north eastern frontier of France. Like his father before him, young Durkheim expected to become a rabbi. His training began early in Hebrew and Old Testament and the Talmud. His Jewish parents nurtured their son's ambition in the strongly homogeneous and cohesive community of Jews. The Jewish minority status and his early contact with the disastrous Franco-Prussian War made a major impression upon Durkheim, which is reflected in his constant fascination with the study of group solidarity. He was confirmed (Bar Mitzvah) at the age of thirteen, but having shortly thereafter fallen under the persuasive influence of a Catholic teacher, Durkheim experimented with his religious sensibilities, eventually while still a teenager, gave up any affiliation with organized religion and became a passive agnostic, unable to settle in his own mind whether or not God exists and what religious tradition was true.

A brilliant student in the College d'Epinal, he received many honors and prizes for his budding scholarship as a young intellectual. On his third attempt, he passed his entrance examinations to the prestigious Ecole Normale Superieure and was admitted in 1879. Early on in his student life, his peers recognized Durkheim's brilliance and in congenial fashion and custom, he was nicknamed the "metaphysician" owing to his propensity to philosophize upon every possible topic of conversation.

Among his classmates and fellow university students were such notables as Henri Bergson, Jean Jaures, and Pierre Janet. Though his primary training was in philosophy, his strong personal interest was in politics and sociology. Because he was so astute in the application of his fledgling scientific skills of political and social analysis and partly because of his rebellious demeanor vis-a-vis the more traditional ways of doing things at the Ecole, Durkheim was not always in favor with the university establishment. Upon graduation he taught philosophy in several provincial Lycees in the neighborhood of Paris, the University, from 1882 to 1887. Determined in his professional growth, Durkheim took a leave of absence from teaching to do further study in Germany from 1885-1886, primarily in Berlin and Leipzig where he was specially impressed with the scientific precision in the experiments of the renowned psychologist Wilhelm Wundt.

During this time, Durkheim began to publish articles, first on the German academic life and then critical articles on various kinds of scholarship thereby gaining considerable recognition from the French academy. In 1887, he was appointed to the faculty of

the University of Bordeaux where the first course in social science
in all of France was created for him to teach. Shortly thereafter,
he married Louise Dreyfus, a Jewish girl from a strong traditional
family. They had two children, Marie and Andre. Little is known
about family life except that Louise seems to have been a strong
and supportive wife and encouraging mother.

Durkheim alongwith Max Weber must be credited with founding the modern phase of sociological theory. It began with his
first book, *Division of Labor*, submitted as his French doctoral
thesis at the Sorbonne alongwith his Latin doctoral thesis on
Montesquieu in 1893. Durkheim established a broad framework
for analysis of social systems that has remained central to sociology and anthropology to the present day. The focus of his work
was on the nature of the social system and the relation of that system to the personality of the individual. The French philosopher
Rousseau, a protagonist of "democratic individualism," influenced Durkheim greatly, especially Rousseau's famous concept of
the *volonte generale* which provided a conception of social solidarity directly dependent upon neither politics nor economics. As
reflected in his close ties with Rousseau as well as Descartes,
Durkheim was strongly rooted in French intellectual history and
was admittedly close to Saint-Simon and Auguste Comte as well
as to his university teacher, the noted scholar Fustel de Coul-
anges. Durkheim's genius was somewhat indicated in his ability
to strike an intermediary position between British empiricism and
utilitarianism of Spencer and German idealism of Hegel and
others. To a great extent, modern sociology is a product of the
synthesis of elements that have figured most prominently in these
two traditions. Two years after his monumental work on the
Division of Labor (1893), he published his second major study,
The Rules of Sociological Method (1895), completing his Bordeaux trilogy in 1897 with his incomparable *Suicide*.

Because of the tremendous impact Durkheim was having in
French universities and given the increasing numbers of France's
finest young intellectuals who began to cluster around him, Durkheim became convinced that a literary forum was necessary
both to accommodate the burgeoning of sociological scholarship
and to further enhance the already accelerating recognition sociology was receiving across the spectrum of the French academy.
For this purpose, Durkheim founded in 1898, while at Bordeaux,

the *L'Annee Sociologique*, a scholarly journal under his own editorship that became the organ of research, debate, and discussion among not only Durkheim and his immediate followers but of all accepted sociological work going on in France.

Four years later and as every one was anticipating, Durkheim was called to the Sorbonne, Paris's great university and headquarters of the French intelligentsia. The chair created for him in 1902 was in sociology and education, and though education was soon dropped from his prestigious title, Durkheim remained interested in the application of sociology to the field of education throughout his career.

Though he continued to publish scholarly research in *L'Annee Sociologique*, he concentrated most of his energies in teaching and discussions with the legion of young sociologists he would train over the remainder of his career. His final and in many respects provocative book came fifteen years after his previous study and ten years after going to the Sorbonne, entitled, *The Elementary Forms of the Religious Life* (1912). It was the ripe harvest of a long process of intensive cultivation. Religion, once a major passion for him in childhood, became once again a major pre-occupation, not so much as an unwitting participant but as a scrutinizing observer.

The tragedy of the First World War was a very great blow to France, and Durkheim, a man so much committed to the understanding of social solidarity, felt the strain acutely. Half of his class from his Sorbonne student days were killed in combat. Keeping the university activities going in the name of truth and scholarship ' became increasingly difficult. Distraction, anxieties, despair over loss of friends, students, relations, and colleagues intensified. And, just before Christmas, 1915, Durkheim was notified that his only son, Andre, had died in a Bulgarian hospital of wounds taken in battle. The pride and hope of Durkheim had been shattered by the ravages of war. The loss was too great to bear, his health failed, and in less than two years at the age of fifty-nine, Durkheim died on November 15, 1917. He was a giant among men yet demoralized by the loss of his son killed in battle, a battle to ensure social stability and the way of life of the French people.

MAJOR THEORIES

Social Order and Social Facts

As already mentioned above, Durkheim lived through a very turbulent period in French history—the disastrous war with the Prussians, the chaos and socio-political turmoil which inevitably followed, and the instability and internal conflicts of the Third Republic. His overriding concern as a moral man and scientist was with the social order. Though very differently perceived, social order also constituted the primary focus of attention from both Auguste Comte and Herbert Spencer. Not unlike his fore-bearers in this fledgling science of society, Durkheim believed that the traditional sources of morality upon which the social order was built, especially religion, were no longer viable or valid without serious and rational alterations. The new source of moral integration, so necessary for the establishment and stability of society, would be found in the discipline designed to scientifically analyze social order, stability, and continuity, viz., that of sociology. His program of study was concerned with the sources of social order and disorder, the forces that make for regulation or deregulation in the body social.

Durkheim clearly understood that *order* in a concrete system of contractual relations in which the market figured prominently, could not be accounted for in the terms set forth by Herbert Spencer's monumental but misdirected works. Durkheim's initial orientation to the study of society was two-fold—i.e., substance and method. The substantive aspect concerning the problem of order in a type of system we might call economic individualism may be found in his *The Division of Labor in Society* (1893). The methodological framework for all of his subsequent work was developed in his *The Rules of Sociological Method* (1895). What so distinctively sets Durkheim apart from his forebearers is not just the development of a scientific method utilized in monumental studies of labor, suicide, and religion, but due to his successful analysis of social facts while facing up to the methodological problems of using empirical research in a scientific study of society.

From the outset, Durkheim's orientation toward the study of society required that economic and psychological reductionism be eschewed in deference to the *sui generis* quality of social facts,

collective "ways of acting, thinking, and feeling that present the
noteworthy property of existing outside the individual consciousness." Social facts, argues Durkheim, are not merely manifestations of economic realities analyzable using marketing graphs
and tables, nor are they merely characteristic manifestations of
psychological realities which must be analyzed by studying individual personalities. Social facts are first and foremost "things"
which are social in nature. And, therefore, a science of the social
facts is needed to correctly analyze them. There are four major
characteristics of social facts: (1) they have distinctive social
characteristics and determinants which are not amenable to explanation on either the biological or psychological level; (2) they
are external to the individual; (3) they endure through time out-
lasting any set or group of individuals; and (4) they are, in Durkheim's own words, "endowed with coercive power, by virtue
of which they impose themselves upon him, independent of his
individual will".

Durkheim, in the development of his scientific method, was
insistent that the study of social facts cannot employ the method
of introspection—sociology is neither metaphysical philosophy
nor subjectivistic psychology. Sociologists must seek objectivity.
Facts, he argued, can be gathered by observing external and immediately visible phenomena, e.g., religious affiliation, marital
status, suicide rate, economic occupation, etc. Institutions, says
Durkheim by way of illustration, are real facts because they have
an external existence apart from individuals and provide constraints upon their social constituents. Sociology, therefore, can
be defined as the science of institutions, of their genesis and their
functions. Social facts, of which institutions are constituted, must
be treated as "things", as empirical phenomena, not as concepts.
"Things," he argued in an extended passage in his The Rules of
Sociological Method, "include all objects of knowledge that cannot be conceived by purely mental activity, those that require for
their conception data from outside the mind, from observations
and experiments, those which are built up from the more external
and immediately accessible characteristics to the less visible and
more profound."[1]

If sociology is minimally defined as the study of institutions,
and institutions are constituted of social facts, then sociology is
fundamentally the study of social facts, such as public morality,

family and religious observances, and rules of professional behavior. These realities are what Durkheim thought of as social
facts and the study of these is the proper dominion of sociology.
Diametrically opposed to Spencer's radical individualism and
nominalism, Durkheim supported an equally radical sociological
realism in which the only ultimate social reality is found in the
group, not in the individual. As we have seen, for Durkheim,
social facts are irreducible to individual facts so that in social
life, some facts, the uniquely "social facts, are inexplicable in
terms of and-irreducible to either psychological or physiological
analysis." Since social facts impose themselves upon the individual and control him by force from without, their nature is different from that of the individual facts. We can restrain our impulses,
emotions and habits, for their process is centrifugal. But the
process of social constraint is centripetal. "The former are elaborated in the individual consciousness and then tend to exter-
nalize themselves; the latter are at first external to the individual,
whom they tend to fashion in their image from without."[2]

This strong position nurtured a concern of Durkheim in what
he called the collective conscience or consciousness which implied
both mental and moral qualities. His intention in the use and
analysis of the collective mental and moral phenomena approaches
modern conceptions of the role of culture in social life, especially as employed by social and cultural anthropologists. Within
this framework, Durkheim developed the concept of social integration—the convergence of moral and mental elements in maintaining social order. One major element of integration is the
extent to which various members interact with one another. Participation in rituals, for example, is likely to draw members of
religious groups into common activities that bind them together,
or work activities that depend on differentiated yet complementary tasks bind workers to the work group. The stronger the
credo—political, religious, intellectual—of a group, the more
unified it is likely to be, and therefore better able to provide an
environment that will effectively insulate its members from per-
turbing and frustrating experiences.

Social facts, explained Durkheim, and especially moral rules,
become effective guides and controls of conduct only to the extent that they become internalized in the consciousness of individuals, while continuing to exist independently of individuals.

Constraint, Durkheim says, is a moral obligation to obey a rule—
society is "something beyond us and something in ourselves." A
significant focus in Durkheim's study of order is that constraints,
whether of laws or customs, come into play whenever social
demands are being violated. These sanctions are imposed on
individuals; they channel and direct their desires and propensities.
A social fact can, hence, be defined in this context as "every way
of acting, fixed or not, capable of exercising on the individual an
external constraint." Radical individualism, like economic affluence, explains Durkheim, "deceives us into believing that we
depend on ourselves only." As is evident, Durkheim's general
interest in order and constraint led him directly to a study, not
only of affluence and labor, but of suicide and religion.

Social Solidarity
Durkheim's sociological realism was a frontal attack upon Spencerian individualism and much of what it stood for. Comte's social
physic had been closer to a true portrayal of reality than Spencer's
apologia for the individual vis-a-vis society. Durkheim meant to
show that a Spencerian approach to the social realm did not stand
up before the court of evidence or the court of reason even if it
was well received by the liberal intelligentsia of England and
much of Europe as well as America. Modern society, reasoned
the French sociologist, seems to contain the potentialities for
individualism *within* social regulation.

The theories relating to social solidarity were developed in his
first book, *The Division of Labor in Society* (1893). However,
before we discuss the forms of solidarity, a few concepts have to
be explained. A crucial concept in Durkheim's theory of solidarity
is the collective conscience which is the sum total of beliefs and
sentiments common to the average members of society and forming a system in its own right. This collective conscience, a distinct
reality which persists through time and unites generations, is a
product of human similarities. "It is, thus, an entirely different
thing from particular consciences, although it can be realized
only through them. It is the psychical type of society, a type which
has its properties, its conditions of existence, its mode of development, just as individual types, although in a different way."[3]
The strengths and independence of the collective conscience are
strongest when similarities among individuals in society are most

pronounced. The collective conscience is so strong and accentuated in primitive societies that the common conscience blankets individual differences. The strength of the collective conscience is indicated by such things as drastic reactions against violations of group institutions, e.g., the severe criminal law and constraints against mores in primitive society.

Durkheim also distinguished between two types of law—repressive and restitutive. The former is punitive and severely punishes any breach of social rules. It invokes a passionate reaction because crime is thought of as an offence against collective conscience. The restitutive law, on the other hand, is cooperative and its only aim is to restore things to order when a misdeed has been committed. The rules with a restitutive sanction either do not totally derive from the collective conscience, or are only feeble states of it. Whereas repressive law corresponds to the heart, the centre of the collective conscience, restitutive law corresponds to a special domain of the collective order. Thus, "the relations governed by cooperative law with restitutive sanctions and the solidarity which they express, result from the division of social labor."⁴ Since they correspond to special tasks, they are peripheral to common conscience. Therefore, the rules which determine them cannot have the transcendent activity or superior force which governs the repressive laws.

Durkheim identified two forms of solidarity: mechanical and organic.

Mechanical solidarity is a solidarity of resemblance. People are homogeneous, mentally and morally; they feel the same emotions, cherish the same values, and hold the same things sacred. Communities are, therefore, uniform and non-atomized. Durkheim suggested that mechanical solidarity prevailed to the extent that "ideas and tendencies common to all members of the society are greater in number and intensity than those which pertain personally to each member." He explained that this solidarity grows only in inverse ratio to personality. Solidarity, he suggested, which comes from likeness "is at its maximum when the collective conscience completely envelops our whole conscience and coincides in all points with it." Thus, a society having a mechanical solidarity is characterized by strong collective conscience. Since crime is regarded as an offence against common conscience, such a society is also characterized by repressive law which multiplies punishment to show the force of common sentiments.

Whereas mechanical solidarity arose from similarities of individuals in primitive society, organic solidarity on the other hand develops out of differences rather than likenesses between individuals in modern societies. Individuals are no longer similar, but different; their mental and moral similarities have disappeared. A society having organic solidarity is characterized by specialization, division of labor and individualism. It is held together by the inter-dependence of parts, rather than by the homogeneity of elements. It is also characterized by the weakening of collective conscience and restitutive law. Organic solidarity, as Durkheim envisioned it, develops out of differences rather than likenesses and it is a product of the division of labor. With the increasing differentiation of functions in a society come differences between its members. Durkheim came to realize that only if all members of a society were anchored to common sets of symbolic representations, to common assumptions about the world around them, could moral unity be assured. Without them, any society was bound to degenerate and decay. With the emergence of division of labor in society, owing to a complex of facts such as increased population, urbanization, industrialization, and with its concomitant rise in dissimilarities of individuals in society, there was an inevitable increase in interdependence among society's members. And, as noted earlier, when there is an increase in mental and moral aptitude and capabilities, there is a decrease corollary in the collective conscience.

The two forms of solidarity correspond to two extreme forms of social organization. Archaic societies (primitive societies as they were once called) are characterized by the predominance of mechanical solidarity whereas modern industrial societies, characterized by complex division of labor, are dominated by organic solidarity. It must, however, be noted that Durkheim's conception of the division of labor is different from that envisaged by economists. To Durkheim social differentiation begins with the disintegration of mechanical solidarity and of segmental structure. Occupational specialization and multiplication of industrial activities are only an expression of a more general form of social differentiation which corresponds to the structure of society as a whole.

Mechanical solidarity societies come first in time. According to Durkheim, "it is an historical law that mechanical solidarity which first stands alone, or nearly so, progressively loses ground, and that organic solidarity becomes, little by little, preponderant. But when the way in which solidarity of men becomes modified, the structure of societies cannot but change. The form of a body is necessarily transformed when the molecular affinities are no onger the same."[5]

Now, how does this change occur? In other words, what are the causes of division of labor? Economists explain the division of labor as a rational device contrived by men to increase the output of the collectivity. Durkheim rejects this explanation as reversal of the true order. To say that men divided the work among themselves, and assigned everyone a different job, is to assume that individuals were different from one another and aware of their differences *before* social differentiation. Durkheim also oppsses "contractualists" like Spencer who stressed the increasing role of contracts freely concluded among individuals in modern societies. To Durkheim modern society is defined first and foremost by the phenomenon of social differentiation, of which contractualism is the result and expression. He also considered and rejected the search for happiness as an explanation, for nothing proves that men in modern societies are happier than men in archaic societies. Moreover, since division of labor is a social phenomena, the principle of the homogeneity of cause and effect, demands an essentially social explanation.

Durkheim insists that division of labor, a social phenomenon, can only be explained in terms of three social factors—the volume, the material density and the moral density of the society. The volume of a society refers to the size of the population and material density refers to the number of individuals on a given ground surface. Moral density means the intensity of communication between individuals. With the formation of cities and the development of communication and transportation, the condensation of society multiplies intra-social relations. Thus the growth and condensation of societies and the resultant intensity of social intercourse necessitate a greater division of labor. "The division of labor varies in direct ratio with the volume and density of societies and, if it progresses in a continuous manner in the course of social development, it is because societies become regularly denser and generally more voluminous."[6] As societies become more voluminous and denser, more people come into contact with one another; they compete for scarce resources and there is rivalry everywhere. As the struggle for survival becomes acute, social differentiation develops as a peaceful solution to the problem. When individuals learn to pursue different occupations, the chances of conflict diminish. Each man is no longer in competition with all; each men is in competition with only a few of his fellows who pursue the same object or vocation. The soldier seeks military glory, the priest moral authority, the statesman power, the businessman riches and the scholar scientific renown. The carpenter does not struggle with the mason, nor the physician with the teacher, nor the politician with the engineer. Since they pursue different objects or perform different services, they can exist without being obliged mutually to destroy one another. The division of labor is thus, the result of the struggle for existence.

"Social differentiation, a phenomenon characteristic of modern societies, is the formative condition of individual liberty. Only in a society where the collective consciousness has lost part of its overpowering rigidity can the individual enjoy a certain autonomy of judgement and action. In this individualistic society, the major problem is to maintain that minimum of collective consciousness without which organic solidarity would lead to social disintegration."[7] When Durkheim's study of the division of labor was written, analysis of the social limitations on personal freedom was relatively underdeveloped, making his study one of the most important contributions to the rise of sociology to academia and scientific respectability. Holding fast to his rejection of any explanation of social phenomena in terms of merely individual motivations and while stressing his argument that social phenomenon must be explained on the social plane, Durkheim accounted for the emergence of advanced or organic societies on the basis of the growing "volume" of society. He pointed out that expansion both territorially and demographically increased the physical density of the population and, therefore, added to its social density (i.e., greater communication and interaction). This insight marked a breakthrough for all of sociology.

FUNCTIONALISM AND METHODOLOGY

From his earliest works on social solidarity, Durkheim acknowledged Comte to be his master. They both stressed the centrality
of empiricism and the significance of the group in determining
individual conduct. Durkheim rejected Spencer's individualistic
conception of society, opposing the idea that the social order is
derived merely from the competition and struggle for existence
between and amongst free individuals. However, and unfortunately, he did accept Spencer's idea of social evolution, causing some
necessary modifications of his theory by later disciples. Throughout his methodological considerations, Durkheim continued to
affirm that explanations of social life must be sought from within
society itself. Reductionism must be foiled at all costs. For
example, Durkheim illustrated the fact that the source of all
obligation lies outside every individual, and, since the collective
life is not derived from the individual's life, he believed that the
"determining cause of a social fact should be sought among the
social facts preceding it and not among the states of the individual consciousness."

Durkheim rejects the assumption that the ultimate explanation
of collective will emanates from human nature in general and
that, therefore, sociological laws are only a corollary of the more
general laws of psychology. Social processes are distinct in that
they are external to the individual and independent of his will.
Durkheim insists that social phenomena cannot be reduced to
individual phenomena. A whole is not identical with the sum of
its parts; society is not a mere sum of individuals. To argue that
the first origins of social phenomena are psychological because
the only elements making up society are individuals is like saying
that organic phenomena (human) can be explained by inorganic
phenomena since living cells are only molecules of matter. The
system made up of individuals "represents a specific reality which
has its own characteristics. Of course nothing collective can be
produced if individual consciousnesses are not assumed, but this
necessary condition is by itself insufficient. These consciousnesses
must be combined in a certain way; social life results from this
combination and is, consequently, explained by it. Individual
minds, forming groups by mingling and fusing, give birth to a
being, psychological if you will but constituting a psychic indi-

viduality of a new sort."[8] Thus Durkheim contends: "Since their essential characteristic consists in the power they possess of exerting, from outside, a pressure on individual consciousness, they do not derive from individual consciousnesses, and in consequence sociology is not a corollary of psychology."[9]

Within this setting, sociological analysis, Durkheim believed, must utilize the comparative method as the only acceptable approach to social facts. The comparative method was not for Durkheim a branch of the discipline of sociology, it is the discipline. He wanted to utilize the merits of the English philosophy of John Stuart Mill whose notion of "concomitant variation" Durkheim found informative and helpful. This method holds that if a change in one variable, e.g., rate of suicide, is accompanied by a comparable change in another variable, e.g., religious affiliation, then the two changes may be causally related directly or linked through some basic social facts, such as degree of group solidarity.

Durkheim's methodology consisted of formulating rules to help single out social facts. Three primary rules for any scientist were: (1) Preconceptions must be eradicated—"He must throw off, once and for all, the yoke of these empiric categories which from long continued habit have become tyrannical". (2) Every sociological investigation must be of a group of phenomena defined in advance by certain external characteristics, i.e., social facts existing on the basis of external aspects; and (3) social facts must be considered independently of their individual manifestations. This last one is his main rule in all sociological analysis—the independence and irreducibility of social facts.

In his second book, *The Rules of Sociological Method* (1895), Durkheim introduced a refinement of his concept of the collective conscience. He emphasized that the aggregation, interpretation, and fusion of individual mentalities generate a kind of psychic unity distinguishable from individuals themselves. The collective product—society—is not equal to the sum of its parts—individuals. That is why Durkheim insisted that the analysis of group behavior begins with collective phenomena, and not with individuals. Therefore, he reasoned to his university colleagues, there is no more continuity between psychology and sociology than between psychology and biology. Sociology has its own subject and its own methodology—"the group is a reality *sui generis*" he was fond of saying.

His use of law in his analysis of social order made Durkheim particularly sensitive to ideas and the reciprocity between the collective conscience and social ideals. Social ideals bring into being the collective conscience and the collective conscience in turn generates social ideals. Ideals arise from reality, to be sure, but go far beyond it; the human concept of ideal society is part of social reality and requires sociological study. Religion, law, morals, economics—in these major social systems are both values and ideals. Social ideals, Durkheim explained, constitute the collective conscience as it exists independently of individuals themselves. We see here evidence not so much of a change as a subtle shift in emphasis in Durkheim's theory of the collective conscience from the level of group psychology to the world of ideas, supplying the very contents of the ideas of individuals. Here is strong evidence of Hegel's influence on Durkheim during his student days.

Durkheim's fascination with causality in method led him to a functional approach to the study of social phenomena. Functionalism for Durkheim was his alternative to both Comte's and Spencer's teleological method in which social facts were thought to be sufficiently explained when their specific usefulness in terms of meeting human desires was brought out. The task of functional analysis is to clarify how institutions and other social phenomena contribute to the maintenance of the social whole. Functionalism's usefulness in analysis of complex organizations led Durkheim to a classification of societies according to their degree of organization, a side-line interest of his throughout his career and suggestive of Spencerian influence in social evolution.

Durkheim established the logic of the functional approach to the study of society by establishing a clear distinction between historical and functional types of enquiry and between functional consequences and individual motivations. "The determination of function," says Durkheim, "is necessary for the complete explanation of the phenomena... To explain a social fact is not enough to show the cause on which it depends; we must also show its function in the establishment of social order."[10] Thus, Durkheim established certain fundamental guiding principles for the explanation of social facts: (1) In explaining a given social phenomenon, we must seek separately the efficient cause which produces it and the function it fulfils. (2) The function of a social fact cannot but be social and therefore it ought always to be sought in its relation to some social end. In his employment of functional analysis and the comparative method, Durkheim distinguished his perspective from either the study of historical origins and causes or the probing of individual purposes and motivations. He always contended, however, that a comprehensive explanation of sociological phenomena would utilize both historical and functional analysis

Suicide

Durkheim's third book, *Suicide* (1897), a major theory of social constraints relating to collective conscience, is cited as a monumental lankmark in which conceptual theory and empirical research are brought together. He used considerable statistical ingenuity considered remarkable for his times. His use of statistical analysis was for two primary reasons: (1) to refute theories based on psychology, biology, genetics, climatic, and geographical factors, and (2) to support with empirical evidence his own sociological explanation of suicide. In this study, Durkheim displayed an extreme form of sociological realism. He speaks of suicidal currents as collective tendencies that dominate some very susceptible individuals and catch them up in their sweep. The act of suicide at times, Durkheim believed, is interpreted as a product of these currents. The larger significance of *Suicide* lies in its demonstration of the function of sociological theory in empirical science.

Durkheim rejected the various extra-social factors such as heredity, climate, mental alienation, racial characteristics and imitation as the cause of suicide and arrived at the conclusion that suicide which appears to be a phenomenon relating to the individual is actually explicable aetiologically with reference to the social structure and its ramifying functions which may (a) induce, (b) perpetuate, or (c) aggravate the suicide potential. Durkheim's central thesis is that suicide rate is a factual order, unified and definite, for, each society has a collective inclination towards suicide, a rate of self-homicide which is fairly constant for each society so long as the basic conditions of its existence remain the same.

Based on the analysis of a mass of data gathered on many societies and cultures, Durkheim identified three basic types of suicide:

1. *Egoistic Suicide:* Egoistic suicide results from the lack of integration of the individual into his social group. Durkheim studied varying degrees of integration of individuals into their religion, family, political and national communities, and found that the stronger the forces throwing the individuals on to their own resources, the greater the suicide rate in society. For example, regardless of race and nationality, Catholics show far less suicides than Protestants. This is because, while both faiths prohibit suicide, Catholicism is able to integrate its members more fully into its fold. Protestantism fosters spirit of free inquiry, permits great individual freedom, multiplies schism, lacks hierarchic organizations and has fewer common beliefs and practices. Catholicism, on the other hand, is an idealistic religion which accepts faith readymade, without scrutiny, has a hierarchical system of authority and prohibits variation. Thus "the superiority of Protestantism with respect to suicide results from its being a less strongly integrated church than the Catholic church."[11] This conclusion is confirmed by the case of England, the Protestant country where suicide is least developed. This, Durkheim reasons, is because the Anglican church is far more powerfully integrated than other Protestant churches, has the only Protestant clergy organized in a hierarchy and has a highly developed traditionalism which more or less restricts activity of the individual.

Family, like religious group, is a powerful counter agent against suicide. Non-marriage increases the tendency to suicide, while marriage reduces the danger by half or more. This immunity even increases with the density of the family. In other words, contrary to the popular belief that suicide is due to life's burdens, Durkheim insists that it diminishes as these burdens increase. Small families are unstable and short-lived; their sentiments and consciences lack intensity. But large families are more solidly integrated and act as powerful safeguards against suicide. Again, contrary to the common belief that great political upheavals increase the number of suicides, Durkheim contends that great social disturbances and popular wars rouse collective sentiments, stimulate patriotism and national faith, and force men to close ranks and confront the danger, leading to a more powerful integration of the individual into his community, thus reducing the rate of suicide. Durkheim writes:

...as collective force is one of the obstacles best calculated to

restrain suicide, its weakening involves a development of suicide. When society is strongly integrated, it holds individuals
under its control, considers them at its service and thus forbids
them to dispose wilfully of themselves. Accordingly it opposes
their evading their duties to it through death. But how could
society impose its supremacy upon them when they refuse to
accept this subordination as legitimate? It no longer then
possesses the requisite authority to retain them in their duty
if they wish to desert; and conscious of its own weakness, it
even recognizes their right to do freely what it can no longer
prevent. So far as they are the admitted masters of their destinies, it is their privilege to end their lives. They, on their
part, have no reason to endure life's sufferings patiently. For
they cling to life more resolutely when belonging to a group
they love, so as not to betray interests they put before their
own. The bond that unites them with the common cause attaches them to life and the lofty goal they envisage prevents
their feeling personal troubles so deeply. There is, in short,
in a cohesive and animated society a constant interchange of
ideas and feelings from all to each and each to all, something
like a mutual moral support, which instead of throwing the
individual on his own resources, leads him to share in the
collective energy and supports his own when exhausted.[12]

2. *Altruistic Suicide:* This kind of suicide results from the
over-integration of the individual into his social group. An individual's life is so rigorously governed by custom and habit that
he takes his own life because of higher commandments. Examples
are legion: women throwing themselves at the funeral pyre of
their husbands (known as *sati* in India); Danish warriors killing
themselves in old age; the Goths jumping to their death from
high pinnacles to escape the ignominy of natural death; suicide of
followers and servants on the death of their chiefs. As opposed
to these obligatory altruistic suicides, there are optional varieties
which do not require suicide but praise self-sacrifice or ultimate
self-renunciation as a noble and praiseworthy act. Japanese Hara-
kiri, self-immolation by Buddhist monks, self-homicide by army
suicide squads and self-destruction in Nirvana under Brahminic
influence (as in the case of ancient Hindu sages) illustrate other
variants of altruistic suicide. In all these cases, the individual
seeks "to strip himself of his personal being in order to be engul-
fed in something which he regards as his true essence. . . . While
the egoist is unhappy because he sees nothing real in the world
but the individual, the intemperate altruist's sadness, on the con-

trary, springs from the individual's seeming wholly unreal to him.
One is detached from life because seeing no goal to which he
may attach himself, he feels himself useless and purposeless; the
other because he has a goal but one outside this life, which henceforth seems merely an obstacle to him."[13]

Durkheim believed that his analysis of military suicide lent
support to his conclusion. He rejected the popular conception
which attributes military suicide to the hardships of military life,
disciplinary rigor and lack of liberty. While with longer service
men might be expected to become accustomed to barrack life,
their commitment to the army and aptitude for suicide seem to
increase. While military life is much less hard for officers than
for private soldiers, the former accounts for greater suicide rates
than the latter. Above all, volunteers and re-enlisted men who
choose military as a career are more inclined to commit suicide
than men drafted against their will. This proves that where altruistic suicide is prevalent, man is always ready to sacrifice his
life for a great cause, principle or a value.

3. *Anomic Suicide:* This results from normlessness or deregulation in society. Although this kind of suicide occurs during
industrial or financial crises, it is not because they cause poverty,
since crises of prosperity have the same result, but because they
are crises of the collective order. Every disturbance of social equilibrium, whether on account of sudden prosperity or instant
misfortune, results in a deregulation and a greater impulse to
voluntary death.

Durkheim attributed anomic suicide to unlimited aspirations
and the breakdown of regulatory norms. Man's aspirations have
consistently increased since the beginnings of history. There is
nothing in man's organic structure or his psychological constitution which can regulate his overweening ambitions. Social desires
can be regulated only by a moral force. Durkheim views the
collective order as the only moral force that can effectively restrain the social and moral needs.

However, occasionally this mechanism breaks down and normlessness ensues. Durkheim writes:

> But when society is disturbed by some painful crisis or by
> beneficent but abrupt transitions, it is momentarily incap-
> able of exercising this influence; thence come the sudden rises
> in the curve of suicides. ... In the case of economic disasters,

indeed, something like a declassification occurs which suddenly casts certain individuals into a lower state than their previous one. Then they must reduce their requirements, restrain their needs, learn greater self-control. All the advantages of social influence are lost so far as they are concerned; their moral education has to be recommenced. But society cannot adjust them instantaneously to this new life and teach them to practice the increased self-repression to which they are unaccustomed. So they are not adjusted to the condition forced on them, and its very prospect is intolerable; hence the suffering which detaches them from a reduced existence even before they have made a trial of it."[14]

Thus any abrupt transitions such as economic disaster, industrial crisis or sudden prosperity can cause a deregulation of the normative structure. That is why, Durkheim reasons, anomie is a chronic state of affairs in the modern socio-economic system. Sudden changes upset the societal scale instantly but a new scale cannot be immediately improvised. Collective conscience requires time to reclassify men and things. During such periods of transition there is no restraint on aspirations which continue to rise unbridled. "The state of deregulation or anomie is thus further heightened by passions being less disciplined, precisely when they need more disciplining." Overweening ambition and the race for unattainable goals continue to heighten anomie. According to Durkheim, poverty protects against suicide because it is a restraint in itself: ' the less one has the less he is tempted to extend the range of his needs indefinitely."

In analyzing the consequences of anomie, Durkheim showed that there was a high rate of anomic suicide among those who are wealthy as well as among divorced persons. Sudden upward changes in the standard of living or the breakup of a marriage throws life out of gear and puts norms in a flux. Like economic anomie, domestic anomie resulting from the death of husband or wife is also the result of a catastrophe that upsets the scale of life. Durkheim also points to a number of factors that contributed to anomie in modern society. "Economic progress has largely freed industrial relations from all regulation, and there is no moral strong enough to exercise control in the sphere of trade and industry. Furthermore, religion has lost most of its power. And government, instead of regulating economic life, has become its tool and servant."

Theory of Religion

Durkheim's last major book, *The Elementary Forms of Religious Life* (1912), is often regarded as the most profound and the most original of his works. The book contains a description and a detailed analysis of the clan system and of totemism in the Arunta tribe of Australian aborigines, elaborates a general theory of religion derived from a study of the simplest and most "primitive" of religious institutions, and outlines a sociological interpretation of the forms of human thought which is at the heart of contemporary sociology of knowledge.

Durkheim began with a refutation of the reigning theories of the origin of religion. Tyler, the distinguished English ethnologist, as well as Spencer himself supported the notion of "animism', i.e., spirit worship as the most basic form of religious expression. Max Mueller, the noted German linguist, put forth the concepts of "naturism", i.e., the worship of nature's forces. Durkheim rejected both concepts because he felt that they failed to explain the universal key distinction between the sacred and the profane, and because they tended to explain religion away by interpreting it as an illusion, that is, the reductionistic fallacy. Moreover, to love spirits whose unreality one affirms or to love natural forces transfigured merely by man's fear would make religious experience a kind of collective hallucination. Nor is religion defined by the notion of mystery or of the supernatural. Nor is the belief in a transcendental God the essence of religion, for there are several religions such as Buddhism and Confucianism, without gods. Moreover, reliance on spirits and supernatural forces will make religion an illusion. To Durkheim it is inadmissible that systems of ideas like religion which have had such considerable place in history, to which people have turned in all ages for the energy they needed to live, and for which they were willing to sacrifice their lives, should be mere tissues of illusion. Rather, they should be viewed as so profound and so permanent as to correspond to a true reality. And, this true reality is not a transcendent God but society. Thus the central thesis of Durkheim's theory of religion is that throughout history men have never worshipped any other reality, whether in the form of the totem or of God, than the collective social reality transfigured by faith.

According to Durkheim, the essence of religion is a division of

the world into two kinds of phenomena, the sacred and the profane. The sacred refers to things human beings set apart, including religious beliefs, rites, deities, or anything socially defined as
requiring special religious treatment. Participation in the sacred
order, such as in rituals or ceremonies, gives a special prestige,
illustrating one of the social functions of religion. "The sacred
thing," wrote Durkheim, "is *par excellence* that which the profane should not touch and cannot touch with impunity." The
profane is the reverse of the sacred. "The circle of sacred objects,"
continued Durkheim, "cannot be determined once for all. Its
existence varies infinitely, according to the different religions."
Accordingly, Durkheim defines religion as a unified system of
beliefs and practices relative to sacred things, that is to say, things
set apart and forbidden—beliefs and practices which unite in one
simple moral community called a Church, all those who adhere
to it." Beliefs and practices unite people in a social community
by relating them to sacred things. This collective sharing of beliefs, rituals, etc., is essential for the development of religion. The
sacred symbols of religious belief and practice refer, not to the
external environment or to individual human nature but only to
the moral reality of society.

Instead of animism or naturism, Durkheim took the "totemism" among the Australian tribes as the key concept to explain
the origins of religion. Ordinary objects, whether pieces of wood,
polished stones, plants or animals, are transfigured into sacred
objects once they bear the emblem of the totem. Durkheim writes:

> Totemism is the religion, not of certain animals or of certain
> men or of certain images, but of a kind of anonymous and
> impersonal force which is found in each of these beings, with-
> out however being identified with any one of them. None
> possesses it entirely, and all participate in it. So independent
> is it of the particular subjects in which it is embodied that it
> precedes them just as it is adequate to them. Individuals die,
> generations pass away and are replaced by others. But this
> force remains ever present, living, and true to itself. It quickens
> today's generation just as it quickened yesterday's and as it
> will quicken tomorrow's. Taking the word in a very broad
> sense, one might say that it is the god worshipped by each
> totemic cult; but it is an impersonal god, without a name,
> without a history, abiding in the world, diffused in a count-
> less multitude of things.[15]

Totem, Durkheim explained, refers to an implicit belief in a mysterious or sacred force or principle that provides sanctions for violations of taboos, inculcates moral responsibilities in the group, and animates the totem itself. The emphasis, in keeping with his overall emphasis upon social analysis of social phenomena, was upon the collective activities as the birthplace of religious sentiments and ideas.

According to Durkheim, the essence of Totemism is the worship of an impersonal, anonymous force, at once immanent and transcendent. This anonymous, diffuse force which is superior to men and very close to them is in reality society itself. Durkheim maintains:

> There is no doubt that a society has everything needed to arouse in men's minds, simply by the influence it exerts over them, the sensation of the divine, for it is to its members what a god is to his faithful. For a god is first a being whom man imagines in certain respects as superior to himself, and on whom he believes he depends, whether we are speaking of personalities like Jacob, Zeus, or Jahweh, or of abstract forces like those which come into play in totemism. In either case, the believer feels that he is obliged to accept certain forms of behavior imposed on him by the nature of the sacred principle with which he feels he is in communication. But society also maintains in us the sensation of a perpetual dependence, because it has a nature peculiar to itself, different from our individual nature, and pursues ends which are likewise peculiar to itself; but since it can attain them only through us, it imperiously demands our cooperation. It requires that we forget our personal interests and become its servants; it subjects us to all kinds of inconveniences, hardships, and sacrifices without which social life would be impossible. So it is that at every moment we are obliged to submit to rules of conduct and ideas which we have neither made nor willed and which are sometimes even opposed to our most fundamental inclinations and instincts.
>
> Society awakens in us the feeling of the divine. It is at the same time a commandment which imposes itself and a reality qualitatively superior to individuals which calls forth respect, devotion, adoration.[16]

Moreover, Durkheim claims that just as societies in the past have created gods and religion, societies of the future are inclined to create new gods and new religions when they are in a state of exaltation. When societies are seized by the sacred frenzy, and when men, participating in ritualistic ceremonies, religious services, feasts and festivals, go into a trance, people are united by dancing and shouting and experience a kind of phantasmagora. Men are compelled to participate by the force of the group which carries them outside of themselves and gives them a sensation of something that has no relation to every day experience. During such moments of sacred frenzy and collective trance, new gods and new religions will be born.

Durkheim believed he had solved the religious-moral dilemma of modern society. If religion is nothing but the indirect worship of society, modern people need only express their religious feelings directly toward the sacred symbolization of society. The source and object of religion, Durkheim pointed out, are the collective life—the sacred is at bottom society personified. Therefore, a secular sociological explanation of religion could sound something like this—the individual who feels dependent on some external moral power is not a victim of hallucination but a responsive member of society. The substantial function of religion, said Durkheim, is the creation, reinforcement, and maintenance of social solidarity. He argued that religious phenomena emerges in any society when a separation is made between the sphere of the profane—the realm of everyday utilitarian activities—and the sphere of the sacred—the area that pertains to the numerous, the transcendental, the extraordinary.

Religion, as Durkheim saw and explained it, is not only a social creation, but is in fact society divinized. Durkheim stated that the deities which men worship together are only projections of the power of society. If religion is essentially a transcendental representation of the powers of society, then the disappearance of traditional religion need not herald the dissolution of society. Furthermore, Durkheim reasoned that all that is required for modern men now was to realize directly that dependence on society, which before, they had recognized only through the medium of religious representation. "We must," he explained, "discover the rational substitute for these religious notions that for a long time have served as the vehicle for the most essential moral ideas". On the most general plane, religion as a social institution serves to give meaning to man's existential predicaments by typing the individual to that supra individual sphere of transcendent values which is ultimately rooted in his own society.

Society of Morality
From the very beginning of his professional career Durkheim has
given sustained and penetrating attention to the moral dimension
of human behavior. Indeed, a scholar of passionate commitment
to moral values, he was pre-occupied with establishing and ela-
borating a science of morals. This does not mean an attempt to
extract ethics from science but to establish the science of ethics.
Moral facts, Durkheim insisted, are like any other phenomena;
"they consist of rules of action recognizable by certain distinctive
characteristics. It must, then, be possible to observe them, describe them, classify them, and look for the laws explaining
them."[17] While every man is entitled to follow a given moral principle, the scientists must adopt "a complete freedom of mind. We
must rid ourselves of that habit of seeing and judging which long
custom has fixed in us; we must submit ourselves rigorously to
the discipline of the methodological doubt."

What are the most important characteristics of morality? The
first and foremost characteristic of morals is their relativism.
Morality is a function of society; it makes sense only in relation
to a given collective order. This view is in sharp contrast to Immanuel Kant's position which attributes to morality a "categorical imperative," a universality and a deeply embedded sense of
"oughtness" in human nature that transcends immediate culture
or locality. In refuting Kant's theory of morality, Durkheim de-
clares that morals are relative to the diversity of social organization.

Thus the source of morality is society, and there is an indis-
soluble bond between man and society. "It is impossible to desire a morality other than that endorsed by the condition of society
at a given time. To desire a morality other than that implied by
nature of society is to deny the latter and, consequently, oneself. . . . Society is the end of all morality. Now (1) while it transcends the individual it is immanent in him; (2) it has all the
characteristics of a moral authority that imposes respect. . . .
Society transcends the individual's consciousness. It surpasses
him materially because it is a result of the coalition of all the
individual forces. By itself this material superiority would not be
enough. The universe also surpasses the individual materially,
but is not on that account called moral. Society is something more
than material power; it is a moral power. It surpasses us physi-

cally, materially and morally."[18] But all this does not mean that there is no room for conflict between individual and society. However, Durkheim feels that the individual does not rebel against the social system as a whole but against one or more aspects of it; indeed, it is precisely his conformity with many other aspects of the system that provide the rebel with the motive force to rebel.

Durkheim defines morality as "a system of rules of conduct". Since all techniques are governed by rules, he hastens to differentiate between moral rules and other rules of technique in terms of two distinct properties.

(a) Obligation or duty: "Moral rules are invested with a special authority by virtue of which they are obeyed simply because they command".

(b) Desirability: "The notion of duty does not exhaust the concept of morality. It is impossible for us to carry out an act simply because we are ordered to do so and without consideration of its content. For us to become the agents of an act it must interest our sensibility to a certain extent and appear to us as, in some way, desirable."[19]

Thus, a combination of the obligatory and the desirable make up morality. Durkheim is astutely aware that at times there may be divergence or even tension between the two elements. Indeed, he felt that the moral crisis afflicting the society of his day was attributable to a system that placed greater emphasis upon the desirable than upon the obligatory. When the feeling of obligation is relegated to the background or when "the old duties have lost their power without our being able to see clearly and with assurance where our new duties lie" a moral crisis develops in the collective order.

Durkheim identified three elements of morality: (1) the spirit of discipline; (2) attachment to social groups; and (3) autonomy and self-determination. First, morality is not simply a system of customary conduct, it is a system of commandments based on authority which imposes respect. The essence of morality is authority which regulates human conduct as well as provides the individual with "determinate goals". "Through the practice of moral rules we develop the capacity to govern and regulate ourselves, which is the whole reality of liberty. Again, it is these same rules that, thanks to the authority and force vested in them, protect us from those immoral and amoral forces besetting us on every hand."[20] Secondly, as Durkheim sees it, morality begins only in so far as we belong to a human group. He insists that "man is complete only to the extent that we feel identified with those groups in which we are involved." Thirdly, morality involves a kind of autonomy ingrained in collective order. It is not an autonomy that comes to us at birth, prefabricated from nature; rather, we fashion it ourselves to the extent we achieve a more complete knowledge of things. While we are an integral part of the world and to some measure the product of things, "we can, through science, use our understanding to control both the things that exert an influence upon us and this influence itself. In this way, we again become our master."[21]

According to Durkheim, there is no conflict between legal authority and individual liberty. On the contrary, liberty is the product of regulation. "I can be free only to the extent that others are forbidden to profit from their physical, economic, or other superiority to the detriment of my liberty. But only social rules can prevent abuses of power."[22]

Durkheim felt that contemporary world is only feebly ruled by morality. The greatest part of man's existence takes place outside the moral sphere. Economic functions have become most elaborate and varied but occupational ethics exists only in the most rudimentary form. Individuals are primarily motivated by self-interest and are not inclined to thwart and restrain themselves. The family can no longer perform this restraining role since it has abdicated most of its conventional functions. The territorial groups such as the village or city are too narrow and cannot reach out to regulate the ever-increasing spheres of occupational affairs. A society composed of an infinite number of unorganized individuals constitutes a veritable sociological monstrosity. The state is too remote from individuals and poorly equipped to supervise the specialized economic tasks. Durkheim is convinced that an effective moral or juridical regulation of the social order is possible only through well organized occupational groups, or corporations as he called them, which are "formed by all the agents of the same industry, united and organized into a single body." Durkheim concludes: "A nation can be maintained only if, between the State and the individual, there is intercalated a whole series of secondary groups near enough to the individuals to attract them strongly in their sphere of action and drag them, in this way, into the general torrent of social life."[23] Only occupational groups are fit to fill this role, and "that is their destiny." Whenever a group is formed, a moral life appears with it. The new occupational groups constitute "a moral power capable of containing individual egos, of maintaining a spirited sentiment of common solidarity in the consciousness of all workers of preventing the law of the strongest from being brutally applied to industrial and commercial relations."[24] Durkheim tells us that such corporations existed in Medieval European countries and the Roman empire. Members of each group looked upon themselves as members of the same family; they shared a common god, a common cult and a common cemetry; they held common banquets, codified rules to guarantee occupational ethics and served as mutual aid and insurance cooperatives. However, they failed to survive mainly because of excessive state control. Durkheim feels that there is desperate need for such corporate bodies today. But today's occupational groups must be adapted to modern economic conditions; they should not be limited to the city; they must institute codified rules to regulate economic life. Moreover, the State and the corporations must be distinct and autonomous, each with distinct functions.

Crime and Punishment

Durkheim defines crime simply as the violation of an imperative or prohibition. In the sociological sense of the term, it is simply an act prohibited by the collective consciousness. Every society at any given moment of its history has a collective morality, and crime is simply an act that offends the collective sentiment. Therefore crime can only be defined from the outside and in terms of the state of the collective consciousness. Law and morality vary from one social type to the next and from one historical period to another. Practices once tabooed may become acceptable later and customs once sanctioned may be defined as morally wrong at a later date.

Durkheim refutes the popular assumption that crime is pathological, or an example of social morbidity. He insists that crime is normal. Crime has always been present in all societies of all types; a society exempt from it is utterly impossible. "To classify crime among the phenomena of normal sociology is not to

say merely that it is an inevitable, although regrettable phenomenon; it is to affirm that it is a factor in public health, an
integral part of all healthy societies."[25] To admit the morality of
crime is to admit that there will always be some violations that
offend the collective consciousness. Even a society of saints, a
perfect cloister of exemplary individuals, is not exempt from it.
Although crimes, properly so-called, may be unknown in such
"spiritual" societies, faults which appear venial to the layman
will create there the same scandal that the ordinary offence does
in ordinary consciousness and invoke the same kind of punishment. However, crime may, on occasion, assume abnormal forms,
especially when its rate is unusually high.

According to Durkheim, crime is not only normal, it is also
necessary: "it is bound up with the fundamental conditions of
all social life, and by that very fact it is useful, because these
conditions of which it is a part are themselves indispensable to
the normal evolution of morality and law."[26] Crime brings about
needed changes in society; it implies that the way remains open
to necessary changes and in certain cases it even prepares these
changes. "Where crime exists, collective sentiments are sufficiently
flexible to take on a new form, and crime sometimes helps to
determine the form they will take."[27] Thus there is a vital link
between deviance and progress. "To make progress, individual
originality must be able to express itself. In order that the originality of the idealist whose dreams transcend his century may
find expression, it is necessary that the orginality of the criminal,
who is below the level of his time, shall also be possible. One
does not occur without the other."[28] This is the only way we can
explain the progressive changes brought about by such great
moral innovators as Socrates, Buddha, Jesus or Gandhi who
rebelled against the system but for the reconstruction of a new
moral code.

Now, if crime is normal and necessary, then the criminal is no
longer "a totally unsociable being, a sort of parasitic element, a
strange and unassimilable body, introduced into the midst of
society. On the contrary, he plays a definite role in social life.
Crime, for its part, must no longer be conceived as an evil that
cannot be too much suppressed."[29] Indeed, there are types of crime
the very existence of which is a sound indication of the healthy
nature of the social order.

Having thus outlined a theory of crime, Durkheim has offered a theory of punishment. Durkheim rejects the classic interpretations which claim that the purpose of punishment is to prevent the repetition of the guilty act. If crime were a disease, its punishment would be its remedy. However, since crime is normal, and not pathological, punishment cannot be a cure for it. Durkheim insists that the purpose of punishment is nothing rational or utilitarian as simple deterrence or *quid pro quo*, or anything like rehabilitation. The purpose and meaning of punishment lie in what Durkheim calls "passionate reaction" of a community to violation of its customs or laws which has offended the collective consciousness. So the function of punishment is to satisfy the collective consciousness which, having been offended, demands reparation, and the punishment of the guilty is the reparation offered to the feelings of all. The roots of punishment lie not so much in a community's desire to do something about the offender as in its desire to do something for itself; punishment, therefore, is a kind of vengeance exercised by the collective consciousness to satisfy itself. Durkheim maintains that the essence of punishment has not changed in modern society. "Punishment remains for us what it was for our ancestors, a means of regaining the sense of collective good through passionate reaction, through vengeance, and through vicarious expiation for the sin of having contained in the community the individual maldoer. The continuity of crime and punishment lies in the fact that it is through crime and punishment, in their spasmodic eruptions, that a community is able to reaffirm, give emotional intensity to support of the community's most fundamental values."[30]

Durkheim in Retrospect
Durkheim carved out a special field of study for sociology, established a sound empirical methodology and laid the foundation of structural functionalism, the dominant school of sociological theory today. Although critics have characterized his emphasis on collective consciousness as a belief in an occult or as angelic transcendentalism, few have surpassed his sociological realism or matched his substantive contribution to the many concerns of theoretical sociology. In the words of Rossides:

Durkheim deserves a pre-eminent place in the history of sociological theory. By repudiating the teleological and psychological evolutionism of Comte and Spencer and by developing the empirical method that they had espoused but had practised so poorly, he helped to recast the entire tradition of sociological positivism. Despite Durkheim's devastating critique of the main sociological tradition, he gave to sociology the functional method, which extended the range and depth of empirical investigation far beyond anything that social science had hitherto attained. Furthermore, he identified a realm of subject matter that was, while natural, distinct from the rest of nature. His functionalism, which broadly speaking was synonymous with his concept of "comparison" or the identification of variables in a cause-effect framework, employed both qualitative and quantitative concepts and techniques. His concept of the subject matter of sociology, though focused on the topics he analyzed in his major works, included an interest in developing a scientific basis for ethics, education, and the family and brought him into contact with the disciplines of history, philosophy, and anthropology. The genius of Durkheim's empirical method lay in the fact that, unlike British or American empiricists, he refused to dissolve his subject into individuals or particulars. He insisted that the totality of social phenomena formed a structural entity that must be studied in its own right. If he dissected society for purposes of study, he did so in terms of nonpsychological variables or "social facts"—beliefs, sentiments, symbols, and interaction. In this process of analytical dissection he always insisted that these social facts had meaning and reality only as part of a general system of collective existence.

If there is a single idea which constitutes the central theme of Durkheimian sociology, it is the primacy of society over the individual. This idea which Durkheim maintained all his life has several meanings. First and foremost, it means that individual is born of society, and not society of individual. Society is *sui generis*, not simply an assemblage of individuals. The priority of the whole over the part means also the irreducibility of the social entity to the sum of its elements, the explanation of the elements by the entity and not of the entity by the elements. It also implies the historical precedence of societies in which the individuals resemble one another and in which individual consciousness is entirely external to itself, over societies whose members have acquired both awareness of their individuality and the capacity to express it. Finally, it also implies the necessity of explaining individual phenomena by the state of the collectivity, and not the state of the collectivity by individual phenomena. That the primacy of society over the individual is the corner-stone of the sociology of Durkheim may be illustrated with reference to his major works. For instance, division of labor, to Durkheim, is the disintegration of mechanical solidarity. Morality is a product of the social order, and punishment of deviance is a reparation offered to collective consciousness. Suicide is not entirely an individual phenomenon; the rate of suicide varies with the degree of social integration. And, above all, Durkheim's theory of religion postulates that men worship society transfigured by faith.

Durkheim's contribution to the development of modern sociology is matched by no one save possibly that of his German contemporary Max Weber. His contributions fell into three general categories— (1) he provided the essential principles of structural and functional analysis in sociology; (2) he furnished a highly pertinent critique of psychologistic methods in the study of society; and (3) introduced such key concepts as anomie, social integration, and organic solidarity. In spite of the profundity of his contributions, Durkheim was accused of having an overly anti-individualistic approach to the study of social phenomena. He was faulted because he appeared to be mainly concerned with the taming of the individual impulse and the harnessing of the energies of individuals for society's purposes. As we have seen, Durkheim was acutely aware of the danger of the breakdown of social order as his experience of the Franco-Prussian War and its aftermath suggested. He also realized that total control of component social actors by society would be as detrimental as anomie and deregulation. Throughout his life and in spite of the overstated criticism, Durkheim attempted to establish a balance between societal and individual claims. Yet, his work was marred by his acceptance of certain evolutionary doctrines. Evolutionism, as suggested earlier, appears in his theory of growth from mechanical to organic solidarity, in the assumption of necessary stages in social organization, and in the view that contemporary primitive societies represent earlier periods of evolutionary development. Nevertheless, unlike Comte and Spencer, Durkheim was not dominated by evolutionary ideology. Without doubt, Durkheim shaped French sociology. His influence before the Second World War was insignificant, but following Talcott Parsons' *The Structure of Social Action* (1937) in which Durkheim was fully and admirably introduced to American sociology, his influence flourished. By the 1950s he had become along with Weber the major influence in America and all Europe.

6

GEORG SIMMEL

LIFE AND TIMES

In the person of Georg Simmel (1858-1918), Germany produced her first sociologist to gain international reputation. He was both a philosopher and sociologist, possessing a catholic interest, breadth of knowledge, and felicity of writing style unsurpassed by any master of social theory of that time. A truly Renaissance Man, Simmel has been praised for his genius and sparkling brilliance while criticized for his lack of consistent, coherent system of thought. No sociologist has a more bi-partisan evaluation by his peers than has Simmel. While some thought of him as a great philosopher-sociologist, others labelled him a journalistic gadfly popularizing but still cavalier about the science.

Simmel was born in Berlin on March 1, 1858. A truly cosmopolitan and urban figure, Simmel had no experience of nor love for the rural folk Germany was populated with during his time. For him, the library, the symphony, the art gallery, the salon were his forte, circles of intellect and culture in a flourishing and burgeoning city of the arts, science, and culture. The youngest of seven children, Simmel was the son of a prosperous businessman, a Jew converted to Roman Catholicism and a stern practical mother, a Jewess converted to Lutheranism. Though a baptised Lutheran at infancy, Simmel renounced his faith while still a university student, but like many youthful converts to agnosticism, he retained an intense interest in religion.

While still just a lad, his father died and his guardian, a well-to-do owner of a music publishing house cared for his needs. Through his parents and his guardian, Simmel was tied to the intellectual *milieu* of Berlin, associating freely and easily with the intelligentsia, the artistic community, and the bearers of German high culture. Simmel had no special concern for the social and political issues and problems of the day but was totally immersed in the cultural affairs of Berlin and the European community. He had a pronounced disdain for crude and vulgar displays amongst the working people. His mood has been characterized as a kind of "spiritual aristocratism." Early in Simmel's academic career, his loyal guardian died, leaving Simmel a considerable fortune which allowed him to live an independent life of leisure as an intellectual and man of culture.

As a student, Simmel's interests led him to a thorough study of cultural history, folk psychology, the history of art, and philosophy. Unlike most students of the day who travelled about from one German university to another until they sat for the degree examinations, Simmel took all of his studies at the University of Berlin where in 1881 he sustained a defence of his doctoral dissertation on Immanuel Kant, winning a prize for excellence. In spite of his early successes in scholarship, Simmel's professional advancement was bafflingly sluggish. In 1885, he became a *Privatdozent*, an unpaid lecturer and tutor who received only student fees for private instructions. He was a brilliant public lecturer, attracting large crowds not only of university students but of professors and the cultured intelligentsia of Berlin as well. In spite of all, sixteen years passed before Simmel was even promoted to the rank of *Ausserordentlicher Professer* which, though higher than private tutor, is nonetheless non-stipendiary and still essentially outside the university community of scholars. Reasons are several and complex for Simmel's difficulties. Anti-Semitism at the time ran rather high in Germany and even infiltrated the academy in spite of efforts to hold it back. Simmel's breadth and fluidity of knowledge was disturbing to the academy which revered specialization rather than catholic interests regardless of the brilliance of the scholar in question. His intellectual circles ran larger and were more in number than propriety dictated within the academy. Very popular with the cultured intelligentsia and skilled in the ways of high society, Simmel never expressed bitterness over his lack or belated acceptance within academia.

With many books and hundreds of scholarly and popular articles to his credit, Simmel was very active in scholarly circles in spite of the delay in his professorship, being a co-founder with Max Weber and Ferdinand Tonnies of the German Sociological Society. He began his teaching career lecturing in philosophy and ethics. Soon after, he began to concentrate more of his attention upon the sociological aspects of ethics and social philosophy. Finally, he resolutely turned his attention to courses in sociology per se, being the only university faculty teaching the discipline in any German university of the time. During this period, 1890, he married a German intellectual and writer on philosophical topics. Gertrud provided Simmel with a home which became a meeting place for Berlin's intellectual elite, a gathering place for men and women distinguished in letters, in the arts, and in the high culture of Berlin. Without a bonafide university forum for his ideas, his parlor and drawing room became the forums for Simmel. Eventually, Simmel was promoted to Professorship at the University of Strassbourg in 1914 at the age of fifty-six. Ironically the University suspended classes that year owing to the turmoil of war and tumult of political uncertainty. Before the university was able to re-establish a semblance of order and commence classes once again, Simmel died of liver cancer on September 28, 1918, never having taught a class as Professor of Sociology at the University of Strassbourg.

A tragic story when viewed from outside, Simmel never let bitterness or despair over his lack of academic success adversely affect his cultural, social, or intellectual life. Throughout his life, he maintained a serious interest in the arts, admired and wrote about Rodin, entertained Rilke in his home, published a book on Goethe, and was a personal friend of Stefan George. During his academic life, he wrote thirty-one books and over two hundred and fifty scholary and popular articles. About mid-way through his academic career such as it was, early in the 1900s he turned his attention more towards the cultured intellectuals and somewhat away from the more specialized pursuits of the pure scholarly community of the university.

MAJOR THEORIES

Perspective on Human Culture
As Georg Simmel reached adulthood, he came under the conflicting and often competing world views of the nature of man

and society at the time. Coming under the sway of late eighteenth century Enlightenment optimism about social progress, he wrote of the constantly growing freedom of the individual that has resulted from the continuous development of societal complexity and heterogeneity. Nevertheless, he also fell under the persuasiveness of the turn-of-the-century pessimistic German philosophy of alienation, writing as he did that the development of modern society also involves the progressive alienation of the individual from his culture. More so than any other intellectual writer of the time, Simmel reflected both influences in his published works, both scholarly and popular.

While a strong exemplar of high culture himself, Simmel nevertheless regarded modern condition of alienation as the result of the growth of money economy, the profession and specialization of cultural development. Each aspect of culture, he explained, gains a momentum of its own, such that it develops a multiplicity of specialized elements that are increasingly unrelated to other aspects of culture as well as to the total unity of the personality. Simmel argued persuasively that individuals cannot relate meaningfully to this vast multiplicity of cultural objects, but neither can they ignore them. Individuals, therefore, and necessarily suffer—they suffer a kind of cultural alienation and the impoverishment of their personalities as creative, meaningful wholes. In the words of Simmel:

> Society strives to be a whole, an organic unit, of which the individuals must be mere members. Society asks of the individual that he employ all his strength in the service of the special function which he has to exercise as a member of it; that he so modify himself as to become the most suitable vehicle for his function. Yet the drive toward unity and wholeness that is characteristic of the individual himself rebels against this role. The individual strives to be rounded out in himself, not merely to help to round out society. He strives to develop his full capacities, irrespective of the shifts among them that the interest of society may ask of him. This conflict between the whole, which imposes the one-sidedness of partial function upon its elements, and the part, which itself strives to be a whole, is insoluble.[1]

Among the modern culprits responsible for this growing alienation is the inevitable and from the point of view of urbanization and industrialization, the necessary division of labor. Division of labor, Simmel explains, severs the creator from the creation so

that the latter attains an autonomy of its own. By virtue of this
gradual emergence of the reification or objectification of cultural
products; which is necessarily accentuated by the division of
labor, there is a concomitant increase in alienation between the
person and the products he makes or shares in making. Unlike
the artist, the producer can no longer find himself within his
product, rather, owing to the distancing from his creative efforts
brought about by the division of labor, he actually loses himself in
the product itself. He encounters the bafflingly dialectical realization that while the cultural universe is objectively made by individuals in time and space, he nevertheless perceives it as a world
he never made. This sounds very similar to the theory of alienation by Marx. But there is a crucial difference: for Marx, alienation can be resolved in a future society based on communism,
for Simmel, the contradiction flowing from the antimony of life,
hence alienation, is eternal and ineradicable.

Simmel's analysis of metropolis and mental life provides an
accurate insight into his view of modern society. For the sake of
self-preservation modern man tends to develop a defensive reserve
around his personality which protects him from the overwhelming social forces that threaten to engulf him. "The metropolitan
type of man—which, of course, exists in a thousand individual
variants—develops an organ protecting him against the threaten-
ing currents and discrepancies of his external environment which
would uproot him. He reacts with his head instead of his heart.
In this an increased awareness assumes the psychic prerogative."[2]
Individuals living in today's mass society acquire what Simmel
calls the 'blase attitude' which involves antipathy, repulsion,
unmerciful matter-of-factness and utmost particularization. This
attitude precludes them from interacting with other men as full,
emotional and concerned human beings. And precisely because
in their everyday life men interact with one another in the most
rational, matter-of-fact and impersonal way their psychic system
is largely unaffected by the disruptive consequences of structural
disintegration and de-institutionalization.

Simmel wrote a great deal about the psychological and social
consequences of the development of money economy. He saw a
close relationship between the existence of money economy,
rationality and individualism. Money permits rational calculation
and impersonal transaction; replaces personalties with impersonal

relationships; it stimulates the growth of large and purposive groups; it reduces all relationships to the pecuniary principle of sheer exchange value, and transforms the whole world into an arithmetic problem. As money becomes "the most frightful leveller", man becomes a calculating machine devoid of all emotions, sentiments and symbolism. "Money, with all its colorlessness and indifference, becomes the common denominator of all value; irreparably it hollows out the core of things, their individuality, their specific value, and their incomparability."[3]

The human mind, Simmel points out, creates a variety of products that have an existence independent of both their creator and those who create them. As Simmel saw it, the individual in modern society is very much in need of such things as art and science, religion and law, in order to attain personal autonomy from social entrapments and to realize his own personal purposes for existence. In this matrix of entrapment and autonomy, technology in modern society creates what Simmel calls "unnecessary" products to fill "artificial" wants the same way modern science generates "unnecessary" knowledge, a type of knowledge without particular value but rather is simply the by-product of the autonomous expansion of scientific activities.

Much of Simmel's time was spent analyzing the problematical situation which modern man finds himself in as a result of these converging trends of autonomy and entrapment. Though man finds himself surrounded by a multiplicity of cultural elements, he realizes upon encounter and reflection that these cultural paraphernalia are neither blatantly meaningless nor fundamentally meaningful for his existence. On the one hand, they oppress the individual because he cannot fully assimilate them, while on the other hand, he cannot reject all cultural forms because they belong at least potentially to the sphere of his own cultural development. "The cultural objects," Simmel was quick to point out in his *Philosophie des Geldes*, "become more and more linked to each other in a self-contained world which has increasingly fewer contacts with the subjective psyche and its desires and sensibilities."[4] As man becomes freer by virtue of technological mechanization he becomes more entrapped by the necessary interdependency n society fostered by this technology. Human freedom creates cultural modes of existence which in turn capture their creator.

Simmel supported the liberal view of historical patterns of the day. Cultural, social, industrial, and technological differentiation involves, explained Simmel, a shift from homogeneity to heterogeneity, from uniformity to individualization, from absorption in the predictable routine of a small traditional world to participation in a wider world of multifaceted involvements and open possibilities. Within the movement of modern history, Simmel believed that a case could be made for the operation of an identifiable trend, a trend towards a progressive liberation of the individual from the bonds of exclusive attachment and personal dependencies. And, said he, all of this happening in spite of the increasing dominion of man by cultural products of his own creation. In modern society, Simmel pointed out, an individual is a member of many rather specified groups of individuals and activities. No one of these groups can possibly involve and control the totality of his life and personality. "The number of different circles in which individuals move," Simmel explained in his *Sociologie*, "is one of the indices of cultural development." This specific point Simmel not only dwelt upon laboriously in his writing but exemplified in his own personal life, the empirical evidence for corroborating the theory. Complex involvements in numerous and decidedly different kinds of cultural and social circles contribute to increased self-consciousness, Simmel felt. As the individual escapes the dominion of the small circles and groups which imprison or stifle the development of his personality, he becomes increasingly aware of a personal sense of individual freedom, a genuine encounter with liberation of spirit. Within the modern world, the forms of "subordination" and "super-ordination", key concepts for Simmel, take on a rather interesting flavor. No longer is the individual able to be totally dominated by others in any group, no matter how central to the individual life. Whatever domination is able to continue in the modern world, it is fundamentally specified and limited to circumscribable parameters of influence.

But Simmel was not only optimistic about human culture in the modern world as influenced by his adopted British and French philosophies of social progress he also, in his characteristically dialectical fashion, has drawn from the sober philosophies of cultural pessimism among the German intellectuals of the day as well as from Karl Marx himself. From the pessimistic perspective, Simmel writes of the enduring dualism which he believed inherent

in the relationship between the individual and the objective
cultural values of his social milieu while at the same time, explained Simmel, these very values which are so sought after threaten
to engulf and to subjugate the individual. More specifically, the
division of labor, while it constitutes the origins of a differentiated
cultural life, in its own way actually subjugates and enslaves the
individual who is "cultivated"

Methodology

Throughout Simmel's analysis of social life, he never dealt with
the social actions of individuals themselves; rather he concentrated
his time and attention upon the relationship of individuals to
each other especially as related to and affecting social structures
and processes. Though not an uncritical adherent to the reigning
philosophy of social evolution and progress, there does exist
much evidence in Simmel's early writings that the mode of reasoning applied to the issues of the day was taken from Spencer and
Darwin. Short of an outright acceptance of Spencerian belief in
the progressive development of human society, Simmel does reflect
the belief in a progression from the primitive immersion of group
life to the autonomous individuality of man in modern society.
This mind-set was especially evidenced in his two books of the
1890s *On Social Differentiation* and *Introduction to the Science
of Ethics*.

In spite of these social Darwinian tendencies in his early writings, Simmel decisively and articulately rejected Spencer's and
Comte's conception of sociology as an all-embracing "synthetic"
science, a queen of the sciences under which all other scientific
endeavours are subsumed. To be a real and usable science of
society, Simmel argued, sociology must not claim to do everything
but rather must claim to do one thing well. Sociology must have
a well-defined subject matter admitting of scientific analysis.
While taking Durkheim to task, Simmel also believed that society
could not be understood as merely a psychic entity independent
of individual minds. Yet, he was not willing, on the other side,
to argue for the naively individualistic position which negated
the real importance of the social group. The dialectics of the
individual in society was an enduring focus of Simmel's work.
He was never tired of analyzing the dynamic interconnectedness
and the conflicts between the social units. Throughout his work,

he stressed both the connections and the tensions between the individual and society. The linkage, Simmel pointed out, between the individual and society is a social process. "The total content of life", he wrote in his *Sociologie* (1908), "even though it may be fully accounted for in terms of social antecedents and interactions, must yet be looked at the same time under the aspect of singularity, as oriented toward the experience of the individual."[5]

Without doubt Simmel probably derived much of his sociological method from Darwin and Spencer in his analysis of interaction, functional relations, and reciprocal dependencies. But, during his mature writing and research years, Simmel came increasingly under the influence of the distinguished German philosopher, Immanuel Kant. Having rejected Marx and the positivism of social Darwinism, Simmel was influenced in a variety of ways by Hegel, Schopenhauer, and the existentialist Nietzsche. His later philosophy of life resembled that of his friends Husserl and Bergson, and his philosophy of history and culture was colored by his contact with the German philosopher of history, Dilthey. But most of his methodology became an example of modified Kantian principles, especially Kant's theory of knowledge. The guiding theme appeared in Kant's work on the concept of knowledge, where Kant has argued persuasively that the realm of nature, the sensible world, is organized by the human understanding in accordance with certain *a priori* principles of knowledge. Kant argued that mankind would never be able to attain immediate knowledge of things in themselves as they in sheer actuality really are, but rather human knowledge could only be a knowledge that was mediated through certain fundamentally natural categories—categorical imperatives—such as time and space. In this framework, knowledge becomes usable only when it is being filtered through a categorizing apparatus. Historical knowledge, then, is knowledge filtered through mental categories and is a product of selecting, categorizing, and constructive thinking. Historical knowledge is never merely a given, something to be discovered; rather, it is a human creation, a result of intentional construction. Therefore, the science of historiography, Simmel said in agreement with Kant, can never limit itself to the gathering of facts. The precise distinction between social forms and social contents, a characteristic of all of Simmel's work, is derived from his reading of Kant, as is his insistence that "abstractions alone produce science out of the complexity or the unity of reality."

Donald Levine calls Simmel's method "causal resolution" and explains it as "the approach in which the investigator moves from subject to subject, ascertaining the meaning of each by disclosing its form." He continues:

> On the basis of observations drawn from the most diverse provinces, the sociologist is to intuit forms of interaction which are constant or recurrent. "That which is similar among complex phenomena is lifted out of them, as if by taking a cross-section, while what is dissimilar, that is the contents, the interests, is ignored." Then the sociologist is to determine just what that form of relationship means in social life by defining its essential characteristics and derivative properties and examining its range of variability: how it arises and develops, what modifications it undergoes because of particular contents it may embody, and under what conditions it increases or decreases."[6]

Subject Matter of Sociology

Though Simmel understood that the comparative method in scientific analysis of group behavior was the core ingredient in sociological methodology, he personally preferred to avoid large-scale analyses such as in Durkheim, choosing rather to restrict most of his work to an investigation of what he called "interactions among the atoms of society", but what today is called "microsociology".

During Simmel's time, there were two distinct schools of thought concerning the nature of society: sociological realism which regarded society as a real entity, and sociological nominalism which thought of society as a fictitious abstraction. The former viewpoint conceived of society as a great being, with a mission to fulfil and with the ability to create such things as custom, religion, law, language and the like. The second perspective assumed that society is a fiction and that individuals alone are real. Carried to its logical extreme, this perspective, Simmel feels, would reduce society to an aggregate of indivisible material atoms.

Simmel not only made a self-conscious attempt to reject the organicist theories of Comte and Spencer, but he also outright opposed both "realist" and "nominalist" schools of thought seeking rather a middle path. For Simmel, society is neither a great collective being, nor a fictitious entity, rather it exists in the process of interaction among social units, both individuals and groups. He supported the conception that society consists of a web of patterned interactions and that the task of a genuinely scientific sociology was to study the forms of these interactions as they occur and re-occur in diverse historical periods. In his view, society consists of an intricate web of multiple relations between individuals who are in constant interaction with one another. However, it must be remembered that Simmel rejected the psychological interpretation of interaction; but presented a positive conception of interaction as social action which has a certain unity based on observable behavioral regularities, and the nature of association. Thus for Simmel, the major field of study for the student of society is *sociation*, that is, the particular patterns and forms in which men associate and interact with one another.

Highly critical of those, like Comte and lesser minds, who tried to claim a privileged seat for sociology as queen above all other scientific endeavours, Simmel was practical and realistic. To claim that sociology is the panacea for all social ills is naive and dangerous. Science must study dimensions or aspects of phenomena rather than global totalities. The legitimate subject matter of sociology, Simmel never tired of pointing out, lies in the description and analysis of practical forms of human interaction and their crystallization in group characteristics: "Sociology," wrote Simmel, "asks what happens to men, by what rules they behave, not insofar as they unfold their understandable individual existences in their totalities, but insofar as they form groups and are determined by their group existence because of interaction."[7]

Simmel distinguished three different forms of sociology: (1) General sociology which is the study of a social phenomenon or problem in developmental terms, for example, Simmel's study of the expansion of the group and the development of individuality and freedom. (2) Philosophical sociology, which is his philosophy of the social sciences and the study of epistemological and metaphysical aspects of society. Philosophy, for Simmel, was not one of the many disciplines; nor was it confined to a particular subject matter. Rather "it is a distinct mode of treating any given subject matter, characterized by receptiveness to the totality of being and at the same time expressive of a fundamental attitude or world orientation on the part of the philosophizing person."

(3) Formal sociology which is a classification and analysis of forms of sociation, to which we will return later.

Levine divides the numerous sociological problems considered by Simmel into three basic categories: social processes, social types and developmental patterns. Simmel has analyzed a number of social processes such as superordination-subordination, conflict, cooperation, competition and reconciliation in terms of their form, content and social consequences, and with examples from everyday experience and history. He also singled out a number of social types, analyzed the categories of social interaction into which they enter and their essential personal qualities. The types considered by Simmel include the aristocrat, the miser, the non-partisan, the coquette, the poor man and the stranger. The term, developmental patterns, "refers to historical processes, processes of genesis or transformation" and covers a whole gamut of studies that deal with the development of social organizations over a period of time.

Formal Sociology

Georg Simmel is regarded as one of the founders of formal sociology, an approach which classifies and analyzes patterns of interaction, differentiating between their form and their content. He identified and discussed countless forms of social interaction, or sociation as he preferred to call it, insisting that they have peculiar modes of existence and structural configuration. Indeed, he viewed, as we saw earlier, forms of sociation as the proper subject matter of sociology.

Simmel's contribution to formal sociology may be analyzed under four major headings:

1. *Distinction between form and content*

As Simmel explained and exemplified it, formal sociology isolates form from the heterogeneity of content of human sociation, and generalizes it at a higher level of abstraction. Individual drives, purposes and other motive powers constitute the content of interaction, whereas forms of interaction may be thought of as basic structural configurations or abstract, analytical aspects of social reality, and not concrete entities. Throughout his analytical enterprise, his study of the nature and kinds of social interaction, Simmel distinguishes between form and content, a conceptual tool

which he put to good use. Form is that element in social life that
is relatively stable and patterned, predictable and universally
present, whereas content is conspicuously variable from time to
time and place to place. From the beginning of his work, Simmel
argued with the German idealists that the analysis of social forms
is a legitimate undertaking because it requires a systematic study
of the actual structure of society. A particular war, a great man
of history, a revolution or a social movement may be a unique,
historically specific event. However, what is important from a
sociological perspective is not their uniqueness, but the uniformities underlying the phenomena of wars, revolutions and leadership. And for Simmel, the forms of social interaction constituted
the peculiar domain for sociological investigation and analysis.
This position he put forth in answer to those historians and other
representatives of the humanities who denied that a science of
society could ever come to grips with the novelty, the irreversi-
bility, and the uniqueness of historical phenomena.

As the persistent elements of interaction, form provides the
structure which makes it possible for contents to be related.
Speaking of contents, Simmel asserts that "the mere sum . . . (of)
disconnected . . . elements is mere material." Form, therefore,
can best be recognized by the task it performs. First, form relates
a number of contents to each other in such a way that they constitute a unity. "In any forming, a multiplicity of elements is
synthesized into a unity." Second, as a number of contents are
given form, they are separated from other contents. Third, but
not as an operation that is distinct from the others, form imparts
a structure to the contents it relates.[8]

It has been suggested that Simmel's use of the term "form"
was unfortunate since it carried a rather weighty philosophical
connotation at the time which he did not intend. If he had employed today's popularly used term, "social structure", he might
very well have fared better amongst his sociology peers. In spite
of it all, such modern terms as status, role, norms, and expectations as elements of social structure are very much at one with
Simmel's work in the field of human interaction. In his formal
analysis of social phenomena, certain features of a concrete
character are analytically extracted from sheer reality which are
not readily observable unless such a perspective is applied to
them. Once this has occurred, it becomes possible, says Simmel,

to compare phenomena that may be radically different in concrete content yet essentially similar in structural arrangement.

2. *Forms of Sociation*

When individuals interact with one another, they establish some
type of reciprocal relationship or sociation which may vary from
a fleeting encounter of no great significance to a long lasting relationship of deep involvement. Simmel identified numerous forms
of sociation to which he devoted considerable work. We will touch
upon three of the most important forms of sociation; dyad, triad,
and superordination-subordination.

   In analyzing the dyad, the simplest sociological unit of two,
Simmel describes how many general forms of sociation are realized in it in a very pure and characteristic fashion. Moreover, the
limitation to two members is a condition under which alone several forms of relationship exist; monogamous marriage is a case in
point. Simmel emphasizes that the significant difference between
the dyad and larger groups consists in the fact that the dyad
has a different relation to each of its two elements than have larger
groups to their members. The dyad is not an autonomous, super-
individual unit in relation to its participants. "Rather, each of the
two feels himself confronted only by the other, not by a collectivity above him. The social structure here rests immediately on
the one and on the other of the two, and the secession of either
would destroy the whole. The dyad, therefore, does not attain
that super-personal life which the individual feels to be independent of himself. As soon, however, as there is a sociation of three,
a group continues to exist even in case one of the members drops
out[9]."

   The addition of a new member or the transformation of a dyad
into a triad brings about profound structural changes. For
example, the arrival of a child cements the relationship between
couples. Indeed, in many simple societies childbirth alone makes
a marriage perfect or insoluble. The third element, the child,
closes the circle by tying the parents to each other, strengthens
the union of the two and produces a new bond between them.
"The dyad represents both the first social synthesis and unification, and the first separation and antithesis. The appearance of
the third party indicates transition, conciliation, and abandon-
ment of absolute contrast although, on occasion, it introduces
contrast[10]."

The triad differs from a dyad in that it has a potential existence independent of each of its members. The departure of a member does not automatically dissolve the group; also it is possible for two members to form a coalition against the third member. In this triadic constellation, there are three basic roles which the third party can take: (1) non-partisan mediator who seeks to be objective and not favor either side but help them reconcile their differences; (2) *tertius gaudens* or being the third party who actually enjoys the conflict of the other two parties and seeks to use it for his or her own advantage; and (3) divide and rule type of role in which the third party deliberately instigates conflict between the other two parties in order to promote his or her advantage.

Simmel used his mode of analysis of dyad and triad not only to explain patterns of interaction in everyday life but also forms of political alliances, historical constellations and pressure group situations. For example, he traced the beginning of the British House of Commons to the "incessant splits, abuses, power shifts, and clashes," between the crown and the great barons who ultimately had to turn to a third element drawn from among free men, countries and cities to provide a source of unity and stability. Similarly today, the super-power rivalry, the shifting alliances and the emergence of the Third World may be analyzed in terms of Simmel's insights.

Simmel's essay *Superordination and Subordination* which discusses the third major form of sociation is a classic. Writing about Simmel's sociology of power, Walter reports: "Power in the form of subordination and superordination is a constitutive force without which society would lose its coherence. Superiority and subordination are found in every human association and they are by no means necessarily subsequent to the formation of society. It is rather one of the forms in which society comes into being". Social solidarity is not a necessary condition on which power must depend; on the contrary, a power relation may be "the *cause* of a commonness which in the absence of it could not be attained and which is not predetermined by any other relation among its members."[11]

Domination of some form is a logical and structural necessity; however, the societal form of superordination designates a readiness on the part of the superordinate to be bound by his own

dictates. Simmel insists that the relationship between a subordi-
nate and a superordinate is reciprocal, rather than one of implicit
obedience by the former and absolute domination by the latter.
Even in extreme forms of domination, there is a reciprocal interaction, Simmel insists. Referring to the whole rulership relation
between the one and the many, Simmel explains that the ruler
and the subject mass do not enter the relationship "with an equal
quantum of their personality." The ruler invests his entire personality; the ruled invest only fragments. "The more individuals there
are to rule, the slighter the portion of each which is dominated'

3. Social Types

Simmel's inventory of social forms was complemented by a gallery
of social types constructed for analytical purposes. The social
type is a conception abstracted from the structural components
of a particular social relationship and involves the essential qualities of the person as well as the awareness and expectation of the
status-role involved. Along with his classical study of "the stranger," Simmel described in great detail such diverse types as
"the mediator," "the poor," "the adventurer," "the miser," "the
man in the middle," "the modern cynic" and the "renegade."
Simmel's argument is interesting and persuasive—the type becomes what he is, through his relations with others who assign
him a particular position and expect him to behave in specific
ways. His characteristics are seen as attributes of the social structure, e.g., the poor are a social type who emerge only when
society recognizes poverty as a "special" status and assigns
specific persons requiring assistance to that category. Similarly,
on the stranger, Simmel wrote: "to be a stranger is naturally a
very positive relation; it is a specific form of interaction. The
inhabitants of Sirius are not really strangers to us, at least not in
any sociologically relevant sense: they do not exist for us at all;
they are beyond far and near. The stranger, like the poor and
like sundry "inner enemies", is an element of the group itself.
His position as a full-fledged member involves both being outside
it and confronting it . . . elements which increase distance and
repel, in the relations of and with the stranger, produce a pattern
of coordination and consistent interaction."[12]

It must be noted here that the forms found in social reality are
never pure—every social phenomenon contains a multiplicity of
formal elements.

4. *The Significance of Numbers*

Simmel's approach to the study of society is reflected in his classic analysis of the effects of sheer numerical size on the forms of sociation. In small groups, members typically have a chance to interact directly with one another. As the size of the group increases, its members become more unlike one another. Beyond a certain size, individualism and structural differentiation develop. Face to face interaction is replaced by formal arrangements consisting of offices, written rules and well defined tasks and responsibilities. Whereas interaction in small groups involves the total personality of individual members, participation in large groups is weak and restricted to a segment of personalities. Coser has effectively summarized Simmel's position on size as follows:

> Although through its formal arrangement the larger group confronts the individual with a distant and alien power, it liberates him from close control and scrutiny precisely because it creates a greater distance among its members. In the dyad, the immediacy of the *we* is not yet marred by the intrusion of structural constraints, and, it will be remembered, in the triad two members may constrain the third and force their will upon him. In the small group, however, the coalitions and majorities that act to constrain individual action are mitigated by the immediacy of participation. In the large group, the differentiated organs constrain the individual through their "objective" powers, even though they allow freedom from the group through segmental rather than total involvement.[13]

In spite of his emphasis on numbers, Simmel cautioned that individuals must not be treated in sociological analysis as free-standing entities—"social atoms," nor as merely social organs devoid of their integrity as persons. It is not true, said Simmel, that reality can be identified only with the smallest units that compose wholes. Society, rather, is much more than the individuals composing it; in fact, society's true significance is revealed in its contrast with the sum of individuals. Simmel was emphatic that, from a sociological perspective, society is an objective unity expressed in what he called the "reciprocal" relations among its human elements.

Dialectical Approach

A fundamental philosophical orientation rooted in dialectical thinking informs all of Simmel's writings. He wrote extensively on the dynamic inter-connectedness and the conflict between individuals, between individual and society, between social groups and between elements of culture. Simmel's dialectical approach may be analyzed in terms of three main emphases:

1. *The Principle of Dualism*
This is based on the assumption that the subsistence of any aspect of human life depends on the co-existence of diametrically opposed elements. Simmel wrote: "Man's position in the world is defined by the fact that, in every dimension of his being and his behavior, he finds himself at every moment between two boundaries. This appears as the formal structure of our existence, manifesting itself in continually new content in the manifold provinces, activities, and destinies of human life. We feel that the content and value of each hour stand between a higher and a lower, every thought between a wiser and a more foolish, every possession between a more extended and a more limited, every deed between a greater and a lesser measure of meaning, and morality."[14]

Unlike Comte, Simmel could not conceive of a Golden Society free from tensions, clashes and feuds; a conflict-free society is impossible. Conflict and consensus, order and disorder, war and peace constitute a part of the eternal dialectic of social life. They are like two sides of the same reality, both natural and inevitable.

2. *Forms of Interaction*
Simmel applies the principle of dualism to the relationship between individual and society and to various forms of sociation. Lewis Coser has neatly summed up Simmel's position as follows:

> "According to Simmel, the socialized individual always remains in a dual relation with society: he is incorporated within it and yet stands against it. The individual is, at the same time, within society and outside it; he exists for society as well as for himself: "(Social man) is not partially social and partially individual; rather, his existence is shaped by a fundamental unity, which cannot be accounted for in any other way but through the synthesis or coincidence of two logically contradictory determinations: man is both social link and being for himself, both product of society and life from an autonomous center." The individual is determined at the same time as he is determining; he is acted upon at the same time as he is self-actuating."[15]

Similarly, Simmel insisted that "sociation" always involved

both harmony and conflict, both attraction and repulsion, both love and hatred. All human relationships experience this dialectical tension, this intrinsic ambivalence. For Simmel, there is no empirically demonstrable group of individuals which is entirely harmonious, devoid of tension and conflict. In his researches, he therefore made a point of distinguishing between social appearances, relationships as they appear to others outside the group, and social realities, relationships as they exist within the interacting unit.

3. Positive Functions of Conflict

At a time when conflict was generally regarded as disruptive and dangerous, Simmel focussed his attention on the positive functions of conflict. Using his skilful writing style and analytically interpretive talents, Simmel enjoyed demonstrating that popular assumptions about social relationships, often held to be obvious, were frequently incorrect, as his discussions of the mutuality of superior-subordinate relationships, for instance, demonstrated. He also illustrated the error in the commonly held belief that conflict between individuals or within a group is a totally negative process destructive of social relationships and group unity. For example, his analysis of conflict as a form of sociation showed how it may promote social unity as well as disunity. He contended that all social relationships have both positive and negative elements, attraction and repulsion, harmony and disorder. Purely positive, harmonious, and lasting social relationships, says Simmel, are inconceivable. Conflict functions to bring into the open negative feelings, which, if suppressed, might continue to build and contribute to greater social disruption. It also permits a more realistic appraisal of social relationships and of areas of agreement and disagreement by the participants.

Simmel argues convincingly:

> If every interaction among men is a sociation, conflict—after all one of the most vivid interactions, which furthermore, cannot possibly be carried on by one individual alone— must certainly be considered as sociation. And in fact, dissociating factors—hate, envy, need, desire – are the causes of conflict; it breaks out because of them. Conflict is thus designed to resolve divergent dualisms; it is a way of achieving some kind of unity, even if it be through the annihilation of one of the conflicting parties. ··· Conflict itself resolves the tension

between contrasts. The fact that it aims at peace is only one, an especially obvious, expression of its nature: the synthesis of elements that work both against and for one another.[16]

Simmel took great pains to spell out the positive functions of conflict. Even though a particular conflict situation is distasteful, even disastrous, for the individual, it may be beneficial to the community as a whole. Competition between two businessmen reduces the risk of monopoly and strengthens the economy. Even in the most antagonistic games, opposing teams are drawn into a social system based on a common set of rules and standards. Warfare brings the feuding nations together as each nation seeks to understand the language, culture and social system of the other. Conflict with an outside group enhances the unity of the in-group by reinforcing 'we—feeling', loyalty, and conformity to norms; conflicts try intimate relationships as well as confirm and strengthen them. Simmel also pointed out that conflict between groups is a major causal determinant of the development of group organization and organizational complexity.

Rejecting the notion that conflict is a temporary phase which is eventually transformed into unity, Simmel insisted that peace and conflict are reciprocally intertwined in historical reality. Neither peace nor conflict is the ultimate manifestation of historical reality; they exist as equal. Just as conflict is transformed into peace, it is equally possible for peace to be transformed into conflict.

Simmel suggested four ways in which conflict may be terminated: (a) Disappearance of the object of conflict, that is, the contending parties are deprived of the object of their conflict, often by a third party. (b) Victory, which results from the superiority of one party over the other, is the "simplest and most radical way of getting from fight to peace." (c) Compromise, whereby the two parties agree to divide or otherwise share the object of conflict. In situations where the object cannot be shared, the parties may agree to symbolic compromise. (d) Conciliation, based on a purely subjective orientation, the meaning of conciliation is summarized in the dictum, "forgive and forget." Whereas compromise represents an objective sharing of the prize, conciliation involves a change of heart.

Simmel in Retrospect

As discussed above, Simmel was a cultured intellectual who

enjoyed the genteel culture of Berlin's high society while contributing much to the academic community by writing and exemplifying the qualities of educated refinement. He was a full
participant in both the university culture and that of Berlin. Yet,
in a real sense, he was marginal to both. The benefit accruing
from this marginality was a kind of emotional and intellectual
distance which enabled him to exercise his analytical skills unim-
peded by institutional commitments. His use of formal sociology—a kind of geometry of social space—provided him with a
preliminary map which others after him would find helpful in
locating and predicting the mores of social actors who are caught
in a web of group relationships.

Simmel founded no school of thought and his reputation seems
to have died with him. Nevertheless, the distinguished German
sociologist, Ferdinand Tonnies, praised his work and Durkheim
published one of Simmel's essays in the *L'Annee Sociologique*.
With Weber, Simmel was a co-founder of the German Sociological Society in 1910 and was greatly esteemed by Weber. In the
United States, Simmel's works were translated and acclaimed
noteworthy by such sociologists as A.W. Small, Ezra Park, Bur-
gess, Spykman and others.

During his lifetime, Simmel received criticism from Durkheim
for his too artificial separation of the concepts of form and content. Durkheim had maintained in his own work that sociological
abstractions should be established according to the "natural
division of facts" or they become "fantastic constructions." Max
Weber, while supportive of Simmel and even employing some of
his ideas, was critical of him for methodological reasons, particularly for the lack of clear distinction between subjectively
intended and objectively valid meanings. And Sorokin also criticized Simmel's methodology, suggesting that he made subjective
interpretations without being aware of them. Despite these criticisms, however, Simmel has made a profound and lasting impact
upon sociological theory and at the same time called attention to
sociology from the cultured elite of Berlin and Germany which
proved helpful to the furtherance of the science within the university. Today, "interaction" remains a key concept in sociological
analysis, as well as such concepts as social structure, social process, social status, and social roles—all owing to the genius of
Simmel's sociological insights and imagination. During the last

period of his life, Simmel shifted his interest to the philosophical campus of Bergson, the French process philosopher, and to the German existentialist, Frederick Nietzsche, concentrating his attention to the celebration of the ever-renewing stream of vital energy. In his last book, particularly, *Lebensanschauung*, he indulged in a kind of "lyrical exaltation of life and its continuous flow of vital energy."[17] The irony of Simmel's life is that those works of his which he did not consider sociological in the strictest sense, such as his writings on aesthetics, art, music, drama, and high culture, are today judged of greater sociological value than his formal sociology. And, in recent years, Simmel has again become the focus of admiring disciples and sociological enthusiasts, bringing forth new translations of his books.

7

MAX WEBER

LIFE AND TIMES

Unquestionably, Germany has produced a disproportionately large number of great scholars since the Reformation and before, and the field of sociology has claimed a healthy share. War and economic depression seem not to have adversely affected such development, rather, if anything, they have been a positive factor in the rise of distinguished sociologists. Max Weber (1864-1920) is undoubtedly the greatest among them.

During the rule of Bismarck, the eldest of seven children was born to elder Max Weber and his wife, Helene, on April 21, 1864, a son they christened Max. Both were from a long line of Protestant refugees from Catholic persecution. Little Max's parents represented a diverse personality and worldview with mother Helene, a devout Calvinist with strong spiritual commitments to hard work and duty to God and man, while father Max was an outstanding lawyer in Berlin with deep secular ties to the National Liberal Parliament of which he was a deputy. Though both parents were dedicated to the work ethic, she was motivated by religious commitments while he was a striving entrepreneur of an unabashedly secular turn of mind. On the surface, the home seemed happy and stable, the common meeting place of many of Germany's most distinguished intellectuals. Elder Max, after working for a time in the city government of Berlin, assumed the position of magistrate in Erfurt (little Max's birthplace), only to return again to Berlin as a city councillor and member of the Prussian House of Deputies to the German Reichstag. The household was markedly bourgeois and culturally refined, but behind the veneer of domestic harmony was an ideological and psychological tension which caught young Max in the middle. He was plagued with mental anguish from his earliest years of recollection, unable to reconcile the competing and conflicting personalities and worldviews of his two parents. Coupled with this family drama was Weber's troubled mind resulting from the political turmoil in Germany at the time.

In keeping with his family's station in society and in view of the expected place he would assume in the German intelligentsia, Weber received an excellent formal education in languages, history, and the classics. Exceptionally bright, Weber was nevertheless a difficult student—sickly, shy, withdrawn, often rebellious in the face of legitimate authority. A ravenous reader, Weber advanced quickly, entering the University of Heidelberg at age eighteen where from 1882 to 1886 he read law, passing the bar in 1886 after intermittent study at Berlin and Gottingen. The intermittent years at Berlin and Gottingen also included a compulsory year in the military service which he served at Strasbourg coming under the influence of an aunt who was nearby. Where mother had failed to stir her son's religious interest, the aunt succeeded. During this time, Weber read deeply in theology, especially the American divine of the day from Yale Divinity School, William Ellergy Channing. His enduring respect and admiration for the Protestant virtues seem to date from this important period in his formative years.

Except for the terms of leave for military service, Weber lived with his parents. In 1889, he took doctor's degree in medieval commercial law, specializing in legal history with a study of Roman agrarian law. The following year, the *Verein Fur Sozialpolitik* commissioned him to investigate the social and economic plight of the East German agricultural worker. During this time he also worked as a barrister (lawyer) in the Berlin courts, and soon was named *Privatdozent* (lecturer) in law at the University of Berlin. In 1893, Weber married Marianne Schnitger, the daughter of a locally distinguished physician in Berlin, a happy match that thrived well through the good and bad years of Weber's life. The next year, 1894, he was named Professor of Economics at the University of Freiburg followed by a similar post in 1896 at Heidelberg. Maintaining a frantic work load in the midst of growing tensions with his father, Weber's health finally failed in July of 1897 with a nervous breakdown. His father died in August following a severe dispute with young Weber. For five years, Max Weber found himself unable to sustain intellectual or professional work, unable even to read. Resigning his Heidelberg chair, he travelled throughout Europe, spending time for rest and treatment in a sanatorium. Never fully able to maintain a professional position or academic output of his earlier years, living the life of a private scholar in Heidelberg, Weber eventually in 1903 became associate director of the *Archiv Fur Sozialwissenschaft Und Sozialpolitik.*

His intellectual and emotional struggles seem never to have been resolved, for he attempted to combine political realism with a genuine nationalism often in the guise of a critic of the German government. While deeply committed to ethical problems and the cultural significance of the ongoing power struggle in the Germany of his day, he never ceased being a scientifically motivated analyst of power politics. The struggle centered around his desire to develop a conceptual method of historical knowledge able to bridge historical description and sociological theory. The tension, unresolved, finally was the motivating force in Weber's intellectual genius.

During the First World War, he was a director of nine army hospitals at Heidelberg. As a consultant to the German armistice commission at Versailles he participated in the drafting of the memorandum on German war guilt, also serving as an advisor to the commission that prepared the draft of the Weimar Constitution. In 1910, Weber had with Tonnies and Simmel founded the German Sociological Society. Following the War, Weber lectured a term each at the universities of Vienna and Munich in 1919, having already put the finishing touches on his works in the sociology of religion consisting of the individual studies of China, Hinduism, and ancient Judaism. On the 14th of June, 1920, Max Weber died. Burdened with unresolved tensions and anguish from childhood, plagued with failing nerves and bad health, Weber worked tenaciously for the development of a scientific method for the study of human society. A man of deep ethical and value-laden commitments, Weber believed that if done well, sociology could maintain a scientific posture in the pursuit of all and any human action without bias. To that commitment of a humanistically refined scientific science of human behavior,

156 SOCIOLOGICAL THOUGHT

Weber gave his life, producing works of genius yet unsurpassed in their excellence and boldness of analysis and style.

MAJOR THEORIES

SOCIOLOGY: STUDY OF SOCIAL ACTION AND RELATIONSHIP

From the outset, Weber was obsessed with the possibility, even the necessity, of analyzing human actions and relationships scientifically. Yet, he recognized, more than many of his contemporaries, that a scientific approach to human behavior must *enter into* the subject-matter for an authentic analysis. "The central question for sociological theory," Berger and Luckmann point out, "can be put as follows: How is it possible that subjective meanings *become* objective facticities?"[1] In an attempt to emphasize the fundamental centrality of the sociological task posed in this question, they have juxtaposed two complementary statements from the giants, Durkheim and Weber. From Durkheim, we read: "The first and most fundamental rule is: consider social facts as things."[2] Then, to counterbalance the point, Weber has written: "Both for sociology in the present sense, and for history, the object of cognition is the subjective meaning-complex of action."[3] For better than a century, sociology has worked within the parameters of these two perceptions of what the science can do and what its legitimate subject-matter is. Both perceptions are incontrovertible. Society consists of qualities of 'objective facticity' and is unquestionably constituted of activities which express 'subjective meaning.' "It is precisely the dual character of society in terms of objective facticity and subjective meaning," Berger and Luckmann insist, "that makes its reality 'sui generis'."[4]

For Weber, the combined qualities of 'action' and 'meaning' were the 'central facts' for sociology's scientific analysis. Webei defined sociology as "a science which attempts the interpretive understanding of social action in order thereby to arrive at a causal explanation of its course and effects."[5] The technical category of 'action' described in Weber's work is all human behavior to which an actor attaches subjective meaning. "Action is social," explains Weber, "in so far as, by virtue of the subjective meaning attached to it by the acting individual, it takes account of the behavior of others and is thereby oriented in its course." The refinement and utilization of this technical category of 'action' provided Weber with an objective facticity necessary to apply his other subjective category called 'meaning,' a term which refers to the rationalized reasons put forth by an individual as explanation for specific actions. "In no case," explains Weber, "does it (meaning) refer to an objectively 'correct' meaning or one which is 'true' in some metaphysical sense." To offset the false accusation that the term was value-laden, Weber proposed the term "nonmeaningful behavior," defined as "reactive behavior to which no subjective meaning is attached" to cover all other forms of human action, a term which, admittedly, covered a large range of social action.

What intrigued Weber was the actually assigned 'reasons' for identifiable behavior given by actors themselves. These behavior complexes, oriented by individuals within specifiable socio-historical settings, were the subject of sociological analysis. In the absence of assigned 'meanings' by the individuals, the actions are meaningless and thus outside the purview of sociology. The behavioral complex or matrix fell into one of four types in Weber's work:

(a) Zweckrational action or rational action in relation to a goal.
The actor determines the goal and chooses his means purely in terms of their efficiency to attain the goal.

(b) Wertrational action or rational action in relation to a value. Here means are chosen for their efficiency but the ends are determined by value. The action of a captain who goes down with the sinking ship or that of a gentleman who allows himself to be killed rather than yield in a duel are examples.

(c) Affective or emotional action. Here emotion or impulse determines the ends and means of action as in the case of a mother who slaps her child or a player who throws a punch at a partner in a game.

(d) Traditional actions where both ends and means are determined by custom. Rituals, ceremonies and practices of tradition fall in this category.

Modern Western society, Weber's primary concern, has, regrettably says Weber, become inordinately dominated by goal-oriented rationality, replacing the earlier preference for traditional and value-oriented behavior. The origins of this radical shift in assigned meanings from values to goals touches every aspect of modern social life—politics, economics, law, interpersonal relationships—and has resulted from the sustained application of a means-to-ends utility in human behavior.

Always with his feet planted firmly on the ground, Weber never let the science forget that its simple overriding responsibility was the analysis of the objectively identifiable acting individual. "Interpretive sociology," explains Weber, "considers the individual and his action as the basic unity, as its 'atom.' The individual is . . . the upper limit and the sole carrier of meaningful conduct . . . Such concepts as 'state,' 'association,' 'feudalism,' and the like, designate certain categories of human interaction." Hence, Weber concludes, "it is the task of sociology to reduce these concepts to 'understandable' action, that is without exception, to the actions of participating individual men."[6] Weber's distinctiveness and his indisputable mastery of the science centers upon his tenacious pursuit of the mutual orientation of social actors and the 'understandable' motives of their behavior. Whereas Durkheim believed that the successful acceptance of sociology as an authentic science was predicated upon its recognition as a science of 'things' like any other science, though the 'things' of sociology were human action, Weber placed emphasis elsewhere. The shortcomings of Durkheim's attempts at vindicating scientific sociology are self-evident when he blatantly disregarded "assigned meanings" by individuals and societies to the various behavioral complexes. To reduce human behavior to merely objective fact is essentially to misrepresent that behavior, for thinking rational individuals purposely attribute specifiable reasons to their complex action-patterns. But Weber appreciated the distinction between the natural sciences and social sciences and used it to the advantage of sociology. Sociology under Weber boldly asserts its uniqueness and distinctiveness from the physical sciences.

Sociologists study humankind—their behavior and their explanations of behavior—therefore necessarily bringing to their subject-matter a special kind of understanding or participatory cognitive reflection (verstehen). Weber countered the naive claim that there are identical methodological procedures employed in all sciences. Finally, Weber argued persuasively that "because indivi-

duals in a social situation undergo certain experiences, the sociologist cannot avoid including in his purview the psychological
causes and effects of these experiences".[7] Unlike Durkheim, Weber
wanted to enter into the subjective dynamics of human behavior
in order to grasp more fully its intended purpose or meaning as
thought of and perceived by the acting individual himself.

Weber, who was as insistent about the absolute distinctness of
science and philosophy as he was about the differences between
the social and the natural sciences, placed the core of his scientific
work and credibility upon his insistence that knowledge "about
nature" and knowledge "about human beings" were categorically
incomparable. "Knowledge about nature", Rossides explains in
the Weberian tradition, "is a question of causal behavior and no
more" "knowledge about human beings", he points out, "is concerned with meaning as well as with causation."[8] So, from Weber's
argument about the subjective nature of social facts, the scientist
is obliged when analyzing human behavior to pay attention to the
value frames of reference which bear upon the actions of thinking
people. Since behavior is value-oriented, social facts can only be
understood in terms of the origins and functions of these values
within behavioral contexts.

Of course, for Weber, the ability to grasp the subjective quality
of human behavior is dependent upon the scientist's ability to
interpret the causal meaning of human action. "A correct causal
interpretation of a concrete course of action", wrote Weber, "is
arrived at when the overt action and the motives have both been
correctly apprehended and at the same time their relation has
become meaningfully comprehensible."[9] In order that he might
more precisely identify and analyze what he considered to be the
matrix of meaningful action within human behavior, Weber coined the concept "social relationship" to describe patterned human
interaction which is intentional, meaningful and symbolic. The
precision in the development of this concept was quite refined.
Identifying six types of social relations designated as "modes of
orientation of social action", Weber thought of these as "patterns
of human behavior attributable to the recognition of normative
expectations." The six types have been briefly identified and defined by Larson in the following way: "(1) *Usage* described behavior performed simply to conform to a style or pattern, e.g.,
social etiquette; (2) *Custom* described habitual practices with roots

in antiquity; (3) *Rational Orientation* designated that variety of
social action which is the consequence of actors orienting themselves to one another on the basis of "similar ulterior expectations," e.g., mutual self-interest; (4) *Fashion* described social action
which is the result of adherence to contemporary fad; (5) *Conven-
tion* designated that type of social action performed in recognition of strong moral obligation in the manner of Sumner's 'mores',
and (6) *Law* described that type of social action performed in
recognition of codified expectations and restrictions."[10]

Because Weber conceives of "sociology as a comprehensive
science of social action", the struggle to arrive at and maintain a
scientifically justifiable stance vis-a-vis behavior is necessarily
organic, not static. "The scientists' goal", Aron explains in a
major treatise on Weber, "is to arrive at propositions of fact or
at relations of causality or at comprehensive interpretations that
are universally valid."[11] Aron then points out that this approach
to scientific research suggests that science itself is reasoned action
tending towards a goal, viz., "universally valid truth." Yet, he
explains, the goal itself is a value-laden determination, viz., "the
value of a truth demonstrated by universally valid facts." Thus,
he concludes, forcing Weber's logic to its terminus, "scientific
behavior is, therefore, a combination of rational action in relation
to a goal and rational action in relation to a value." Science, then
in the Weberian tradition, is an instancing of the rationalization
process in search of truth thought to be of value in itself.

Quick to defend sociology as a science yet distinct from the
natural sciences, Weber never ceased making much of the distinction between a physical scientist who studies non-human entities
and social scientists who study human behavior. For the latter,
the subject-matter is the *human subject* whereas for the former the
subject-matter is the *non-human object*. Because the social scientist
studies human behavior and in view of the fact that common
language is replete with terms applied to such behavior, Weber
was particularly conscious of the need for refined and precise
technical nomenclature in sociology. The rich breadth and depth
of human emotion and behavior makes any attempt to analyze and
understand them susceptible to misinterpretation or distortion.

Sociological Methodology
Weber's methodology, of course, depends upon his conviction

that the social scientist can 'understand' 'meaningful' social 'relationships.' Weber used the term "sympathetic introspection" to designate the core of this approach. "For the verifiable accuracy of interpretation of the meaning of a phenomenon", wrote Weber, "it is a great help to be able to put one's self imaginatively in the place of the actor and thus sympathetically to participate in his experience."[12] Thus, if the sociologist is to "interpretively grasp" the 'meaning' of human behavior, he must come to grips with the causal motivation behind the action itself. "A motive," explains Simpson, in this context is thought by Weber to be "a complex of subject meaning which seems to the actor himself or to the observer an adequate ground for the conduct in question."[13] Beyond "sympathetic introspection" in Weber's methodology is another complementing analytical device called the "typological analysis." Though a later section is given over to a careful discussion of this concept, we should here outline its characteristics. As an aid to research rather than "conclusive interpretations", Weber thought of the ideal types as a categorizing process enabling the scientist to contrast "actual types" with their common ideals. Whereas the former types were limited to historical circumstances, "the ideal type was," explains Larson, "an attempt to deal with the problem of the historical relativity of conceptual types by means of the construction of a limited number of terms which could be used as constant generalizable abstractions".[14] Simpson has given us a cogent commentary on the nature and purpose of the ideal-type as a methodological instrument in the following: "As far as individual social action is concerned the sociologist seeks to arrive at an understanding of individual motives, in groups he seeks to arrive at motives which are typical of the group. In both cases the sociologist seeks to arrive at ideal types which establish what the action of individuals or groups would be if it were strictly rational, unaffected by errors or emotional factors, and if, furthermore, it were completely and unequivocally directed to a single end. Actual behavior of individuals and groups is then studied as a deviation from such ideal-typical behavior."[15]

Weber was particularly interested in the possibility of identifying those intervening factors preventing the actual facts from actualizing the ideal type. Essentially the ideal-type in the hands of the sociologist is, according to Julien Freund, an orthodox Weberian, "able to measure the gap between the ideal-typical objectively possible action and the empirical action, and ascertain the part played by irrationality and chance or by the intrusion of accidental, emotional and other elements."[16] Weber's real interest was in grasping the total life-situation, the "sit sez leben," of the acting subject in order that the 'ideal,' 'actional,' and 'gap' dimensions to human behavior might more clearly be understood as meaningful action. This Weber thought of as the 'organic' school of sociology which he described in some detail: "(Organic sociology attempts) to understand social interaction by using as a point of departure the 'whole' within which the individual acts. His action and behavior are then interpreted somewhat in the way that a physiologist would treat the role of an organ of the body in the 'economy' of the organism, that is from the point of view of the survival of the latter . . . this functional frame of reference is convenient for purposes of practical illustration and for provisional orientation. In these respects it is not only useful but indispensable. But at the same time if its cognitive value is overestimated and its concepts illegitimately 'reified,' it can be highly dangerous . . . in certain circumstances this is the only available way of determining just what process of social action it is important to understand in order to explain a given phenomenon. But this is only the beginning of sociological analysis as here understood".[17]

One of the major sources of the traditionally oriented sociologists like Durkheim who readily thought in static categories of 'things' for objective analysis was Weber's incessant harping upon the necessary incompleteness of all modern science. "Nothing," explains Aron, "is more alien to Weber's way of thinking than the image so dear to Auguste Comte of a science which possesses the essential and has set up a closed and definitive system of fundamental laws."[18] The organic school relied heavily upon an evolving, dynamic, and organic science—incomplete necessarily due to the evolving nature of its own subject matter, i.e., "science is its own evolution." Particularly in the realms of history and culture, accumulated knowledge is socio-historical in context growing out of the perpetual formulations and reformulations of questions about humanly experienced 'reality.' New and re-phrased questions necessarily grow from the onward movement of history. "Insofar as history-reality renews the curiosity of the historian or sociologist, it becomes impossible to conceive of a complete history or sociology. "To speak in the manner of Max Weber," says Aron, "history and sociology could only be complete if human evolution were at an end. Humanity would have lost all creative capacity for the science of human achievement to be definitive."

Nowhere is this organic dynamism of history and society more concretely evidenced than in the particularized behavior of individual persons. By focussing upon the ideal-actual continuum bridged by the 'gap' factors, Weber hoped his action schema would facilitate the identification of the causes of human behavior. Weber was intentionally super-sensitive to the inevitable variations in individual person's responses to identical situations, choosing to respond to the challenge of identifying which factors—rational or emotional—would prove paramount in any given set of circumstances. "Any regularities in interhuman conduct," Martindale reminds us, "represent no more than the stabilization of behavior in terms of rationality, ethical fixity, emotionality, or habit."[19]

With the advent of the twentieth century came also a revival of Kantian philosophy in Germany and elsewhere. The gap between the German idealists and the English and French positivists was no less a challenge to Weber than the ideal-actual gap of methodological interest. Kant had laid down a metaphysical mandate which survived several centuries and functioned well again as scientists and philosophers joined in argument that values per se necessarily separate the material world (matter) from the spiritual (spirit). While agreeing with the positivists that social and cultural 'things' can be objectively analyzed and causally understood in terms of methods comparable to those in the natural sciences, he nevertheless sided with the German idealists who argued persuasively and vehemently that human behavior, because of the dynamics of meaning and ideas, necessarily required a subjective understanding from within the action and not outside. Weber felt, to the distress of both Kantian idealists and the Franco-English positivists, that 'verstehen' or internal understanding was no less scientific than any other science; rather, he contended that the social sciences were in a particularly advantageous position, for whereas both natural and social sciences must study factual things by objective observation, only the social sciences must also study social facts from *within* through reflective self-awareness and introspection. Verstehen does not displace scientific methodology and authenticity; it supplements, augments, enhances, and contributes to scientific analysis of human behavior.

The refinement of Weber's use of the term 'action' to mean specifically human behavior to which individuals attach subjective meaning greatly facilitated both the focussing of the sociologist's range of subject matter and nurtured the growth of specialized nomenclature within the social sciences. Weber's unrelenting emphasis upon the meaning 'dynamic', operative within behavior saved him from the foibles of the radical behaviorists who refused to concede that behavior could be studied scientifically in terms of actor-attributed meaning of action. Though in the 1920s and 1930s, behaviorism held the day, particularly in America, the neo-Weberians such as MacIver and Znaniecki have recovered much of the ground again for Weber's methodology. In his final treatise, Weber reaffirmed his definition of sociology as a "science which attempts the interpretative understanding of social action in order thereby to arrive at a causal explanation of its course and effects."[20] Today, we would say with the phenomenologists that Weber attempted to understand action from the actor's point of view as, for example, in religious behavior we attempt to understand the faith from the believer's point of view. The interpretation of human action in terms of attributable subjective meaning— behavior in terms of meaning-giving values—is the task of authentic sociology.

With the use of this methodology, Weber managed to weave himself creatively through the Scylla of positivism (natural and social sciences are essentially the same) and the Charybdis of historicism i.e., the realms of "kultur und geist" (culture and history) are beyond the sciences due to the diversity and unidentifiable factors affecting human action. Weber struggled to vindicate his science (proceeding from abstraction and generalization) while demonstrating an effective analysis of observable behavior from within the meaning-motivations of the actor. Sociology, he believed, holds in productive and creative balance "the value-bound problem choices of the investigator and the value-neutral methods of social research.'[21]

Of course, the "meaning of meaning" has given many a metaphysician a bit of a tussle, and even with Weber, there was the awareness of the concept's slippery nature. In an extended quote,

we encounter Weber's most refined attempt at its clarification
for sociological use :

"The word *meaning*," he writes, "may refer first to the actual
existing meaning in the given concrete case of a particular actor,
or to the average approximate meaning attributable to a given
plurality of actors ; or secondly to the theoretically conceived
pure type of subjective meaning attributed to the hypothetical
actor or actors in a given type of action. In no case does it refer
to an objectively correct meaning or one which is "true" in some
metaphysical sense. It is this which distinguishes the empirical
sciences of action, such as sociology and history, from the dogma-
tic disciplines in that area, such as jurisprudence, logic ethics,
and aesthetics, which seek to acertain the 'true' and 'valid' meanings associated with the objectives of their investigation."[22]
Within the framework of an interpretive-meaning approach to
social facts, Weber says that the grounds on which the scientist
says he understands can be either 'rational' (logical and mathematical) or 'emotionally empathetic' or 'artistically appreciative'
in nature. "In his methodology," says Rossides, "Weber insisted
on a steady interplay between theory and fact, a cardinal principle of Enlightenment philosophy." "Yet", continues Rossides,
"(Weber) differed from the Enlightenment and its heirs in his
belief that the purpose of that interplay is not to uncover social
reality, but to render portions of it amenable to human understanding and control."[23]

In summary : from the outset, Weber had hoped to demonstrate the scientific capabilities of sociology by adhering to the
multi-verification axiom of the physical sciences. Thus, he attempted in countless ways and on numerous occasions to demonstrate that history can be written as a rational science based on
repetitive verification and confirmation. He argued that historical
and sociological statements can accurately describe facts which
reflect definite reality, i.e., human behavior, in terms of the meaning assigned to it by the actors themselves. "Weber's ambition,"
Aron explains, "was to understand how individuals have lived in
different societies as a result of different beliefs..."[24]

Science and the Place of Values

To the positivist, values are forbidden subject matter. For the
idealist, they negate the possibility of a science of human beha-

vior. For Weber, values are precisely the subject-matter and make possible a truly scientific study of human actions. He is unquestionably the leading spokesman for what is usually labelled the value-free approach in sociology. There is no paradox or irony in Weber's dual contention that 'values' make human behavior meaningful and value perspectives are neccs arily forbidden to the scientist. To deny the possibility of a science of human action because 'values' are inextricably a part of the scientist as person is an affront to the rational man's ability to articulate and then hold in suspension his own value commitments. Yet, vis-a-vis the idealist, for the positivist to dismiss the study of values in human behavior is to abandon the *sine qua non* of all human behavior, for values express meaning which makes behavior rational. Within this dilemma, i.e., scientific method and value judgements, Weber worked out his profoundly insightful methodology. Shils and Finch have succinctly summarized the refined Weberian positon in the following statement :

"The scientific treatment of value judgements may not only understand and empathetically analyze the desired ends and the ideals which underline them; it can also 'judge' them critically. This criticism can...be no more than a formal logical judgement of historically given value judgements and ideas, a testing of the ideals according to the postulate of the internal *consistency* of the desired end. It can assist (the acting person) in becoming aware of the ultimate standards of value which he does not make explicit to himself, or which he must presuppose in order to be logical...As to whether the person expressing these value judgements *should* adhere to these ultimate standards is his personal affair; it involves will and conscience, not empirical knowledge."[25]

From the outset, Weber, himself well trained in the German philosophical tradition of Kantian idealism, took issue with the positivists who wished to ignore the value base of all human decisions. To pretend otherwise is to make the scientist look either naive or shallow. "There is no absolutely 'objective' scientific analysis of culture or of social phenomena," wrote Weber, which is "independent of special and 'one-sided' viewpoints according to which. . .expressly or tacitly, consciously or unconsciously. . .they are selected, analyzed and organized for expository purposes."[26] Objective knowledge of the natural world must forever remain an outside acquaintance and physically observed phenomena, but

with human nature (behavior-action-motivation-rationality-cau-
sation-will), we can with care reach inside the motivational and
emotional factors of action and grasp the essence of human behavior. "Social facts," Weber argued to the end, "are in the last
resort *intelligible* facts." Through 'verstehen,' the social scientist
can pierce through the subjective meanings to the values behind
all and each human action motivated by rational and emotional
elements. "A sociology of the chicken yard," writes Coser, "can
only account for regularities of behavior. . . . A sociology of human
grounds," he continues, "has the inestimable advantage of having
access to the subjective aspects of action, to the realm of meaning and motivation."[27] From this vantage point, scientists can be
optimistic and aggressive in their efforts to come to a grasp of
the human mystery of behavior. From this perspective, Weber's
definition is vindicated as "that science which aims at the interpretive *understanding* (verstehen) of social behavior in order to
gain an explanation of its causes, its course, and its effects."[28]

Weber, too often misunderstood by his peers, agreed with the
historicists and idealists of German metaphysics who argued that
the "facts of human behavior are not 'givens' or data, but the
non-necessary creations of history."[29] The relationship between
values and science Weber wished to establish as a creative and
self-conscious balance vis-a-vis antagonism (idealists) and alienation (positivists). Scientists cannot choose whether or not to make
value judgements for, as Rossides points out, "values are what
prompt science." Rather, realizing that science itself is a value of
western culture, scientists must either be self-consciously aware of
their own value-commitments and judgements or else they are not.
If the scientist wishes to remain scientific in his analysis of human
action, he will be as rigorous in his self-scrutiny of value-pre-
suppositions as he is in the scrutiny of social facts. "Values," Rossides continues, "are focussed and clarified by logical analysis,
and the means for attaining them are found by determining the
causal sequences in the factual determination for the simple
reason that reason and facts have no necessary relation either to
each other or to values." Weber addressed himself to an extended
explanation in a major essay which seems appropriate to quote
from at this point :

> Today one usually speaks of science as 'free from presupposi-
> tions.' Is there such a thing? It depends upon what one under-

stands thereby. All scientific work presupposes that the rules of logic and method are valid; these are the general foundations of our orientation in the world; and, at least for our special question, these presuppositions are the least problematic aspect of science. Science further presupposes that what is yielded by scientific work is important in the sense that it is 'worth being known.' In this, obviously, are contained all our problems. For this presupposition cannot be proved by scientific means. It can only be *interpreted* with reference to its ultimate meaning, which we must reject or accept according to our ultimate position towards life."[30]

Then Weber goes on to say that

"science 'free from presuppositions,' in the sense of a rejection of religious bonds, does not know of the 'miracle' and the 'revelation.' If it did, science would be unfaithful to its own 'presuppositions.' The believer knows both, miracle and revelation. And science 'free from presuppositions' expects from him no less—and no more—than acknowledgement that if the process can be explained without those supernatural interventions, which an empirical explanation has to eliminate as causal factors, the process has to be explained the way science attempts to do. And the believer can do this without being disloyal to his faith"

Inevitably, Weber's early exposure to politics and his fascination with it while deeply committed to scientific objectivity brought him into a serious struggle with the two warring and hostile camps of German social science. Weber's initial writings were grossly misunderstood for many too readily assumed that his value-free (werfrei) sociology meant that he disallowed any personal views of the sociologists upon his field of study, vigorously suppressing such personal perspectives."This," explains Abraham, "was far from what Weber had in mind. What he was violently opposed to was the growing tendency among academic people to use their platform for propaganda and partisan purposes. (Weber) thought that this was not only prostituting one's intergrity but was fatal to any kind of genuine scholarship."[31] Of course, Weber was well known for his own deeply held positions as a scholar in search of truth yet a passionate apostle of the liberal ideals of society. Indeed one of the persistent tensions operative in Weber's personal life was his dual attraction to both practical politics and to scholarship—feeling deeply the political and cultural significance of historical and sociological investigations—insisting nonetheless in the absolute distinctiveness, of the two professions, politics

and academia. His tensions were particularly evident in his fostering of a professional class of politicians to run the German
administrative machine. Condemning Bismarck for failure to
nurture a professional class, Weber attributed the German debacle
to the weak government brought on by political dilettantism. His
personal commitment to and his universal demand for the test of
scientific objectivity without reference to one's own personal biases "caused the schism in the social sciences in Germany" for
"the weakness of many of the professions in German universities,
against whom he (Weber) inveighed with all the power he could
command, was precisely their failure to be objective in this
sense…" While arguing that neither scientific nor philosophical
analyses could solve the disputes arising out of ethical and cultural values, he did argue that "empirical scientific investigation
could lead to the discovery of the ultimate motive of human behavior, which," he believed, "would serve as a preliminary to an
adequate causal explanation of historical events…"[32]

Because history and sociology are created values and are understood in reference to values, a science of human culture might
fairly be defined as, in Aron's words, "a rational activity whose
goal is to arrive at judgements of fact which will be universally
valid."[33] The challenge is for the development of a universalized
value-judgement using socio-historical instances of human creativity. Aron says the problem is resolvable by distinguishing between value-judgement (werturteil) and value-reference (wertbeziehung). This distinction will help many an aspiring student
of Weber's thought steer clear of needless pitfalls. According to
Aron, judgements are personal and necessarily subjective, dependent upon one's values and beliefs. To declare, for example,
that freedom of speech is a positive value worthy of protection
is a value-judgement. "The term 'value reference', on the other
hand, "simply means that (for example) the sociologist of politics will regard freedom of expression as a matter on which historical subjects have disagreed, as a stake in controversies or
conflicts between men and parties, and he can explore the past or
present political reality by placing it in relation to the specific
value, 'freedom.' For the sociologist of politics, freedom is a
point of reference. The sociologist as such is not obliged to profess belief in freedom." Aron concludes : "freedom need only
be one of the concepts by means of which he selects and organi-

zes a part of the reality to be studied—a procedure which merely implies that political freedom is a value for the men who have experienced it, and therefore a value for the sociologist in organizing the subject matter of his science." Therefore, to be true to the method of Weber, *wertbeziehung* (value relevance) must be thought of as bearing upon the "selection of the problem" but not upon "the interpretation of the phenomenon." Weber never ceased to emphasize the "disjunction between the world of facts and the world of values," as Coser said, "the impossibility of deriving 'ought statements' from 'is statements.' "[34]

In short, consistent with Weber's insistence upon the *sui generis* nature of social facts as value-laden and social scientists as people with value-orientations, he insists that the approaching of "evaluative ideas," since inevitable, must therefore be done with conscious deliberation. For Weber, the intentioned 'suspension' of value-perspectives is possible for the trained scientist. He employs an 'ethical-neutrality' though he himself is not devoid of value-preferences or value-commitments. "Evaluative ideas," explains Rossides, "are not ethical imperatives to be realized, nor are they hypotheses to be proved—they are merely expository aids to help bring interest areas into relief."[35]

Verstehen: Understanding and Meaning
We have already introduced Weber's revolutionary approach to the study of human behavior implicit in his key methodological concept called 'verstehen' which means comprehending or understanding on the level of meaning. The notion of verstehen is based on what Weber perceived as an advantage of the social sciences over the natural sciences. In the natural sciences we can only observe uniformities and deduce generalizations about the functional relationships of elements; comprehension is therefore mediate. In the social sciences, on the other hand, we can understand the actions and comprehend the subjective intentions of the actors; comprehension is immediate. We understand, for instance, why a student is repeating a verse over and over, why a politician makes promises or why the mother rocks her baby. Verstehen makes possible the scientific study of social behavior in two ways: it facilitates direct observational understanding of the subjective meaning of human actions and it facilitates understanding of the underlying motive. MacIver has put it succinctly:

Social facts are all in the last resort *intelligible* facts. When we know why a government falls or how a price is determined or why a strike takes place or how a primitive tribe worships or why the birth-rate declines, our knowledge is different in one vital respect from the knowledge of why a meteor falls or how the moon keeps its distance from the earth or why liquids freeze or how plants utilize nitrogen. Facts of the second kind we know only from the outside; facts of the first kind we know, in some degree at least, from the inside. Why did the citizens turn against the government? Why did the union call a strike? To answer these questions we must project ourselves into the situations we are investigating. We must learn the values and the aims and the hopes of human beings as they operate within a particular situation. There is no inside story of why a meteor falls or why a liquid freezes. We comprehend it as a datum, as the expression of a law and nothing more. It is because on the other hand there is always an inside story, or in other words a meaning, in human affairs that we never attain more than partial or relative truth. Here is the paradox of knowledge. The only things we know as immutable truths are the things we do not understand. The only things we understand are mutable and never fully known.[36]

When Weber combined his notion of 'understanding' with his modified Platonism called 'ideal types,' sociology took a giant step forward in both scientific sophistication and socio-political utility. Whereas social realities under Weber's analysis "must be understood (verstehen) by imagining oneself into the experience of men and women as they act out their own worlds," explain Collins and Makowsky, we understand the complementary "ideal types" to be "the tools for making scientific generalizations out of our understanding of this infinitely complex and shifting world."[37] It was necessary for Weber to refine his methodological skills to handle large and complex social phenomena for he aspired to outline and analyze the entire matrix contributing to the rise of modern industrial civilization. Behind economics, law, politics, and religion, Weber sought to analyze the interconnections of all social behavior so that no rational human act was left out. In such a pursuit, he produced nothing short of an outright sociology of world history. He was not driven by a sublimated metaphysical allegiance but by a sheer obsession with scientific understanding of human existence manifest in behavior. "For Weber," explains Rossides, "*Verstehen* sociology was not a search for the underlying principle of existence, but a conscious search for insights and solutions to the unique and changing problems that human beings face, an orientation that Weber stated epigrammatically when he said that social science has 'eternal youth'."[38] Contending that sociology or any science is unable either to validate metaphysical knowledge or any system of values, Weber's scientific method was posited against both the liberal and Marxist positions which wished to 'use' science to further their own 'value' systems in the name of scientific truth.

In fostering the creative potential of his method, Weber was always ready to assert his position that social facts as human phenomena necessarily involve the action of agents (individuals) who themselves attribute a sense or reason or causal factor to what they are doing. Sociology, then, requires an understanding of that sense of the attributed meaning or reason. In this respect, Weber found himself in the German tradition which claimed Hegel, Dilthey, and Rickert as proponents. When "verstehen" seemed to lose its analytical capability, for example, when the scientist looked at unfamiliar or bizzare behavior, Weber would supplement verstehen with a particularly distinct method of inquiry, viz., causal explanation, a concept to be discussed later. Weber's breadth of knowledge, nôt just in the classics but in philosophy and theology, history and economics, gave him a distinct advantage in terms of reach and grasp of ideas. From the philosopher and cultural historian Wilhelm Dilthey (1833-1911), Weber learned much. Coser has drafted for us a brief synopsis of Dilthey's philosophical perspective which had a particularly important bearing upon Weber's method:

"Dilthey opposed positivism by constructing the outlines of an approach to the data of human culture and human history, which, though meant to be scientific, was wholly at variance with the approach of the natural sciences. Knowledge of the world of man, Dilthey claimed, could only be attained through an internal process, through experience (erleben) and understanding (verstehen), rather than through merely external knowledge. . . . The natural sciences (Naturwissenschaften) can do no more than explain (eklaeren) observed events by relating them to natural laws. In the humanistic disciplines, the Geisteswissenschaften, knowledge is not external but internal. Men are intelligible to us in their uniqueness and individuality."[39]

Weber's uncanny ability to appropriate significant philosophical insights without adopting the whole system of distinguished German philosophy allowed him access to a range of materials in the development of his own unique position. While taking advantage of Kant's profoundly provocative distinction between 'practical' and 'pure' reason and Hegel's distinction between 'state' and 'society,' as well as drawing from Marx's materialistic interpretations, Weber was able like none before or after him to avoid both the dangers of a radical subjectivism and that of an anti-scientific historicism. "Against the view that men's actions have an unintended significance, variously derived from (or imputed to) an Absolute Spirit, the necessities embodied in the organization of production or the struggle for survival, Weber developed his concepts in terms of the meaning that individuals attribute to their action in society."[40] With the aid of Dilthey's notion of 'understanding' and that of his psychiatrist-philosopher friend Karl Jasper's notion of the distinction between 'verstehen' and 'explanation,' Weber moved on to argue that intuitive and causal knowledge are not irreconcilable within the context of (sinn) meaning. Through his efforts to bridge the gap between idealism and positivism, he never faltered in his emphasis upon the scientifically authenticated search for subjective meanings which characterize the action of human behavior.

Causation and Probability
According to Weber sociology must not only interpret social phenomena comprehensively but it must also explain them causally. Weber distinguished two types of causal inquiry: historical causality and sociological causality. "Historical causality determines the unique circumstances that have given rise to a given event. Sociological causality assumes the establishment of a regular relationship between two phenomena, which need not take the form 'A makes B inevitable,' but may take the form 'A is more or less favorable to B'."[41] The former explains how a set of historical constellations or social situations have brought about a particular event. For example, trying to determine the causes of World War I or the Chinese Revolution would be a quest for historical reality. Sociological causality on the other hand seeks to establish a regular connection between a set of variables or phenomena. Thus, instead of identifying the specific causes of World

War I or the Chinese Revolution, sociological causality seeks to single out factors that trigger a war or a revolution. The causal explanation expressed in terms of probability simply states that a set of antecedents are likely to have produced a given historical event. As Aron points out, "it is enough to begin with historical reality as it was, to show that, if some antecedent or other had not occurred or had occurred differently, the event we are trying to explain would have been different as well." It is neither possible nor essential to construct an imaginary chain of events, or reconstruct what could have happened in detail; "the causality between a situation and an event is adequate when we feel that the situation made the event, if not inevitable, at least very probable." Similarly, using sociological causality, Weber sought to explain how a set of values that constituted the Protestant Ethic favored the emergence of modern capitalism.

Within the typological framework, Weber elaborated both historical and sociological types of causality. Since he doubted the possibility of sustained objective empirical certainty in social research, he preferred more realistically to follow "a variety of causal chains" which penetratingly circumscribed the phenomenon under scrutiny. In establishing the right approach to the effective utilization of causation analysis, Weber insisted upon the comparative method, emphasizing the fact that from within his system, sociology is always understood to be the study of the behavior of individuals whether in collectivities of states, nations, or families. All collectivities are comprised necessarily of individual instances of personal action. Collectivities within social science must be distinguished from organisms in the natural sciences for in the latter the interest is on "merely demonstrating functional relationships and uniformities" whereas in the study of social collectivities, "we can accomplish something which is never attainable in the natural sciences, namely the subjective understanding of the actions of component individuals."[42] Because the natural sciences are limited to identifying causal uniformities in objective phenomena, there is no claim nor need to "understand" these objective collectivities. Rather, the emphasis is upon careful external observation and predictable functional relationships established by repetitive observation.

"This additional achievement (in the social sciences) of explanation by interpretive understanding, as distinguished from

external observation, is of course attained only at a price—the
more hypothetical and fragmentary character of its results.
Nevertheless, subjective understanding is the specific characteristic of sociological knowledge."

What Rossides calls the 'fortuitous nature of causation' in
Weber's work is illustrated by Weber's own analysis of the origins
of capitalism. The narrative expresses the variegated matrix out
of which capitalism emerged rather than a neatly descriptive
simplistic cause and effect one-dimensional unilinear explanation.
Rossides says Weber's insistence that "religion, ethics, ideas, and
values be incorporated into causal theory in no way implied that
any version of normative culture was true or inherent in human
nature . . . ."[43] Rather, says Rossides,

"Weber's denial that human nature had inherent propensities,
together with his wide grasp of historical materials, led him
away from general or systematic theory. His nominalism led
him only to limited or historical generalizations . . . His antipathy to systematic sociology also marks his characterization
of capitalism; in Weber's overall theory capitalism emerges
only because of a fortuitous confluence of factors, some new,
some old or dormant, and some ironic and unintentional."

Not choosing to take the easy way out by employing rigidly
doctrinaire methodologies, whether Marxist, positivist, or idealist, Weber argued for, and domonstrated the effective use of,
this multi-dimensional variegated causality in analyzing human
motives and behavior.

THE IDEAL TYPE—ABSTRACTION AND ANALYSIS

A creative confluence of neo-Platonism, Dilthey's historicism,
and Kantian metaphysics gave rise to one of Weber's most distinguished contributions to sociological theory, viz., the ideal
type. Because the development of this methodological device has
proven so effective in Weberian analysis, he has himself taken the
time to record in detail his initial and formative thinking on its
emergence. In an essay entitled, 'Objectivity,' appearing in 1904
in the distinguished *Archiv Fur Socialwissenschaft Und Social-
politik*, Weber wrote:

"We have in abstract economic theory an illustration of those
synthetic constructs which have been designated as 'ideas' of

historical phenomena. It offers us an ideal picture of events on the commodity-market under conditions of a society organized on the principles of an exchange economy, free competition and rigorously rational conduct. This conceptual pattern brings together certain relationships and events of historical life into a complex, which is conceived as an internally consistent system. Substantively, this construct in itself is like a utopia which has been arrived at by the analytical accentuation of certain elements of reality. Its relationship to the empirical data consists solely in the fact that where market-conditioned relationships of the type referred to by the abstract construct are discovered or suspected to exist in reality to some extent, we can make the characteristic features of this relationship pragmatically clear and understandable by reference to an ideal type."[44]

"An *ideal type* is an analytical construct that serves the investigator as a measuring rod to ascertain similarities as well as deviations in concrete cases."[45] It is neither a statistical average nor an hypothesis; rather it is a mental construct, an organization of intelligible relations within a historical entity, formed by exaggerating certain essential features of a given phenomenon so that no one case of that phenomenon corresponds exactly to the constructed type but every case of that phenomenon falls within the definitional framework. In the words of Shils and Finch, "An ideal type is formed by the one-sided accentuation of one or more points of view and by the synthesis of a great many diffuse, discrete, more or less present and occasionally absent *concrete individual* phenomena, which are arranged according to those one-sidedly emphasized viewpoints into a unified *analytical* construct."[46]

Weber developed three kinds of ideal types based on their levels of abstraction: (a) ideal types of historical particulars which refer to specific historical realities such as 'Western city', 'Protestant ethic', or 'modern capitalism': (b) ideal types which refer to abstract elements of the historical reality that are observable in a variety of historical and cultural contexts, such us 'bureaucracy' or 'feudalism'; (c) ideal types "that constitute rationalizing reconstructions of a particular kind of behavior."[47] All propositions in economic theory may be said to fall in this category since they "are merely ideal-typical reconstructions of the ways men would behave if they were pure economic subjects."

Weber, of course, was falsely accused of passing value-judgements upon social phenomena by virtue of using the ideal type.

The ideal type as Weber understood it had nothing to do with moral ideal, for the type of perfection implied in the ideal is purely a logical one and not to be found in pure form in any socio-historical situation. Any social phenomenon has an ideal type, be it a brothel, a house of worship or a market place. "The elementary duty of scientific self-conrol," says Weber, "and the only ways to avoid serious and foolish blunders require a sharp, precise distinction between logically comparative analysis of reality by ideal-types in the logical sense and the value-judgement of reality on the basis of ideals."[48] Furthermore, Weber is insistent that ideal types are decidedly not theoretical hypotheses which must be proved by reduction of the empirical world to universal laws. Weber continues:

> "It is not the 'actual' interconnections of 'things' but the conceptual interconnections of problems which define the scope of the various sciences. A new 'science' emerges where new problems are pursued by new methods and truths are thereby discovered which open up significant new points of view."

Weber never claimed the ideal type to completely exhaust every conceivable empirical structure. Social structures are too complex for that. Weary of attempts at adapting natural science ideas and concepts into the social sciences, Weber's criticisms of the whole field of naturalistic positivism and socio-cultural positivism centered around his belief that socio-historical life of mankind is too "infinite and multifarious" for such reductionism. Weber explains:

> "What the content of the ideal-type, be it an ethical, a legal, an aesthetic, or a religious norm, or a technical, an economic, or a cultural maxim or any other type of valuation in the most rational form possible, it has only one function in an empirical investigation. Its function is the comparison with empirical reality in order to establish its divergences or similarities, to describe them with the most unambiguously intelligible concepts; and to understand and explain them causally."

Weber cautioned against the tendency to treat the ideal typology as a *carte blanche* solution to all social analysis. It is strictly a "methodological device" and is not intended to suggest that social phenomena are essentially rational complexes, though the ideal type is a rational grid for logical observation and analysis. Since the fundamental task of the social sciences is understanding, first

at the level of 'observational understanding' and then at a deeper
level of 'explanatory understanding' Weber has given us a brief
example of the practical application of his ideal type to the study
of religious collectivities. He wrote:

"... the ideal-type is an attempt to analyze historically unique configurations or their individual components by means
of genetic concepts. Let us take, for instance, the concepts
'church' and 'sect.' They may be broken down purely class-
ificatorily into complexes of characteristics whereby not only
the distinction between them but also the content of the concept must constantly remain fluid. If however I wish to formulate the concept of 'sect' genetically, e.g., with reference to
certain important cultural significances which the 'sectarian
spirit' has had for modern culture, certain characteristics of
both become essential because they stand in an adequate
causal relationship to those influences. However, the concepts
thereupon become ideal-typical in the sense that they appear
in full conceptual integrity either not at all or only in individual instances. Here as elsewhere every concept which is not
purely classificatory diverges from reality."

The ideal type concept grew out of a creative convergence of
two of Weber's other key concepts, viz., verstehen and causal
explanation. The ideal type is not, contrary to what German meta-
physicians would have liked it to be, a purely classificatory concept rather than an 'ideal' classification, for the former concept
is reached by "abstraction from a wide range of phenomena with
differing individual characteristics" whereas the latter is intended
"to illuminate what is peculiar to a given cultural phenomenon."[49]
Applied primarily to various types of rational behavior, it is
fundamentally "a model of what an agent would do if he were to
act completely rationally according to the criteria of rationality
involved in his behavior's sense." In such instances, the ideal type
provides a milieu of precise language and procedure for analyzing
specific behavior while aiding in the formulation of theoretical
explanations for behavioral instances which vary from what is
called the "ideal-typical norm."

Sociology of Religion
From early in Weber's life, the impact of the confluence of religious beliefs and political and economic interests within his
family was obvious. A source of personal tension and a marked
strain throughout his life, Weber turned his analytical skills to

an investigation of their fundamental relationships with such thoroughness and creative genius that sociology still looks to his *Protestant Ethic and the Spirit of Capitalism* as the classical study in the field. In this work Weber sought to demonstrate that economic factors do not represent a constant and independent variable to which all others stand in dependence. This, namely the treatment of the economic factor as the paramount and determining influence, Weber believed, was Marx's major weakness and ultimate failure. Weber spent his best and most critical years demonstrating with careful precision and lucid narrative that the essentially economic factors are, as Abraham puts it, "one variable, a very important one, in close relationship with others, affected by them as in fact it in turn can affect them."[50]

The Protestant ethic was for Weber a sub-species of social phenomena within the category 'religion.' And religion, Weber was quick to point out, is decidedly distinct from 'magic,' the former intentionally rational, the latter not. Weber refined a functional definition of magical religion before he turned his attention to rational religion and Protestant Christianity. Magical religions, says Weber, are thoroughly conservative designed to "safeguard the traditions," maintaining the 'taboo' as non-abstract rules of finite specificity, and tend by and large to develop polytheistic and pantheistic world-views. The emergence of rational religion, displacing magicians and shamans with priests and prophets, had an opposite impact upon society with the primary norm being ethics, i.e., "an abstract body of rules governing all conduct under all conditions. . ."[51] "For Weber," explains Rossides, "religion was not rational in the sense of being true or scientifically valid, but rational to the degree that it departed from magic."

The investigation of the relationship between religious values and economic interests was triggered by a number of factors. In the first place, Weber noticed that Protestants, particularly Protestants of certain sects, were the chief captains of industry and possessed more wealth and economic means than other religious groups, notably Catholics. Therefore, he wanted to ascertain whether there is an essential harmony between the Protestant ethic and the spirit of capitalism. He also sought to find out whether and to what extent a cluster of values in the religions of India, China and the Middle East facilitated or hindered the development of capitalism.

Now, in order to overcome the methodological problem of defining Capitalism and Protestant Ethic, Max Weber made use of the concept of ideal type. Protestant Ethic does not refer to any particular theological doctrine but a set of values and belief systems that make up a religious ideal. Capitalism, in its ideal type, is thought of by Weber to be that complex activity designed specifically to maximize profit through the careful and intentional exercise of rational organization and management of production. But capitalism as an economic enterprise designed to maximize profit existed all over the world. However, there is something unique about Western capitalism—the idea of unlimited accumulation beyond the notion of maximum profit and the conviction that the desire for profit must be tempered (mediated) by discipline and science, not by speculation and adventure.

Weber now wished to draw religion and economics under his analytical spell, believing, as he did, that the relationship was complex and multi-dimensional. A prime target for his scrutiny was his ready detection of the mutuality of influences between religion and economics, particularly the empirical fact of social stratification and religious behavior correlations. The initial impetus for Weber's famous work, (1904-1905), *The Protestant Ethic and the Spirit of Capitalism*, centered around two general observations, viz., (1) in countless places in the world great material achievements had resulted from the work of monastic orders dedicated to a life of the spirit, and (2) specifically ascetic Protestant sects were noted for their economic success. "There appeared to (be) a paradoxically positive relationship between ascetic religious belief and economic enterprise . . ."[52] By looking specifically at Calvinism, Weber began to see indisputable signs of causal correlations.

Weber identified a number of values embedded in Protestantism which are in harmony with the spirit of capitalism.[53]

1. *The shift from ritualistic and other-worldly orientation to down-to-earth pragmatism.*
The finite mind of man cannot comprehend the infinite mind of the absolute and transcendent God who created the world for His own glory. Therefore, there is no point in indulging in mysticism; rather, man should seek to understand the natural order. This is essentially an anti-ritualistic attitude that favors the development of science and rational investigation.

2. Changed Attitude Toward Work

Protestant Ethic proclaims work as a virtue, something not only good and desirable but contributing to the glory of God as well. Since Adam and Eve were evicted from the Garden of Eden with the punishment that they should henceforth earn their livelihood with the sweat of their brows, the Catholic ethic regarded work as a punitive necessity, the reminder of the original sin, and hence valued leisure. The Protestant Ethic not only encourages gainful enterprises but also insists that work is a virtue in itself since it contributes to the glory of God.

3. The Concept of Calling

This idea emerged from the Calvinist doctrine of predestination according to which every soul is predestined at birth for heaven or hell and that nothing an individual does in this life can change his ultimate fate. But there are signs by which God indicates to every individual whether he is among the elect, success in life being the most important one. Since every man is anxious to know if he is marked for salvation or damnation, he should select a calling, a vocation, work hard at it and be successful. The economic impact of this doctrine was profound indeed. No longer was it necessary for 'religious' men to take the vow of poverty, enter a monastery, undertake a pilgrimage or indulge in self-torture, some of the Catholic means of salvation popular in the Middle Ages. The new doctrine exhorts men to seek gainful enterprises, accumulate wealth and prove their destiny.

4. The New Attitude toward the Collection of Interest on Loans

The theological doctrine of Catholicism proscribed the collection of interest on loans. This prohibition discouraged the operation, at least open and legal operation, of lending houses and the accumulation of capital. It was in 1545 that Calvin wrote the famous letter giving theological sanction to the collection of interest on loans, thus approving in Calvinism a practice that had been proscribed in Catholicism. This prompted a spurt of economic activity: establishment of lending houses, new investments, and new floating capital.

5. Strictures on Alcoholism

Protestant ethic prohibits the consumption of alcoholic beverages;

there is no comparable theological doctrine in Catholicism. Indeed, prohibition movement in Western societies was always spearheaded by Protestants.

6. Encouragement of Literacy and Learning
Based on the conviction that every man should read his own Bible rather than depend on priestly interpretations, Protestant ethic placed great emphasis on literacy and learning which led to significant breakthrough in the sphere of education, leading to the development of mass education (rather than education of the clergy) and of specialized skills.

7. Rejection of Holidays
The Catholic calendar is full of holy days and almost every holy day is a holiday. This is consistent with the Catholic belief that one needs leisure to honor God with ritualistic celebrations. However, since work contributes to the glory of God in Protestant ethic, there is no need for holy days and celebrations. This means factories and other business enterprises can function seven days a week throughout the year, thus making maximum utilization of capital and other investments leading to greater productivity.

8. Protestant Asceticism
Protestant ethic also incorporates the notion that earthly things and flesh belong to the order of sin and death and therefore, one should abstain from the pleasures of the world. Thus, on the one hand, Protestant ethic exhorts people to "accumulate and accumulate" and on the other hand, it forbids the use of wealth for enjoyment. This means a ceaseless pursuit of profit, not for the sake of enjoying the pleasures of life, but simply for the satisfaction of producing more and more, undoubtedly a condition par excellence for the development of capitalism.

Now having established the essential harmony between Protestant ethic and the spirit of capitalism, Weber turned to other religions to see if there is in them a discernible cluster of values comparable to Protestant ethic that is favorable to the rise of capitalism. He found a variety of non-religious social and economic conditions conducive to the development of capitalism in China and India but the ethical system of Confucianism and the doctrine of Karma in Hinduism were not particularly favorable. Moreover, the combination of religious values that constituted the Protestant ethic was unique: an unusual blend of two apparently inconsistent notions, namely limitless accumulation of wealth and abstention from enjoyment. It would be erroneous to assume that Weber replaced a one-sided economic determinism with a one-sided "ideological determinism." He considered a variety of factors—social, economic, and political—but the confluence of values inherent in religion played a central role in the matrix of inter-relationships. Finally, Weber called scientific attention to three forms of relationships which exist between social organization and religious ideas, and which he believed warranted further investigation. These ideas were as follows: "First, social groups with particular economic interests often show themselves to be more receptive to some religious ideas than to others. For example, peasants typically incline toward some form of nature worship and aristocrats toward religious ideas compatible with their sense of status and dignity. Second, religious ideas lead to the formation of certain groups, such as monastic orders, guilds of magicians, or a clergy, and these groups may develop quite extensive economic activities. Third, the distinction between the elite and the masses is as pertinent to the religious sphere as to others—the gap between the elite and the masses poses a problem with which each of the great world religions has had to cope . . . "[54]

Class, Status, and Power—the Way of Society
From childhood, Weber had been exposed to class consciousness and the daily exercise of status and power. As a scientist, he was never far from these three dimensions in his study of human behavior; stratification, organization, and politics consumed his interests. In the formation of relationships, says Weber, men tend to be attracted to and enter into social relationships with others who share common positions and interests in the areas of economics, politics, and culture. Such clusterings or self-selecting collectivities tend also to exclude those who differ in any of the key fields of interest. Weber's concept of stratification, explain Collins and Makowsky, is essentially "a theory of group formation, a set of hypotheses about the conditions that bring men together into solidarity groups. These conditions are found in the way

men relate to the institutional orders that link groups together into a society".[55]

Weber analytically distinguished three orders within society— economic, social and political—and corresponding to these, identified three dimensions of stratification: class, status and power. On the fundamentals, there was little difference between Weber and Marx in defining class. The crucial characteristics of class are: (1) individuals share a particular causal facet of their lives; (2) these facets are represented exclusively by economic drive in the possession of goods and opportunities for property accrual, and (3) class situation is essentially a market situation. Classes are not communities; they merely represent possible bases for communal action. However, status groups are usually communities. Status situation is determined by a specific, positive or negative, social estimation of honor; it is not necessarily linked with class situation. The highest prestige in a particular social group does not always belong to the richest. Status symbols, special attire, exclusive clubs and unique lifestyles distinguish the status groups.

Parties exist in a social club as well as state; they seek to influence communal action and acquire power. Classes are stratified according to their relations to the production and acquisition of goods whereas status groups are stratified according to the principles of their consumption of goods as represented by special styles of life. The genuine place of classes is within the economic order, the place of status groups is within the social order. But parties live in a house of power.[56]

Denying that a unified theory of social stratification was even possible, Weber went beyond a critical rejection of Marx's simplistic unilinear theory of class. In contrast to the whole naturalistic psychological tradition in which theorists such as Saint-Simon, Comte, Spencer, Sumner and others had tried to explain stratification by direct reference to human qualities, Weber sought to understand the more fundamental complexes of social stratification as they might manifest themselves in forms of legitimate authority and then particularly in bureaucratic organization. The movement in Weber's thought from class to authority to bureaucracy is explainable in view of his infatuation with the nature and function of power. Weber was convinced that a striking quality of modern society was its channeling of legitimate authority

through the bureaucratic coordination of activities for bureau-
cracies are intentionally organized upon rational principles.

Legitimate authority was of special interest to Weber as expressed in conventional social action. He took care to identify and
characterize three ideal types of legitimate authority. They are:

> "(1) *Rational Legitimacy*, resting on a belief in the 'legality'
> of patterns of normative rules and the right of those elevated
> to authority under such rules to issue commands (legal autho-
> rity)"; (2) *Traditional Legitimacy*, "resting on an established
> belief in the sanctity of immemorial traditions and the legiti-
> macy of the status of those exercising authority under them
> (traditional authority)"; and (3) *Charismatic Legitimacy*,
> "resting on devotion to the specific and exceptional sanctity,
> heroism or exemplary character of an individual person, and
> of the normative patterns or order revealed or ordained by
> him (charismatic authority)".[57]

Bureaucracy

Max Weber was the first to give an elaborate account of the
development of bureaucracy as well as its causes and consequences. He attributed the following characteristics to bureaucracy:

1. The principle of fixed and official jurisdictional areas which
are generally ordered by rules. The regular activities associated
with each status are distributed in a fixed way as official duties.
The structure of authority is clearly delineated and strictly de-
limited by rules.

2. The principle of office hierarchy and of levels of graded
authority with a firmly ordered system of super-ordination and
subordination in which there is a supervision of the lower offices
by the higher ones.

3. A division of labor based on specialized functions and responsibilities.

4. A system of written documents ('the files') defining the procedure as well as the rights and duties of people in all positions.

5. Office management based on thorough and expert training.

6. Selection for employment and promotion based on technical
competence, specialized knowledge or skill.

7. Office-holding as a 'vocation.' Official work is no longer a
secondary activity but something that demands the full working
capacity of the official.

8. Provision for pecuniary compensation as a fixed salary.

9. Appointment of employees by higher officials, rather than by election.

10. The system of tenure for life. Normally the position of the bureaucrat is held for life as specified by contract.

11. A clear distinction between the sphere of office and that of the private affairs of the individual. The bureaucratic official is not an owner of the enterprise and therefore not entitled to the use of official facilities for personal needs except as defined by strict rules.

12. The practice of performing specialized administrative functions according to purely objective considerations and the official discharge of business according to calculable rules and 'without regard for persons.'

Weber counts the following among the most important factors contributing to the development of modern bureaucracy: (a) The development of money economy which guaranteed a constant income for maintaining bureaucracy through a stable system of taxation; it also encouraged a pecuniary compensation for the officials and a purely economic conception of the office as a source of the official's private income. (b) The quantitative development of administrative tasks, especially in the field of politics where "the great state and mass party are the classic soil for bureaucratization." (c) Qualitative changes of administrative tasks. Among purely political factors, the demand for order and protection ('police') and for the so-called 'welfare state', and among essentially technical factors, the development of modern means of communication especially the railroads and the mass media, operate in the direction of bureaucratization. (d) The purely technical superiority of bureaucracy over any other form of organization. Weber writes:

> Precision, speed, unambiguity, knowledge of the files, continuity, discretion, unity, strict subordination, reduction of friction and of material and personal costs—these are raised to the optimum point in the strictly bureaucratic administration, and especially in its monocratic form. As compared with all collegiate, honorific, and avocational forms of administration, trained bureaucracy is superior on all these points. And as far as complicated tasks are concerned, paid bureaucratic work is not only more precise but, in the last analysis, it is often cheaper than even formally unremunerated honorific service.[58]

(e) The complicated and specialized nature of modern culture that demands "the personally detached and strictly 'objective' expert, in lieu of the master of older social structures, who was moved by personal sympathy and favor, by grace and gratitude." (f) The rational interpretation of law on the basis of strictly formal conception of 'equality before the law' and the demand for legal guarantees against arbitrariness. This is in contrast to the old form of adjudication that was bound to sacred traditions and characterized by traditionalism, arbitrariness and the personally free discretion flowing from the 'grace' of the old patrimonial domination. (g) The concentration of the material means of management in the hands of the master as exemplified in the development of big capitalist enterprises and the giant public organizations as the modern state or army. (h) The levelling of economic and social differences and the corresponding rise of modern mass representative democracy in contrast to the old democratic self-government of small homogeneous communities.

The inevitable furthering of bureaucratization and rationalization of modern Western economies seemed to Weber inescapable. The modern state—its industry, economics, standard of living— is only possible with the emergence of a rational organization on a large scale. Weber insists:

> Once it is fully established, bureaucracy is among those social structures which are the hardest to destroy. Bureaucracy is *the* means of carrying 'community action' over into rationally ordered 'societal action.' Therefore, as an instrument for 'societalizing' relations of power, bureaucracy has been and is a power instrument of the first order—for the one who controls the bureaucratic apparatus.
>
> Under otherwise equal conditions, a 'societal action,' which is methodically ordered and led, is superior to every resistance of 'mass' or even of 'communal action.' And where the bureaucratization of administration has been completely carried through, a form of power relation is established that is practically unshatterable.

The ruled may be frequently manipulated by the bureaucrat but the former cannot eliminate or replace the bureaucratic apparatus of authority once it exists, for "bureaucracy rests upon expert training, a functional specialization of work, and an attitude set for habitual and virtuoso-like mastery of single yet methodically integrated functions." Weber notes: The objective indispensability of the once-existing apparatus, with its peculiar, 'impersonal' character, means that the mechanism—in contrast to feudal orders based upon personal piety—is easily made to work for anybody who knows how to gain control over it. A rationally ordered system of officials continues to function smoothly after the enemy has occupied the area; he merely needs to change the top officials. This body of officials continues to operate because it is to the vital interest of everyone concerned, including above all, the enemy.

Having granted its virtues and its unquestionable advancement of modern society, Weber was the first to concede the vices of bureaucracy, viz., the inevitable de-personalization of human relationships in government and industry. He refers to the formalism and the rule-bound and cool 'matter-of-factness' of bureaucratic organization, a crypto-plutocratic distribution of power and increasing concentration of the materials of management. Yet, says Weber, it is inevitable, irrepressible, and inescapable.

Significance and Appreciation

Some sociologists are unabashed in their assessment of Weber. "To me," wrote Aron in a candid adoration, "Max Weber is the greatest of the sociologists; I would even say that he is *the* sociologist. I shall not attempt to argue the truth of this opinion, which is affirmed today by the majority of sociologists the world over."[59]

Max Weber domonstrated a vast and profound knowledge of history which he analyzed with a conceptual precision that is unsurpassed by any historian or sociologist to date. The wealth of material contained in his writings, the painstaking study of concrete situations and historical processes, his analysis of the structure of social action, typology of behavior, comparative study of religions as well as economic, political and social systems and his insights into the contemporary processes of rationalization and bureaucratization could well be used by generations of sociologists to come. A prolific writer and original thinker, Weber made extensive use of his knowledge of history, philosophical tradition, religious systems and social structures to refine his concepts and to develop general theoretical schema dealing with a variety of social phenomena. In fhe words of Rossides:

... while repudiating the Anglo-French-American tradition

of monistic naturalistic positivism, Weber also repudiated the German tradition that sought knowledge about human existence in metaphysical analysis. The unique amalgam he created out of these rival traditions may be called *historical positivism*. His contribution to sociological theory may be put into broader perspective by saying that he combined the instrumental concept of the human mind that emerged from the Enlightenment with Vico's maxim that humanity can know the truth about itself because human behavior is a human creation and therefore amenable to human understanding. Basically, Weber's position was that science cannot lead to unified or metaphysical or substantialist knowledge, and that it cannot validate any system of values. His position made him unique and separated him from the essentially metaphysical tradition of modern social science, liberal and Marxian, as well as from all forms of religious and philosophical opposition to science and modernity in general.[60]

Wary of the kind of conceptual reification he observed in the works of Marx and Durkheim, Weber refused to conceptualize *the whole* social reality with its variegated complexity and manifold ramifications. However, he analyzed structures and processes and their inter-relationships and developed a cogent sociological mosaic, giving a coherent image of the whole while retaining the functional independence of the elements. Weber was a man of values but not a man of faith; while he passionately upheld certain values, he insisted on objectivity in scientific enterprises. Although, he founded no schools, he influenced every school and branch of sociology with his erudite studies which are rich in insights, far-reaching in scope and based on a mass of data both historical and contemporary. We may conclude with a quote from Bendix:

"A final assessment of Weber's importance is premature. Comparison of Weber's work with that of Marx and Freud shows that his work lacks the central idea or theorem that could have served as the nucleus for the development of a school, nor does it have the same direct intellectual impact on the modern *weltanschaung* that theirs does. Yet in the development of the social sciences, Weber's influence may in the end surpass that of Marx or Freud . . . He developed a remarkably probing and sympathetic understanding of alike world views, while affirming the cultural significance of his own civilization. Such work may well become increasingly relevant to the generation now growing to maturity, as it must come to terms with a world in which the values of western civilization are challenged."[61]

8

KARL MANNHEIM

LIFE AND TIMES

Though intellectual thought seems to emerge from out of the dark and confusing past and tends to proceed in irregular advance and erratic directions making an easy trail impossible to find or follow, Karl Mannheim's intellectual life (1893-1947), is decidedly bifurcated into two branches co-terminous with two countries—England and Germany. Almost as if he had two separate careers, Mannheim's German period—sociology of knowledge—was spent working out the methodological limitations, epistemological implications, and the substantive application of his science. In the second period of his intellectual life in England, he worked almost exclusively in the field of what has come to be called the sociology of planned reconstruction; here his study of the social structure in modern times predominated. Shils has observed that "Mannheim's early writings expressed his struggle against the inheritance of German idealism and was much influenced by the tradition of historicism and by the Marxist model of society."[1] His German period was spent in revising the epistemology of German idealism "in an instrumentalist direction and constituted a critique of its conception of intellectal history as an autonomously developing sequence of ideas . . ." In his English period, Shils points out, Mannheim "combined macrosociological and microsociological concerns with an explicit interest in social policy. . . ." The study of Mannheim's life is a direct reflection and a classic example of the relationship between ideas and situations.

Of Hungarian and German pedigree, Karl Mannheim was born of middle class Jewish parents in Budapest on the 27th of March, 1893, where as a young boy he attended the humanistic gymnasium of the city. Subsequently, he studied philosophy at the University of Budapest until as the custom of the age dictated he went to Germany in 1912 where he studied in Berlin under Georg Simmel. Returning home as a rather confident, aggressive intellectual, he fell into a reflective group of like-minded youth in Budapest, who formed themselves in 1917 into an organization or club pretentiously named the Free School for the Humanities. This emphasised German idealism in contradistinction to another somewhat comparably composed group of outspoken positivists called the Society for Social Sciences. Though not the acknowledged leader of his group in the Free School, Mannheim did however compose an essay in the fall of 1917 which captured the overall orientation and essence of these pro-German idealists in Budapest. The essay, entitled, "Soul and Culture," began by asserting, as Coser has recounted, "that the time had come for a 'reawakening of spirituality' and that 'European culture now will turn away from the positivism of the 19th century and return to a metaphysical idealism'."[2]

Not surprisingly, Mannheim and the Free School group hinted at the timely decline of Marxism and naturalism, calling for a renewed commitment to the thought forms of their intellectual heroes, Dostoevsky, Kierkegaard, Kant and Meister Eckhart. Simmel's philosophy, particularly his analysis of the 'Tragedy of Culture,' exercised a great influence on Mannheim and his colleagues. Reflecting the New School's quest for a new age which would rise above the naive social sciences of the day with all their optimistic progressivism and positivism, Mannheim and his peers sought to inaugurate a new age based on another source for spiritual sustenance. "The new generation," they argued, "needed to renovate human culture, reaffirm the dignity of the human spirit and save the human soul from materialistic, positivistic, and scientistic shackles."[3] A tall order, but not too big for a group of youthful intellectuals bent on reform.

And then, not without warning or struggle the Hungarian Soviet Republic was proclaimed on March 21, 1919. Initially, the prospects looked good, for virtually all of the Free School group members were placed on the faculty of the Soviet-reorganized

University of Budapest in April of that same year. Even though Mannheim himself refused party membership, he taught philosophy with the party's blessings until the short-lived Communist regime in Hungary fell from power in July, 1919, precipitating the flight from Hungary of all of Mannheim's friends and colleagues who had, however peripherally, been associated with the Communist government. Mannheim fled to Germany and largely abstained from politically revolutionary activities. However, he never severed his connections with socialist intellectuals, and continued to show a certain amount of sympathy for the German labor movement.

Now settled, as best as a refugee can be, in Germany, Mannheim seems to have consciously focussed his attention upon the establishment of an academic reputation and career. He studied in succession, early in Berlin under Simmel, then at Freiburg, and at Heidelberg under Alfred Weber. First, he was given the opportunity, owing to the generosity of his family, of living the life of a 'private scholar' (Privatgelehrte), a life-style known and recognized in Germany as honorable and enviable for a young intellectual. During this time, Mannheim continued to think of himself as a social philosopher dedicated to a cultural revolution against positivism and towards metaphysical idealism. His doctoral dissertation, published in 1922 when he was only twenty-nine years old, was entitled, 'Structural Analysis of Epistemology', which reflected his commitment to philosophical thought and suggested early the future of his work in the sociology of knowledge.

Three years after receiving his doctoral degree, in 1925, Mannheim was named a lecturer (Privatdozent) at the University of Heidelberg, and in 1927 was appointed professor of economics at the University of Frankfurt. Before receiving the Frankfurt invitation, Mannheim married a promising young psychologist, Juliska Lang, who brought to his life a domestic transquility and intellectually stimulating compatibility which mellowed and seasoned him markedly. Mannheim's arrival in Frankfurt, where he was to remain until his flight from the Nazis in 1933 to England, brought him into Germany's center of liberalism. Quiet years they seem to be from the outside, as Mannheim did his best work in the sociology of knowledge. His reputation as a classroom lecturer and as a careful philosopher on social thought grew. His major treatise, now an accepted classic, *Ideology and Utopia*, was written here and his major contributions to the sociology of knowledge became increasingly respected. In 1933, it all came to a halt.

Mannheim's thought was conspicuously influenced early on by the writings of Comte, owing to Mannheim's brief study in Paris, and of Hegel, Hegelianism being in the very air he breathed all over Germany. These thinkers "believed that in the past man had been dominated by the historical process whereas in the future he would gain ascendancy over it."[4] This historicist overtone was enhanced in Mannheim's mind by the deep influence of Karl Marx though Mannheim "deviated from Marxism in asserting that a better society might be achieved by non-revolutionary means and also in de-emphasizing the interpretation of the development of society as being semi-automatic and stressing the importance of conscious political effort." As mentioned earlier, a study of Mannheim's life is in some respects an exercise in the biographical illustration of the sociology of knowledge's fundamental point, viz., thought emerges within the human context reflecting that context in its emergence.

Forced by the Nazi madmen to leave his adopted home, the Jewish social philosopher Mannheim turned his eyes towards a country he knew little about and with which he had virtually no contact during his academic career in Germany. The London School of Economics invited this well-known and respected refugee (twice) to join their faculty as a lecturer and he was later named professor of education at London University. The Anglo-Saxon experience profoundly affected Mannheim, and his intellectual work radically shifted. "The change in Mannheim's style of thought," Coser ventures to comment, "was in effect so deep and decisive that there is a very sharp caesura between the 'German' and the 'British' Mannheim." Later in this chapter we hope to illustrate this new direction away from theoretical and empirical sociology of knowledge and towards the sociology of planned reconstruction, For the moment, we might just comment that whereas Mannheim's German period was linked heavily to Hegel and Marx with special interests in culture change, intellectually and socially initiated and reflected, Mannheim's English period owed a great allegiance to Durkheim with particular attention given to the planning and orchestrating of society's transformations in structure and direction.

Though the English intelligentsia received Mannheim well enough, the sociological establishment *per se* never fully accepted their German idealist. Rather, as in his Free School days in Hungary, Mannheim found himself happily ensconced in a sporting array of curiously divergent English middle class intellectuals, mostly with religious ties and commitments and decidedly conservative. The club called itself the Moot and met regularly to discuss religious issues and the possible role of religion in the planned society of the future. Mannheim, among numerous other contributions, presented a rather lengthy paper before the Moot, which became a quite well-known and respected treatise, entitled, "Towards a new Social Philosophy: A Challenge to Christian Thinkers by a Sociologist." By today's standards, a rather fledgling piece of dialogic work, but at the time it was considered quiet significant in its scope. Mannheim continued to live and teach and write in England until his death in 1947 at the age of fifty-four.

The Sociology of Knowledge
No idea can claim absolute originality and uniqueness, for all thought occurs within the everflowing stream of human consciousness. Every good and lasting idea grows out of a sometime ill-defined but nevertheless real past and emerges into the present not as original but as an insightful, provocative, or challenging notion which, if it proves worthy, will continue on into the future sustaining alterations and modifications as it goes. The history of ideas is, in a real sense, the tracking of ideas within social frameworks—their fledgling past, turbulent present, and uncertain future. And the tracking, to the extent that it is possible and honest, is not merely a discovery and following of good ideas but also and equally a cognizant embracing of the human milieu within which ideas emerge and endure. This duplicity—idea and social milieu—leads us directly into the sociology of knowledge (Wissensoziologie).

Karl Mannheim, considered the father of the scientific perspective or methodology called the sociology of knowledge, neither developed the name nor did he establish a great following. Nevertheless he is considered the founder because of the unquestionable advancements he made in the fields of German idealism and historicism and the refinement of those advancements into a classic work, still unsurpassed, entitled, *Ideology and Utopia*. Generally

speaking, sociologists today understand the sociology of knowledge to be a critical study of "the relationship between empirical,
socio-historical circumstances and knowledge. . .particularly intellectual knowledge, ideas, beliefs, morality, and ideology."[5] In
many respects, this type of research underscores our opening
remarks, viz., the realization that every worthwhile idea, and
related cognition, is not unrelated to the human context within
which it emerges.

Mannheim, like every thoughtful, reflective, intellectual of his
age as in every age, was influenced by identifiable human experiential and ideational factors within his social environment
which happened to be the German intellectual milieu of the late
nineteenth century. Georg Hegel (1770-1831) was the foremost
philosophical theorist of the day in the field of historical studies
and Mannheim leaned heavily upon the Hegelian view of things.
The Hegelians argued persuasively that the correct method for the
study of history was the 'wholistic' approach, i.e., the study of
time-frames of historical events within their own terms and criteria of judgement. Events must be analyzed 'phenomenologi-
cally', that is, assessed and interpreted from the point of view of
the participants of the time. Precluding a later period of history
from passing judgement unfairly upon a previous period by using
criteria alien to the period, the Hegelians convinced Mannheim
that intellectual integrity required a suspension of judgement
other than that which might logically emerge within the time
period of the historical event under consideration. Any facet of
a culture must, necessarily, be analyzed within the total contextual milieu of the time and judged accordingly. Another German
historicist, Wilhelm Dilthey (1833-1911) refined and continued to
advance the neo-Hegelian theory of historical interpretation and
made a significant impression upon the young Mannheim. As he
began to launch out upon ideas and theoretical pursuits, Mannheim focussed his attention precisely upon this constellation of
factors, viz., the relationship between ideas and their human
milieu. He defined the sociology of knowledge "as a theory of
the social or existential conditioning of thought."[6] He was acutely
aware of what most intellectuals took to be a commonplace observation, namely, that ideas and knowledge do not emerge or
endure in a vacuum but rather directly and specifically within an
identifiable place or situation, and are, as he said, literally "bound

to a location". And granted the variability of the strength and
nature of this situational character of ideational processes, the
social circumstances and the historical movements within which
ideas emerge and endure are important components of the ideas
themselves. That ideas occur in time and place any schoolboy
knew, but that the time and place were significant in their own
right in relation to the kind of ideas produced, it took Mannheim
to demonstrate. That social science could address the issue scientifically was for him to substantiate.

In striving to illuminate this 'hidden dimension' of thought and
by attempting to extrapolate the complex relationship between
idea and time/space, Mannheim hit upon the concept of 'perspective' as helpful and informative. Ideas are integrally bound up
with both the historical circumstances and the social contexts
surrounding their appearance within human consciousness. Since
the human mind does not function as a *tabula rasa*, the mind's
ideas and thoughts are bio-sociologically bound up with the
physical and social environment within which the mind functions
and the ideas appear. This inevitability produces an actually
identifiable 'perspective.' In Mannheim's understanding, "perspective . . . is something more than a merely formal determination of thinking. (It) signifies the manner in which one views an
object, what one perceives in it, and how one construes it in his
thinking."[7] The emphasis for Mannheim was upon this notion of
'manner' of seeing the world such that the ideas produced must
be seen in the context of their 'holistic' environment—historical
and social. "Perspective", he continues, "also refers to qualitative
elements in the structure of thought, elements which must necessarily be overlooked by a purely formal logic". To look at ideas
apart from their socio-historical milieu is to miss the preponder-
ance of 'qualitative elements' which have produced and nurtured
the appearance of ideas. Failure to see the 'context' or 'situation'
of an idea results in an affront to the socio-historical nature of
all human consciousness. "It is precisely these factors", Mannheim concludes, "which are responsible for the fact that two
persons, even if they apply the same formal-logical rules, may
judge the same object very differently."

The human circumstance of thought has been recognized more
or less by philosophers from early on in Western thought, and
during the nineteenth century, the study of idea-situation relation-

ships was occurring within the philosophical circles of historicism and Marxism. Mannheim wanted to do even more, particularly in a scientifically sophisticated manner. If sociology of knowledge focussed its attention upon the relationship between "thought and society," then this particular methodology, if such be the case, should be able to demonstrate that the emergence and maintenance of ideas is related to the total human milieu of historical situation and social activity. Mannheim necessarily was interested in, and his methodology was designed for, an interpretation of "individual activity in all spheres within the context of group experience." Fighting both solopcism on the left and idealism on the right, Mannheim attempted to forge a middle road in the idea-situation controversy. No single person, he reasoned, "confronts the world and, in striving for the truth, constructs a worldview out of the data of his (own) experience (alone) . . . " To reiterate, persons do not think in a vacuum and ideas do not appear on a *tabula rasa*. On the contrary, he concluded, "it is much more correct that knowledge is from the very beginning a cooperative process of group life, in which everyone unfolds his knowledge within a framework of a common fate, a common activity, and the over-coming of common difficulties."

In the past decade, American sociology of knowledge, following the tradition of Mannheim, has reappeared under the strong leadership of Peter L Berger, and though revised and refined from its youthful past, the method or perspective is still fundamentally the same—i.e., "reality is socially constructed . . ." Berger and Luckmann, in their book entitled "The Social Construction of Reality", explain that in sociology of knowledge, their analysis depends upon these two key concepts, viz., 'reality' and 'knowledge' as used by the sociologist. These contemporary exponents of the sociology of knowledge define reality as "a quality appurtaining to phenomena that we recognize as having a being independent of our own volition" and in turn knowledge as "the certainty that phenomena are real and that they possess specific characteristics " Thus, as Mannheim saw so early in the development, now Berger sees still as a major need and a significant task—"the need for a sociology of knowledge is . . . already given with the observable differences between societies in terms of what is taken for granted as 'knowledge' comes to be socially established as 'reality'."[8]

Max Scheler, not Mannheim, coined the term 'wissensoziologie' back in the 1920s in Germany. To coin a term and to create a science are not the same, and though the German philosopher made some contributions, Mannheim fathered the science. Yet, because of the particular intellectual and cultural context within which this perspective or methodology was introduced, it remains by and large a peripheral curiosity or oddity within traditional sociological circles.

To understand more fully why the sociology of knowledge has been often perceived by sociologists as a superficial addendum to the history of ideas, we need to take a brief look at the three ideological factors of nineteenth century Germany which so greatly influenced and in some respects stifled the new methodology, viz., Marxism, Nietzscheanism, and historicism. Dilthey's school of historicism was in the German tradition of idealism which immediately preceded the sociology of knowledge. "The dominant theme," in Dilthey's school according to Berger, "was an overwhelming sense of the relativity of all perspectives on human events, that is, of the inevitable historicity of human thought."[9] The fundamental point of the historicists' school of idealism was that no single event in history was truly comprehensible except within the total framework or socio-cultural context of its own situation. This school of thought, particularly expressed in Hegelianism, was profoundly important to Mannheim's own development, as seen in the immediate and direct transferral of key terms in historicism to the sociology of knowledge nomenclature, e.g., "situational determination" (standortsge bundenheit) and "seat of life" (Sitz im Leben). These terms "could be directly translated as referring to 'social location' of thought . . . (such that) the historicist heritage of the sociology of knowledge predisposed the latter toward a strong interest in history and the employment of an essentially historical method."

Throughout the first few years of Mannheim's developmental work in theory and methodology building, he was insistent that contemporary intellectuals come to a thorough grasp of the meaning and implication of the historicists' position. In his major essay on method, he said that "historicism has developed into an intellectual force of extraordinary significance. . . .The historicist principle not only organizes, like an invisible hand, the work of the cultural sciences (Geisteswessenschaften) but also permeates

everyday thinking . . . Historicism is therefore neither a mere fad
nor a fashion; it is not even an intellectual current, but the very
basis on which we construct our observations of the socio-cultural
reality."[10]

The influence is obvious and profound; yet, as Coser has
correctly pointed out, in spite of this high praise, "Mannheim
progressed beyond the position attained by historicist thought; he
built upon the Marxist idea that ways of thinking were tied to
ways of doing, and specified the multiple ties by which systems
of ideas were bound to the Praxis of men located in concrete
social structures."[11] The worthiness and greatness of any idea is
both the soundness of it and the advance it makes over previous
ideas upon the same topic. Mannheim's debt to Marx and Hegel
is clear, but his furtherance of an idea made better is cause for
his renown. He progressed, first beginning by seeing ideas "from
within" and then advanced his understanding of ideas as "responses to determinants emanating from the social structure in which
thinkers were variously enmeshed." He recognized and publicly
owned his legacy in historicism. In many respects, the sociology
of knowledge is a furtherance of historicist relativism and Marxian
Praxis which constitutes a combination or convergence of insights. Hegelian historicism was creatively informed and corrected
by a careful grasp of the Marxian emphasis upon action (Praxis).
All this was "supplemented," explains Coser, "by the program-
matic assertion that systems of ideas need to be understood not
only in terms of their autonomous and inherent development but
also by reference to their embeddedness in social structures . . ."

Mannheim was not the first social philosopher to build upon
the historicism of the German idealism of Hegel's metaphysic.
The most celebrated such builder was Karl Marx who insisted
that belief systems are merely a surface manifestation of the underlying economic structure. Marx, of course, takes this insight—the
supreme dominance of the economic imperative—as his *sine qua
non* explanation for all human action. Mannheim gave Marx's
emphasis upon contextual factors in ideational activity due importance but held back from adopting the economic component
of the worldview of the Marxists. Marx reasoned, from standpoint of his challenge to idealism, that all ideational activities, i.e.,
systems of beliefs, are merely ideologies which can be properly
understood only if they are correctly viewed as rationalizations

of the socio-economic class of their perpetrators. In this manner, Marx sensitized Mannheim's perceptions of ideas and the social context from which they emerge.

As with Marx, so with Mannheim, the danger of a deterministic view of human events was ever present. Mannheim fought against and denied vehemently fairness of the charge. He used the terms "existential determination," not as implying a "mechanical cause-effect sequence" but as characterizing the relationship between "thought" and "social structure." He consistently stressed the need for empirical analysis and verification of any single instance of idea-situation cases, refusing to permit generalizations based on unscientific cause-effect explanations any credence. Yet, his struggles with the problem persisted until he abandoned the methodology of the sociology of knowledge altogether. He searched everywhere for concepts to clarify his position and free him of the "determinism" charge. His use of the Marxian concepts, "substructure and superstructure", illustrate his efforts at vindication. "While he sometimes seems to assert that social forces are necessary and sufficient conditions for the appearance of certain ideas", Coser explains, "he is moved at times to restrict his claim to stressing only facilitating social factors that enable sets of ideas to find expression and to get a hearing."[12]

Shils has pointed out that many of the significant sociological variables Mannheim used in his German period were Marxian in origin, e.g., "declining classes", "ascendant classes", "threatened classes", "newly self-conscious classes", etc. In his major treatise, *Ideology aud Utopia*, Mannheim contended "that 'uprooted' and 'unintegrated' revolutionary groups think intuitively and lay little or no stress on historical development; that liberal-humanitarian strata stress the openness of the future and the progressive realization of ethical values; and that oppressed strata, which are chiliastic, expect immediate and sharply disjunctive changes."[13] Mannheim sensed the inherent dangers in reducing the complexities of idea-situation analysis to simplistic causality. Though he was criticized unfairly for determinism and chided for lack of clarity as to what his position really was, he persisted resolutely in avoiding "the task of causal imputation and of differentiated analysis of the process or mechanism through which ideas and social position are connected. "In the main,"

Shils says, "he committed himself to nothing more than the
assertion that thought is 'existentially connected' (seinsverbunden)
with social position." If criticized he must be, Mannheim would
rather be somewhat ambiguous than simplistic when dealing with
the obvious but illusive relationship between thought and social
context.

Unlike Scheler's somewhat one-dimensional analysis of idea-
situation formations, Mannheim was decidedly more creative and
productive owing to his serious encounter with Marxian thought.
In this encounter, society is understood to be determinative for
both the appearance and the content of human thought processes
(except, of course, in mathematics and in the natural sciences).
In this way, the sociology of knowledge has become "a positive
method for the study of almost any facet of human thought,"
says Berger, America's foremost sociologist of knowledge today.
Mannheim's fundamental concern is with the "phenomenon of
ideology," and, continues Berger, "with the general concept of
ideology the level of the sociology of knowledge is reached—the
understanding that no human thought is immune to the ideologiz-
ing influences of its social context."[14] Mannheim far outdistanced
others like Scheler who ventured into these challenging inquiries
regarding thought-and-situation formations primarily because of
his imaginative convergence of a revised Hegelian historicism
and a reformulated Marxism. From the latter, Mannheim derived
much of his best thoughts, his main proposition being the orthodox Marxian line—"man's consciousness is determined by his
social being." We have already commented upon Mannheim's
employment of the Marxian couplet, "Substructure (unterban)"
which is understood to be "human activity" and "superstructure
(ueberban)" which is understood to be the situation produced by
that activity.

What we have already noted and what must not be forgotten if
we are to understand the reasons for Mannheim's renown is the
fact that in spite of his allegiance to Hegel and Marx, he unquestionably went beyond them both in the development of the sociology of knowledge. Whereas the Marxist line is that society is
bifurcated by class conflict and class interest or by mutual distrust,
"Mannheim thought that the cleavages existed at deeper levels as
well...(he) saw social cleavages not merely as divergences of interest but as divergences of modes of thought, of the categories in

which events are conceived, and even, indeed, of the very
criteria of validity."[15] Within Mannheim's discussions of some of
his key terms, another major German philosopher Nietzsche,
appears, especially on the subject of "false consciousness." He
had developed his own definition and application of the term
particularly in his "analysis of the social significance of deception and self-deception, and of illusion as a necessary condition
of life."[16] The Nietzschean tradition was most profoundly carried on through the twentieth century French philosopher-nove-
list, Jean-Paul Sartre, and not the sociology of knowledge school.
However, his concept of 'resentment' as a generative factor in
certain types of ideation, adapted from Scheler, and his concept
of the "art of mistrust" both are reflected in Mannheim's development and more specifically in recent developments in the
sociology of knowledge both in America and in Germany.

Let us now try to summarize the essentials of Mannheim's
sociology of knowledge:[17]

1. Mannheim defines the sociology of knowledge on the one
hand as a theory and on the other hand as an historical-sociolo-
gical method of research: "as theory it seeks to analyze the
relationship between knowledge and existence: as historical-
sociological research it seeks to trace the forms which this relationship has taken in the intellectual development of mankind."

2. On the one hand, sociology of knowledge seeks to discover
workable criteria for determining the relationship between thought and action. "On the other hand, by thinking this problem
out from beginning to end in a radical, unprejudiced manner, it
hopes to develop appropriate criteria to the contemporary situation, concerning the significance of the non-theoretical conditioning factors in knowledge."

3. Thinking does not occur in a vacuum; it is part and parcel
of the process. Modes of thought are to be understood in terms
of their social origins. It is erroneous to assume that the ideas
that motivate the individual have their origin in him alone or
that they can be adequately explained on the basis of his own life-
experience. "Just as it would be incorrect to attempt to derive a
language merely from observing a single individual, who speaks
not a language of his own but rather that of his contemporaries
and predecessors who have prepared the path for him, so it is
incorrect to explain the totality of an outlook only with reference
to its genesis in the mind of the individual."

4. The single individual does not think: rather, "he participates in thinking further what other men have thought before him." According to Mannheim, "the sociology of knowledge seeks to comprehend thought in the concrete setting of an historical-social situation out of which individually differentiated thought only very gradually emerges. Thus, it is not men in general who think, or even isolated individuals who do the thinking, but men in certain groups who have developed a particular style of thought in an endless series of responses to certain typical situations characterizing their common position."

5. Social thought is necessarily perspectivist thought. Whatever men see in social reality, they organize into perspective which derives from a standpoint located in the historical and social context. One of Mannheim's primary goals was to "assess the angle of vision in which social reality presents itself to man in different social and historical situations."

6. To summarize: "the approach to a problem, the level on which the problem happens to be formulated, the stage of abstraction and the stage of concreteness that one hopes to attain, are all and in the same way bound up with social existence."

7. Just as the sociology of knowledge demonstrates that all human thinking and action is determined by social forces, it also calls for a practical application through which these forces themselves can be acted upon by free agents. As we appreciate better the social context of thought or the perspective in which ideas are presented, it can help, especially through the field of education, the development of freedom and individualization.

Sociology and its Methodology

Mannheim divides sociology into three types on the basis of three functions and methodological planes:

1. *Systematic or General Sociology*
It retraces "the variability of social phenomena to those *basic elements* and *basic concepts* of a more or less axiomatic character which make society possible at all."[18] If social sciences are to initiate fruitful causal inquiries, we must go beyond *ad hoc* concepts which serve as a sort of 'first approximation', and develop abstract, general concepts which help us discover 'common causal factors in the maze of intermittent historical phenomena.'

For example, from the point of view of the historian and the political scientist, a secret society of the so-called primitives, a 'guild' in the middle ages or a modern social club may be totally dissimilar or non-comparable but the moment the sociologist introduces the general concept 'closed group', a common factor emerges and the whole analysis and comparison become meaningful.

2. Comparative Sociology

General concepts in systematic sociology are fruitful only if they "are based on the widest possible expansion of the field of observation, when alone it will be possible to see the various phenomena in their proper proportions and to reduce them to their basic and simplified characteristics. Therefore, the concepts of systematic sociological must grow out of the results arrived at in comparative sociology inquiry." A general theory of power, for instance, must be supplemented by a comparative analysis of different types of power organizations in different cultural and historical contexts.

3. Structural Sociology

It seeks "to explain the general features of human behavior patterns and the universally possible, ultimate elements of society not only *in abstracto*, but also the specific, separate constellations which from time to time they assume in different societies in history." In a language reminiscent of Comte, Mannheim divides structural sociology into two parts: statics and dynamics. "The theory of statics deals with the problem of the equilibrium of all the social factors (not only in the economic ones) in a given social structure. It tries to show what makes different societies work. . . . In dynamic sociology we concentrate on those factors which are antagonistic in their respective tendencies. Here we stress the working of those principles which in the long run tend to a disequilibrium and thus bring about changes which transform the social structure."

Mannheim insists that only structural sociology is capable of a comprehensive synthesis of all the facts assembled by the separate social sciences because it is its function to elaborate and compare social structures as wholes. "It is only the structural view of society which enables us to transcend the stage of a mere cumulative synthesis, by relating the data of the special sciences to our hypothetical conception, which views the functioning of societies as a continuous adjustment of all their parts to one another." But structural sociology is able to do this only with the help of the analytical work done by systematic and comparative sociology and by keeping in constant touch with the various specialized branches of knowledge. "Sociology, therefore, is…on the one hand a clearing house for the results arrived at by the specialized social sciences and, on the other hand, a new elaboration of the materials on which they are based."

The idea of structure always dominated Mannheim's approach to sociology: the structure of social reality, and the position of individuals and groups within this 'structure,' determined thinking and action and guided them into intelligible channels. According to Paul Kacskemeti, structure conceived by Mannheim, has the following characteristics:

(a) Structure is the most *comprehensvie* feature of reality. No component part of society may be said to have structure, and any *partial* phenomenon is to be understood only in terms of the comprehensive structure of the *whole*.

(b) Structure is a dynamic entity. It did not consist of a network of static relationships to which any social conflict was extraneous. Structure, as conceived by Mannheim, always implied plasticity and consisted of the configuration of antagonistic forces.

(c) Structure is an intelligible principle. Although a configuration of antagonistic forces, structure involves not a blind dynamism but goal-directedness because it had a discoverable meaning. "The highest goal and greatest happiness of the individual consisted in being in tune with the creative process which was going on in the depths of the structure."

Mannheim was not a commentator upon the genius of Hegel and Marx. He did appropriate through revision much of what he thought was good in their writings. Whereas Marx professed his life work to be an inquiry "into the connection of philosophy with reality," Mannheim undertook to generalize this program and, as Coser explains, "to analyze the ways in which systems of ideas depend on the social position—particularly the class position—of their proponents."[19] Mannheim's methodology was naturally informed both by Hegelian historicism and Marxian

ideas. As pointed out earlier, he accepted as his starting point
the position of the "probability that all ideas, even 'truths', were
related to, and hence influenced ᵇy, the social and historical
situation from which they emerged." It was his belief that any
serious study of human knowledge must be done within the light
of this statement—ideas emerge within human situations. He
attempted to construct an analytical methodology designed specifically for this purpose. At the outset of his major contribution
to the sociology of knowledge, Mannheim insisted upon this
point as the basic premise. Men, he writes, "do not confront the
objects of the world from the abstract levels of a contemplating
mind as such, nor do they do so exclusively as solitary beings.
On the contrary, they act with and against one another in diver-
sely organized groups, and while doing so they think with and
against each other."[20] By taking such a position, he invaded the
dominion of both the historian of ideas and the philosopher,
claiming, as he did, that without a careful analysis of the situation within which ideas emerge, the ideas themselves cannot
rightly be understood. He did not discourage analysis in the ideas
themselves or, as he said, the study of cultural objects and intellectual phenomena "from the inside" in order to discover their
essential meanings. But an equally valuable and finally indispensable inquiry is that of the sociology of knowledge which attempts
to understand ideas "from the outside" as a "reflection of a
societal process in which the thinker is inevitably enmeshed."
His term for this was "seinsverbunden," meaning that knowledge
is conceived of as existentially or socio-historically determined.

He was determined, and went to great pains, to demonstrate in
his theory and method that human thought is 'situationally relative' (situations-gebunden). His major contention was stated and
re-stated, but his finest and most precise instancing of the theme
of the sociology of knowledge appears in his masterpiece. In it,
Mannheim contends "that not only do fundamental orientations,
evaluations, and the content of ideas differ but that the manner
of stating a problem, the sort of approach made, and even the
categories in which experiences are subsumed, collected, and
ordered vary according to the social position of the observer."
He gives a classic illustration of this fine point: "When, in the
early years of the nineteenth century, an old-style German conservative spoke of 'freedom' he meant thereby the right of each

estate to live according to its privileges (liberties). If he belonged
to the romantic-conservative and Protestant movement he understood by it "inner freedom", i.e., the right of each individual to
live according to his own individual personality....When a
liberal of the same period used the term 'freedom' he was thinking of freedom *from* precisely those privileges which to the old-
style conservative appeared to be the very basis of all freedom....
In brief, even in the formulations of concepts, the angle of vision
is guided by the observer's interests. Thought... is directed in
accordance with what a particular social group expects."

The danger which plagued Mannheim's methodology throughout his German period was that of relativism, the ultimate danger
for the historicists as well. Having established the credibility of
his sociology of knowledge methodology, he was called upon to
demonstrate how his position differed from relativism and why
he should not be criticized for the same reasons that relativism
was condemned. His system did claim that all socio-historical
knowledge was socially determined in both form and content.
If that is the case, what comes of 'truth' and why is the system
not 'relativistic?' "He declared," Timasheff says, "that relativism leads to nihilism—to the position that nothing can be truly
known. To avoid this problem he developed the concept of
relationism, which, in contrast to relativism, analyzes the social
perspective of a body of knowledge, not in order to discredit it,
but rather to understand it better."[21] Unlike relativism which
blatantly denied the possibility of there being any 'truth' and
which insisted that even if there was, there is no 'human' way of
grasping it, Mannheim felt that relationism did not deny the existence of truth or the comprehensibility of human effort; rather it
sought to come as close to truth as possible.

Mannheim was insistent upon the service to truth which his
methodology could render if used properly. He argued further
that rather than impugning the validity of an insight, the sociology of knowledge methodology was able to effectively draw
attention to the fact that the insight is dependent upon, and
confined within, a specific socio-historical context. That insight
is important in order to give proper weight to each instance of
perceived truth. His critics responded that this argument merely
shifted the relativity but did not remove the cause of the charge
against the method. Mannheim's response went something like

this: "Every socio-historical situation is located at a specific point along a unilinear, ever-progressing and never-returning temporal continuum—history. Each situation is therefore unique, and the knowledge to which it gives birth, and which is true within it, is equally unique, bound to its time and place, and relative."[22] But here Mannheim parts company with the seekers after metaphysical truth, for he is not primarily concerned with "the truth of propositions" but rather conceives of truth in socio-historical situations as being "an attribute", and attribute not of discourse but of reality at the moment it is known. Thus, an individual "who is in contact with the living forces of his age has the truth, or better, is in · the truth," not a metaphysical truth subject to propositional testing and verification but one of experiential validity and immediacy. This concept of the truth àt once demonstrates Mannheim's convergence of the ideas of Marxism, historicism, and his Anglo-Saxon legacy of pragmatism. Because of his forced defence of a traditional argument about the relationship of *thought and reality*, he proposed to move his arguments over to a discussion of the relationship between *thought and situation*. "He was interested in the genuineness, rather than in the truth, of a given worldview." Mannheim, though his thought and work took a major shift in direction upon arriving in England, never corrected this basic contradiction which was precipitated by a combination of a persistent idealism and a Marxian negation of idealism. The contradiction in his thought never disappeared. And in terms of his movement into planned reconstruction, he devised a concept which took him beyond resolving the contradiction of his earlier work; the term was "functional rationality," that is, "the organization of series of action in such a way that they are highly calculable and efficient. . . . "[23] In effect, utility replaces truth.

The Process of Democratization

Mannheim underwent a profound reorientation in his work upon departing from Nazi-plagued Germany for the unknown intellectual terrain of England. Having essentially abandoned his steady work in the field of the sociology of knowledge, the work which produced his masterpiece as well as his continental reputation, he devoted himself for the remainder of his life to what he called a "diagnosis of our time" and to the development of a sociology of social planning and of social reconstruction. "His English writings ... differ dramatically from his early contributions", Coser explains, "for the rising tide of fascism threatened to engulf the whole of Europe, and Mannheim felt that no longer did it behove the scholar to stay in his academic tower when all of civilization threatened to fall into the abyss of fascism ... " The transition from the sociology of knowledge to what in England was thought of as macro and microsociological studies of social structure became quickly visible in the Mannheim of the London School of Economics. His interest in personality and culture studies led him to the development of the concept called the "planning of personality" which was never fully developed. He also wrote a book during this time on the intelligentsia in the final section of which he presented an "original analysis of the postulates of the democratic outlook, setting forth for the first time his later more fully developed views about fundamental democratization and the deterioration of the rationality and solidarity of elites."[24] Mannheim was anxious to explore the implications of the inevitable process of 'fundamental democratization.'

"A democratic trend is our predestined fate", Mannheim insists. The trend of democratization in modern societies is inevitable and irreversible. The frequency with which dictatorships supersede democracy is no proof that political reality is becoming less and less democratic in its essence. "Dictatorships can arise only in democracies; they are made possible by the greater fluidity introduced into political life by democracy. Dictatorship is not the antithesis of democracy; it represents one of the possible ways in which a democratic society may try to solve its problems."[25]

Mannheim identifies two essential prerequisites for the maintenance of democracy:

(a) Balance in the structure of society which prevents one or several power groups from exercising excessive pressure to serve their vested interests. A constitution is no substitute for such a balance which must be built into the government machinery as well as reflected in genuine democratic process.

(b) Political mass education of the citizenry. The greatest enemy of democracy is not the enlightened masses but the demagogically exploited and enraged mob.

Mannheim lists nine virtues of representative government:[26]

1. The integration of all social forces
2. Competition in ideas and bargaining
3. The superiority of parliamentary over corporate representation
4. Emotional identification and sense of responsibility
5. Public accountability
6. Assignment of responsibility
7. Flexible policies
8. The constructive use of the opposition
9. The resolution to act

Whereas in the past, political decisions were made by a small group of more or less homogeneous economic and political elites, with universal suffrage, several groups not yet familiar with political reality have become charged with a political function. At the same time believers in the ideal democracy tend to become disillusioned by its actuality. They discover that the majority is not necessarily 'progressive' or 'rational', that the democratic process is extremely slow and that it does not necessarily guarantee international harmony. While democracy fosters individual autonomy and freedom on the one hand, it develops, on the other hand, powerful social mechanisms inducing the individual to give up his autonomy. Mannheim cautions that when groups not yet ripe for political responsibility are suddenly admitted to a share in power, they are more likely to make use of mechanisms of this sort than to stimulate individual freedom.

Mannheim enumerates three fundamental principles of democracy:

1. The essential equality of all human beings. Democracy does not imply a mechanical levelling but the acceptance of the same ontological principle of humanness and equality of opportunity.

2. The autonomy of the individual. Unlike in predemocratic societies in which the social will was determined from above, by the ruling elites, democracy involves the recognition of the vital selfhood of all components of society.

3. Novel methods of selecting and controlling elites.

Now, Mannheim turns to a consideration of the way in which the cultural process as a whole is shaped and influenced by the three fundamental democratic principles outlined above. First, the cultural implications of the principle of equality consist in the changed evaluation of human models. "The authoritarian, pre-democratic mind shuns the idea of process and genesis in favor of static, hierarchically ordered models of excellence. The democratic mind, on the other hand, stresses the plasticity of man."[27] Leaders in democratic cultures are not necessarily charismatic personalities or geniuses with innate greatness; they simply had better opportunities to develop themselves. The democratic ideal of knowledge is thus characterized by unlimited accessibility and communicability. And when certain types of knowledge are accessible only to the elite connoisseurship, the democratized culture has a tendency to devalue them.

Second, the principle of the autonomy of the social units has fostered the creative role of individual consciousness. Predemocratic ages have had no use for discussion; they debarred the individual from questioning traditions. Even the prophets appeared as messengers of God to reinforce sacred tradition. However, as the process of democratization encourages new groups and more and more individuals to interpret reality from their own personal viewpoint, the new era induces spontaneity, creativity, and above all, genuine discussion in which all participants are equally and jointly responsible for the conclusion reached. Responsibility is no longer concentrated in the hands of an absolute monarch, a charismatic leader or a ruling elite; rather it has become a collective function which must be realized anew all the time through conflict and stress, negotiation and reconciliation. "There is no pre-existent pattern of order guaranteed forever in a democratic world; order and integration must always be created anew. This is essential to democracy as a way of life; it is therefore futile as well as thoughtless to condemn democracy in the name of the ideal of order."

Third, although democracy involves an anti-elitist trend, this does not eliminate the distinction between 'elite' and 'mass' altogether. Democracy is characterized not so much by the absence of all elite strata but by a new mode of elite selection and a new interpretation of the elite. Mannheim identifies three forms in which elite selection takes place in modern society: (1) bureaucratic advancement, (2) unregulated competition (e.g. cut-throat competition in political arenas), and (3) class pressures.

The process of democratization involves a lessening of the distance between the elite and the rank-and-file. In predemocratic

cultures, elites were the models of excellence and everything of
value was judged in terms of the standards of aristocracy. Democratic culture recognizes the inner worth of every individual; the
distance from the low social groups is no longer a mark of culture
or superiority. However, "distantiation" is not eradicated in
democracy; it merely assumes a different form. For instance,
whereas traditional authority was hereditary, being centered in
persons or families, democratic authority is conferred only tem-
porarily and conditionally upon certain individuals. "But while
the mythically sanctioned distantiation of persons is absent in
democracy, the fundamental institutions do become 'distantiated'.
They are elevated to symbolic dignity as myths." The prestige,
perquisites and symbolism associated with the office of the President of a republic, for instance, are designed to perpetuate the
mythical role inherent in distantiation.

Planned Reconstruction of Society
Mannheim is convinced that "our society has been taken ill . . . .
We are living in an age of transition from laissez-faire to a planned society. The planned society that will come may take one of
two shapes: it will be ruled either by a minority in terms of a
dictatorship or by a new form of government which, in spite of
its increased power, will still be democratically controlled."[28]
Mannheim rejects the extravagant liberal conception of freedom
understood as the individual's absolute independence of the social
environment. Freedom in the sense of individuals being totally
independent of and unaffected by collective forces is an illusion.
The individual is always moulded to some extent by social environment. Mannheim also rejects the laissez-faire creed, pointing to
its disastrous factual consequences. The assumption that the
social environment may be left to itself so that tensions arising
within it are resolved by spontaneous mutual adaptation and
adjustment of groups and individuals has not worked.
    There is no doubt that every Western nation is moving in the
direction of a kind of planned society, made possible by the new
economics, political and social techniques. The new social techniques are, in the words of Mannheim, "the sum of those methods
which aim at influencing human behavior and which, when in the
hands of the Government, act as an especially powerful means of
social control." They include the new military technique that

allows a great concentration of power in the hands of the few, revolution in transportation and communication facilitating centralized government and control, bureaucratization and the scientific management of large-scale organizations that create key positions of domination, the new science of human behavior which gives the government a knowledge of the human mind which can either be exploited in the direction of greater efficiency or made into an instrument playing on mass emotions, the development of social services, especially of social work, which allows the exertion of an influence that penetrates into people's private lives and the new techniques of propaganda and psychological warfare that seek to manipulate or enslave the greater part of the population. Such modern techniques foster centralization and, therefore, minority rule and dictatorship. They also make planning not only necessary but inevitable.

Planning may be of two types:

1. Totalitarian planning with its two variants, Fascism and Communism.

2. Democratic planning gradually evolved by the progressive policies of the democracies.

Mannheim characterizes totalitarian responses "as those of the panic-stricken mind to a novel problem—an escape into the methods of command, pressure, coercion, and genocide."[29] This method is generally adopted by societies in which the tradition of the military pattern and strict regeneration prevail. Totalitarian societies—both Communist and Fascist—have recognized the necessity of economic, social and political planning. Both conceive of planning as an all-pervasive process which would regulate everything and execute planning by dictatorship. Totalitarian over-regimentation means the rule of a single party, concentration of power in the hands of a few, complete control of mass media, suppression of all freedom, irresponsible use of power by official and non-official gangs, widespread use of propaganda, concentration camps and torture as means of enforcing conformity and above all a dictated culture.

The two variants of totalitarian responses are:

1. *The Pessimistic View of Fascism*
Unlike the Marxists, the Fascists do not believe in the perfecti-

bility of man and have no utopian vision of creating a new social order. Therefore, they tend to indulge in reckless exploitation of the immediate chances to benefit a minority, usually their ruling class or their race. While others are working hard to prevent war, the Fascists believe that war is rooted in human nature and seek to turn out the most efficient soldiers. They replace the methods of political discussion by organized propaganda and ruthlessly use the new social techniques to enslave man. "The Fascist is against growth and improvement because he does not believe in the basic creative powers of man. With this pessimism and skepticism it is possible to use efficient techniques only for further exploitation."

2. *The Utopian Hope of Marxism*
"Where the Fascist has too little, the Communist has rather too much." He has a fanatical faith in the perfectibility of human nature and of the social order. Being over-critical of the existing state of affairs he is eager to scrap everything and start anew. "In diagnosing the inevitability of class war, the Communist takes part in creating it. Through relentless emphasis on the proposition that society can be essentially transformed only by violence, he shatters the environment in which gradual reform could be carried out. By destroying the hopes of the reformers he creates a situation in which nothing can survive but extremist revolutionary or extremist reactionary mentality." Mannheim also believes that the minority who manipulates and controls the masses by means of the new social techniques will never willingly hand over the reigns of power and that no established totalitarian regime can be broken from within; "it takes an external power to unseat it." In olden days when "every man represented one rifle, and every rifle one man", it was possible for the masses to turn against the tyrant. "Today with completely different weapons, the private or semi-official armies of the dictator, together with a centralized government and a vast network of spies, constitute a stronghold against which in peacetime thus far no resistance has ever succeeded." Thus Communism has destroyed all freedom, established a parmanent dictatorship and failed to create the promised social order.

Democratic Planning

Saying that "not all planning is evil", Mannheim makes a distinction between planning for conformity and planning for freedom and variety and, of course he indicates his strong preference for the latter. The only type of planning that is socially beneficial is the one that not only preserves individual freedom but also actually fosters it. Modern society must adopt democratic planning of the free type if it is to avoid the kind of crisis which will thrust the planning of the totalitarian type on us. Democratic planning simply means a greater economy and a more purposeful use of the social techniques. No great society can survive if it only fosters conformity.

Mannheim formulated his concept of democratic planning as follows:

> Our task is to build a social system by planning, but planning of a special kind: it must be *planning for freedom*, subjected to democratic control; *planning, but not restrictions* so as to favor group monopolies either of entrepreneurs or workers' associations, but 'planning for plenty', i.e. full employment and full exploitation of resources; *planning for social justice* rather than absolute equality, with differentiation of rewards and status on the basis of genuine equality rather than privilege; *planning not for a classless society* but for one that abolishes the extremes of wealth and poverty; *planning for cultural standards* without 'levelling down'—a planned transition making for progress without discarding what is valuable in tradition; *planning that counteracts the dangers of a mass society* by coordination of the means of social control but interfering only in cases of institutional or moral deterioration defined by collective criteria; *planning for balance* between centralization and dispersion of power; *planning* for gradual transformation of society *in order to encourage the growth of personality:* in short, *planning but not regimentation.*[30]

The laissez-faire methods have been destructive. In the economic sphere they were responsible for the trade cycle and devastating mass unemployment; also it is slow and wasteful. The age of laissez-faire system has passed. Although Fascism seems to be efficient, "its efficiency is that of the devil." And Communism has been a great disappointment. Neither Dictatorship nor the State seems to wither away. A single party and its bureaucracy have mastered the new social techniques and hence have absolute control over the masses. Mannheim proposed to show a Third

Way incorporating the painful experiences of the last decades
into a new pattern of democracy. It is "a way through reform
and peaceful change, but a way that will demand serious sacrifices
from all. Planning the transition needs to be as decisive as map-
ping out a distant future." Democratic planning or "Planning for
Freedom" is the only way to develop a new social order and to
check the dictatorial tendencies of modern social techniques.
This, Mannheim feels, must be done immediately while the
techniques are still flexible and have not been monopolized by
any single group.

What does this democratic planning consist of? The essential
features are:

1. Coordination of the means of social techniques such as
education, propaganda, administration, etc., or positive choice
between the different and contradictory tendencies presented by
various institutions in society. In contrast to freedom in unplan-
ned societies which to Mannheim is merely the 'possibility of
escape' or negative freedom, democratic planning involves positive freedom or coordination on the basis of a well conceived
plan.

2. "Coordination does not mean creating new facts by bureaucratic command, but the use of the indispensable spontaneous
forces of society in fostering certain desirable aims. It means the
harmonizing of all the spontaneous and vital forces of society by
anticipating the ways in which they are likely to work and the
continuous correlation of the necessary adjustments."

3. "Coordination does not involve the suppression of individuality but, rather, entails differentiation, providing the space
where it may grow and the social stimuli which regularly foster
it."

4. "In the planned societies to come it gradually becomes
necessary to acquire a detailed knowledge of the working of the
forces making for individualization and to rearrange these social
stimuli in such a way that they serve not only particular local
needs but the central aims of a planned community." To determine what kind of social environment is most conducive to a
healthy growth of personality we need all the psychological and
sociological knowledge we can master. Planners must rely on
their knowledge of human motivations, on social sciences that

enable them to predict what arrangement of the environment will bring forth the most desirable, cooperative and productive responses; thus they seek to rearrange and manipulate social environment without resorting to outright coercion. This will not diminish the freedom of the individual who will be encouraged to continue to be a free and intelligent agent.

Democratic planning must meet the increasing demand for social justice; Mannheim believes that it can be done through reform and without revolutionary interference. Democracy must involve tolerance but not at any cost. Tolerance does not mean that we should refrain from taking a stand for what we believe to be true; it does mean however, that everybody should have a fair chance to present his case. It also means faith in peaceful adjustment and a commitment to freedom and democratic control. Mannheim feels, however, that we have carried the attitude of democratic mentality "so far that we ceased to believe, out of mere fairness, in our own objectives." In other words, in our eagerness to be fair to every segment of society we become blind to the concerns of collective good. Mannheim writes:

> Our democracy has to become militant if it is to survive. Of course, there is a fundamental difference between the fighting spirit of the dictators on the one hand, who aim at imposing a total system of values and a strait-jacket social organization upon their citizens, and a militant democracy on the other, which becomes militant only in the defence of the agreed right procedure of social change and those basic virtues and values—such as brotherly love, mutual help, decency, social justice, freedom, respect for the person, etc.—which are the basis of the peaceful functioning of a social order. The new militant democracy will therefore develop a new attitude to values. It will differ from the relativist laissez-faire of the previous age, as it will have the courage to agree on some basic values which are acceptable to everybody who shares the traditions of Western civilization.[31]

Mannheim considered 'planning for freedom' to be the only practical approach to achieve freedom and individualization. Yet, he also recognized the dangers of planning. The greatest danger for him was that the planner, baffled and disillusioned by the difficulty of the right approach, might take the short cut of bureaucratic regulation and totalitarian oppression of the individual. The declaration of Martial Law or Emergency by democratic planners may serve as an example.

It must be remembered that Mannheim's conception of planning differed from the popular image of a planned social order. In the words of Kecskemeti:

> "... 'planning' was for Mannheim a *corrective* to the blind and unregulated workings of the collective dynamic forces of society, rather than a *culmination* of the trend towards collective dynamism. Its function was a hygienic and prophylactic rather than a creative one, Mannheim's concept of planning has nothing to do with the idea (usually associated with 'planned society') of developing a 'blue-print' of a new social order and reshaping society according to its specifications, after one has made a *tabula rasa* of the old unplanned system. Far from proposing to start from scratch, Mannheim envisages planning as proceeding within the institutional framework of mature democracies.[32]

However, the new planning can no longer be a mere hit-or-miss compromise on disconnected issues; it must meet the growing demand for social justice. The totalitarian society is able to undertake effective planning because of a one-party system. If modern democracies are to survive, they must "discover new methods of creating a unified political will by voluntary agreement on the part of rival social groups. Either democracy must invent in the shortest possible time such new techniques, or some form of totalitarianism will win."[33] This is a deep-seated conviction of Mannheim's. If the rival social forces and political parties indulge in excessive competition and carry on the power game to extreme limits, there will be no genuine integration and the democratic system will slip into Fascism. Constructive criticism and genuine cooperation are needed for democracy to work.

Mannheim also cautions that the democratic plan must be consistent and acceptable to a majority. According to Mannheim, "such a majority can be found only in the cénter, excluding both reactionaries who do not want to move at any price, and radicals who think the millennium is just around the corner." However, the center groups must allow for different shades of opinion, stimulate cooperation on basic issues and represent a strong commitment to peaceful methods to facilitate freedom, reform and change. Mannheim's conclusion is frank and forthright:

> It is not worth dying either for a sham democracy that favors only restriction and extremes of poverty and plutocratic wealth, or for a sham planned society in which all human

freedom vanishes forever. Everything, therefore, depends on our imagination and intellectual effort. We must neither accept the existing deterioration of our democratic system as irreversible nor embrace the first chance experiments of reorganization in totalitarian states as the only possible course. Even in politics the *status quo* is instructive only if the analytic mind can disentangle (a) which features have come about through the exigencies of the changing basic structure of society and (b) which are arbitrary answers to a challenge that might be met in some other manner.

Influence and Appreciation

'Planned society' is considered a collectivist slogan, a crowning triumph of the collectivist trend in history. However, strange though it may seem, in Mannheim's case the adoption of the principle of social planning coincided with his loss of faith in the comprehensive structural forces of history and with increased respect for the freedom and dignity of the individual. The planning Mannheim advocates, is for the preservation of freedom, spontaneity and self-realization of the individual. That is why he rejected both Fascist and Marxist systems of planning on the ground that they both rely on coercion and stunt the freedom and self-realization of the individual and recommended a Third Way, the way of a militant democracy.

Mannheim is an optimist who sees a significant role for the science of human behavior in the emerging age of Planning for Freedom. In the past custom and tradition coordinated and integrated social institutions and moulded behavior of the individual. Modern age marked a transition from custom to social science. "So long as custom and tradition worked, there was no need for social science. The science of society emerged when and where the automatic functioning of society ceased to find adjustment. Conscious analysis of the situation and conscious coordination of social processes then became necessary." Mannheim believes that social science serves three key functions in democratic planning: "it will clarify (1) the democratic idea of coordination in contrast to totalitarian regimentation; (2) the making and remaking of human behavior, i.e. social and psychological means of conditioning of man; (3) the pattern of democratic behavior, conscience, and personality as ends of democratic planning."

It is now generally agreed that Mannheim's most significant

contributions lie in the field of the sociology of knowledge. Louis
Wirth has noted:

> Professor Mannheim has sought to trace out the specific con-
> nection between actual interest groups in society and the ideas
> and modes of thought which they espoused. He has succeed-
> ed in showing that ideologies, i.e., those complexes of ideas
> which direct activity toward the maintenance of the existing
> order, and utopias—or those complexes of ideas which tend
> to generate activities toward changes of the prevailing order—
> do not merely deflect thought from the object of observation,
> but also serve to fix attention upon aspects of the situation
> which otherwise would be obscured or pass unnoticed. In this
> manner he has forged out of a general theoretical formulation
> an effective instrument for fruitful empirical research.[34]

But how can we validate a theory which proposes that human
thought is determined by social reality? If we accept the theory,
then we must also admit that the theory itself, being an element
of thought, is the product of objective social forces. As Grunwald
puts it: "No long argument is needed to show beyond doubt
that this version of sociologism, too, is a form of scepticism and
therefore refutes itself. For the thesis that all thinking is existentially determined and therefore cannot claim to be true claims
itself to be true."[35] Similarly, Dahlke pointed to a logical difficulty: "The notion of relativism or relationism, as developed by
Mannheim, is self-contradictory, for it must presuppose its own
absoluteness. The sociology of knowledge . . . must assume its
own validity, if it is to have any meaning." Indeed, any theory
which proposes that all thinking is totally determined by social
factors destroys itself. However, it is doubtful whether Mannheim had such a rigid existential determination in mind. On the
other hand, he emphasized concepts like perspective, freedom
and individualization. Moreover, as Kecskemeti observed, "no
amount of methodological purism can relieve us of the task of
accounting for the historical process as a whole and as defining
our relationship to our culture."

Mannheim's position marked a departure from two aspects of
German idealism: (a) the over-estimation of the role of ideas in
human affairs; and (b) the consequent tendency to assume that
concepts which emerge in various periods of history inherently
evolve from one another in something like a logical continuum.
Mannheim abandoned the image of an autonomous evolution of

ideas and sought to explore the relationship between thought and its social milieu. He concentrated on the social mechanism which intervenes between the roles individuals play and the ideas they espouse. As Bramsted and Gerth have observed: "Even where the social observer is careful to control his personal bias, to argue 'objectively' by not indulging in special pleading and subjective value preferences, his socio-historical background can be shown to condition his ways of thought."[36] And this is exactly what Mannheim set out to show.

Put bluntly, and in the words of Edward Shils, "the sociology of knowledge as practised by Mannheim has found no succession."[37] If by succession we mean a school of thought which regularly and religiously draws attention to and sustenance from the writings of a master, then Shils is correct. That sociology of knowledge is alive and well in Germany and America particularly is certainly true; in the U.S. it is being carried on in a burst of interest and scholarship under the profound leadership of Peter L Berger and others. Mannheim's "influence in this area (especially studies of 'ideology') is a product", says Shils, "less of anything specific he said about the problems of ideology than of the fact that he dwelt on them long and seriously." Mannheim sought to enrich the sociology of knowledge in two ways: "substantive contributions involving 'purely empirical investigation through description and structural analysis of the ways in which social relationships in fact, influence thought", and "epistemological inquiry concerned with the bearing of this interrelationship upon the problem of validity."[38] But, as Coser says, "It would seem that he was considerably more successful in the first endeavor than he was in the second."[39] In spite of the fact that Coser and others argue that Mannheim's British period did not result in scholarship which has endured the ravages of time owing to his naive promise of a synthesis of the idea of planning and reconstruction of a modern futuristic society, Shils does point out that his macro-sociological views of contemporary large-scale society "have had a more receptive audience and a more enduring influence." The man's genius was his creative convergence of historicism, Marxism, and English pragmatism, and his name will forever be recalled in the circles of sociology of knowledge.

9

PITIRIM SOROKIN

LIFE AND TIMES

Russia was able to make a significant contribution to the development of a new science of society in the person of Pitirim Sorokin (1889-1968). Born amongst the Urgo-Finnish-speaking people, the Komi, of the Volgoda Province in the far north country of Russia's forested frontiers, Sorokin emerged as Russia's first distinguished sociologist. Though reared amongst peasant people in a small community nestled in the primeval woodlands of Russia's expansive wilderness, Sorokin exemplified a thirst for knowledge. Three sons were born to his father, a Russian by birth and allegiance. Pitirim's mother died when he was but three years old, and owing to the erratic displays of despair and abuse of his father, the sons ran away when Pitirim was just ten years old. The boys had learned enough of their father's craft as icon painters and woodworkers to eke out a living painting art forms for Churches of the area. But at fourteen, Sorokin was able to win a scholarship, albeit a modest one, to attend the Khrenovo Teachers Seminary where he received training as an elementary teacher for the Orthodox Church's school system.

Sorokin was mocked and teased mercilessly for being an uncouth peasant from the rude back country. But his congeniality with his peers, his capacity for hard work and robust interchanges with his teachers earned him respect and served his ambitions well. Not unlike many masters of sociology before him, Sorokin, though reared in a Christian family and country environment, gave up belief in religion, choosing rather as a professed agnostic to place his confidence in the scientific theories of evolution, becoming an untiring activist in the ensuing Russian Revolution. Again like the masters before him, war and armed conflict between peoples—in this instance the Russo-Japanese War and its subsequent turmoils and political mayhems—contributed substantially to his shifting of allegiances and his commitments to the Revolution.

Yet, unlike many of his youthful peers, Sorokin, possibly because of his personal experience of freedom within his village community, was repelled by the then popular Marxist determinism of social democracy. Rather, he became a most distinguished activist in the cause of the populist Social Revolutionary party. Combining vigorous activism, intellectual acumen, quick-wittedness, and a rural lad's gift at practicality, Sorokin naturally became a regular candidate for the popular public addresses on political issues. His first arrest and imprisonment came on Christmas, 1906, the authorities having been made aware of a planned address by Sorokin on a politically controversial and potentially inflammatory topic. Unlike earlier days when the Czar made imprisonment a grave experience of deprivation and destitution, Sorokin found his few months of confinement not unpleasant but highly informative as a training facility for more expert revolutionary activity. During the time, Sorokin became a respected and well-regarded spokesman for the progressive movement among Russia's radical and intellectual communities. Later on, Sorokin would write his first book on the experience of *Crime and Punishment*, pioneering a new field of research and study in criminology and penology. After four months, Sorokin was released and acclaimed a hero by the Revolution. Under an assumed name—"Comrade Ivan" he recommenced his insurrectionist activities but owing to rising personal dangers and pressures from friends, he returned to Komi for a time of safety, peace, and rest.

In 1909, Sorokin enrolled in the Psycho-Neurological Institute in St. Petersburg where he studied sociology. Later, when political, social, and economic barriers were surmounted, he became a student at the city's university, becoming later a lecturer in sociology back at the Institute. A prolific writer throughout his life, Sorokin was publishing scholarly and popular treatises even as an undergraduate. His first book was published during his junior year at the University. All the while, Sorokin's political activities, especially his public lecturing and political journalism, continued unabated. Arrested and released again in 1913, Sorokin won a first class diploma from the University of St. Petersburg the following year in sociology. As a result of his scholarly achievement and recognition as a promising sociologist, he received a four-year stipend at the University to prepare for his examinations for the Master's degree. Two years later, he earned the Master's degree and was made Privatdozent at the University. The following May, 1917, Sorokin married Elena Petrovna Baratinsky, a helpmate in his scholarly and political activities. In July, 1917, following the Czar's abdication, a Provisional Government was formed by Kerensky, and due to his early distinctions for brilliance in politics and scholarly attainments, Sorokin was made Secretary to the Prime Minister.

Whereas the Czarist authority had plagued Sorokin before, now, the Bolsheviks were determined to beleaguer him with constant surveillance and harassments. All in all, Sorokin was arrested and jailed three times by the Czarists and three times by the Bolsheviks. With the decline of the Czarist government in 1917 came the temporary presence of Kerensky's Provisional Government which was to last briefly. Following its fall, leaving Sorokin without his secretariat to the Prime Minister, he became an active participant in the struggle against communism. As a student; he had participated in the Revolution's rise to prominence, then as a member of the Constituent Assembly, then secretary to Kerensky and editor of the politically liberal left-wing newspaper, *Volia Naroda*. Sorokin's revolutionary experience had led him to radically break with optimistic views of one-directional, material progress. In January, 1918, the Bolsheviks arrested and jailed him for two months. That same year, following a short period of release, Sorokin was arrested again. Only after the intervention of Lenin himself was Sorokin released, his death sentence being commuted to banishment in 1922. Throughout it all, he had been actively engaged in research and writing—especially his two volume-work, *System of Sociology*. Having himself forged the censorship page in his study—a requirement by the Bolshevik communist authorities—Sorokin actually sold 10,000 copies of each volume before his final arrest. The communist government stopped the presses but were unable to recall the sold copies. Amidst Communist protest and anti-Communist Revolutionary support, the University of St. Petersburg awarded Sorokin the Ph.D. in sociology on April 22, 1922, at the age of 33. During this fateful year, there had been a new wave of arrests of members of the non-communist parties among the intelligentsia—Sorokin and his friends in Petrograd being the most conspicuous. Hearing of arrests, Sorokin and his family fled to Moscow but there, upon learning that banishment and not execution was the penalty, he surrendered, leaving Russia with his family on September 23, 1922, never to return. At the personal invitation of Czechoslovakia's President, Sorokin spent a little less than two years there, but, thanks to invitations from abroad, Sorokin began a lecture tour on the Russian Revolution in America, lecturing first at Vassar College. The following year, 1925, he was made visiting professor and then full professor of sociology at the University of Minnesota.

Sorokin spent six years at Minnesota, productive years by professional standards—appreciated by colleagues, admired in the classroom, and writer of many articles and numerous books. Among his more important books at the time were *The Sociology of Revolution* (1925); *Social Mobility* (1927); *Contemporary Sociological Theory* (1928); *Principles of Rural-Urban Sociology* (1929); and a three-volume study, *A Systematic Source-Book in Rural Sociology* (1930-1932). As might have been expected, a call came for a new challenge and a new career in another prestigious institution which Sorokin accepted. In 1930, the President of Harvard University invited Sorokin to come to Cambridge to establish that institution's first department of sociology, himself becoming its first full professor of sociology. Like his Minnesota period, his Harvard period was most productive. Over the next twenty-nine years at Harvard, Sorokin continued to work, research, and publish. But, as his volume of published work continued to increase, his popularity and especially his national visibility began steadily to wane. Though popular with students for his passionate lectures and Revolutionary vignettes, and having been elected President first of the International Institute of Sociology (1936) and then of the American Sociological Association (1964), among colleagues he was often perceived as distant, aloof, or even cranky. He eventually resigned the chairmanship of a department he had reason to be proud of having built, handing over the leadership to, as it turned out, his most popular and distinguished American colleague, Talcott Parsons. Many books were published during the period, the most important being his *Sociological Theories of Today* (1966), published when he was seventy-seven years old. He taught until 1955, and fully retired from university functions at age seventy, was still a vigorous and intellectually stimulating scholar. Friends, family, and admirers kept his life full, and in later years, he came to pride himself in his gifts as a flower gardener almost as much as an author and teacher. He died, still very much the emigre in lifestyle and manner of vision, on February 11, 1968, at the ripe old age of seventy-eight.

MAJOR THEORIES

Sociology: Its Nature and Methodology

Given his rather substantial involvement in the revolutionary ideology in the Russia of his day, on the one hand, and his careful and successful study of society in its scientific mode of approach at the Psycho-Neurological Institute on the other, Sorokin's experience necessarily resulted from the conflicting traditions of Russian intellectual history, viz., populist idealism of the revolutionary party and positivistic and deterministic behaviorism of the scientific community. Early in his writings, he favored the latter position. For example, in 1926, he wrote: "Human conduct is an extraordinary complex phenomenon, determined in an immense variety of cases by inborn reflexes and their stimuli. ..The balance of conduct is achieved by way of self-restriction and complex of struggle of various stimuli and reactions." Following his disenchantment with the Russian Revolution, Sorokin turned away from the behaviorism and positivism supported by the communist ideologues. These positions seemed to have failed because of their bold reductionism of human behavior to simplistic and non-human categories. Subsequently, his career was dedicated to humanitarian methods in sociology and an aggressively outspoken rejection of and attack upon all forms of reductionistic behaviorism.

Sorokin defined sociology as the study of the general characteristics common to all classes of social phenomena including a careful investigation of the relationship between social and non-social phenomena. He referred to general sociology as the study of those properties common to all socio-cultural phenomena and divided it into two parts: structural sociology which deals with the structure of social, cultural, and personality features of the superorganic; and dynamic sociology which investigates "(1) repeated *social processes* and change, together with the uniformities of the how and why; (2) repeated *cultural processes* and change; (3) the processes and changes of personality in its relationships with the social and cultural processes."[1] The study of those properties common to a given class of socio-cultural phenomena, Sorokin labelled as special sociology.

Following the Russo-Polish scholar Leon Petrazucki's logic that if a particular social phenomenon can be divided into *n* sub-classes there must be *n* + 1 disciplines to study them, that is, *n* disciplines to study each of the sub-classes and one more to study that which is common to all of them, Sorokin reasoned. While economics, political science or anthropology, studies a particular sub-class of social phenomena, sociology studies society as a whole as well as the relationship between economy and society, state and society and so on. In a rather formal fashion, Sorokin has refined the parameters of the discipline, itemizing three special domains open and susceptible to sociology. In his *Society, Culture, and Personality*, he defines sociology as the generalizing theory of the structure and dynamics of (1) social systems and congeries (functionally inconsistent elements); (2) cultural systems and congeries; and (3) personalities in their structural aspects, main types, inter-relationships, and personality processes.[2]

During his later years at Harvard, Sorokin kept up his work, serving as a self-appointed critic of major trends in modern society, as for example, the concentration of power in irresponsible hands and the anarchism of sexual norms which he believed to be characteristic of a waning society. At Harvard, his research centered among the modes of behavior antithetical to current values as exemplified in such phenomena as the forms and techniques of altruism, their distribution and social correlates. He believed and worked feverishly in support of the belief that this thrust of research was important if sociology was to prepare society for the likely aftermath of change from the sensual quality of the modern world.

As a strong advocate of what has come to be called the

"integralist school" of sociology, Sorokin wrote a strong treatise on methodology in his volume entitled, *Dynamics*, and also again his *Socio-Cultural Causality, Space, and Time*. The integralist school focussed its attention upon an investigation of social phenomena in three ways: (1) Empirically, social phenomena are studied through sense perception and sensory-empirical observation; (2) the "logico-rational" dimension in which socio-cultural phenomena must be comprehended through discursive logic of human reason; and (3) socio-cultural reality which has its supersensory, superrational, and metalogical dimensions. This latter, Sorokin indicated, is evidenced in the historic religions, absolutist ethics, and the truly great fine arts. "This phase of socio-cultural reality" Sorokin felt, "must be apprehended through the truth of the faith, that is, through a supersensory, superrational, metalogical act of intuition or mystic experience."[3]

Consistent with his integralist philosophy, Sorokin expounded two fundamental methods by which order can be brought into the conglomeration of cultural events, objects and values: causal or functional unity and logico-meaningful method. The former refers to the establishment of the presence of "tangible, noticeable, testifiable, direct interdependence (mutual or one-sided) of the variables or parts upon one another and upon the whole system. If variation A is always followed by B (under the same conditions and in a large enough number of cases so that mere chance is eliminated), we say that they are functionally related."[4] The second type of cultural integration is obtained by the use of "the logical laws of identity, contradiction, consistency: and it is these laws of logic which must be employed to discover whether any synthesis is or is not *logico-meaningful*. Side by side with such logical laws in the narrow sense, the broader principles of "keeping", of internal consistency, must also be used to determine the existence of this higher unity, or the lack of it."[5]

In addition to his researches on cultural dynamics, Sorokin also spent much time in the area of personality studies. His research led him to strongly emphasize the influence of sociocultural environments in shaping the human personality. Carefully avoiding a one-sided "sociologistic" interpretation of human behavior—a danger Durkheim occasionally was not too careful to avoid—Sorokin was concerned particularly about the interdependent and interacting elements of the individual and personality on the one hand and society and culture on the other as integrated totalities or social wholes. Sorokin was earnest in his emphasis upon the pluralism of "selves" in individuals which he believed is a reflection of the pluralism of groups, and the multiple "social egos" of the individual he argued are a consequence of his or her various group memberships. Sorokin also believed that each of the broad socio-cultural systems to be discussed later, viz., ideational, sensate, idealistic, produces characteristic personality types.

Modalities of Interaction

In pondering the complex relationship of these two correlated pairs of social phenomena, viz., individual-personality and society-culture, Sorokin became convinced that "interaction" must be the single most important and determinative unit in terms of which social phenomena should be analyzed, and defined it as "any event by which one party tangibly influences the overt action or the state of mind of the other." "In its developed forms," he contended, "the super-organic is found exclusively in the realm of interacting human beings and in the products of their interaction." Because of his development of the specialized concept of socio-cultural interaction, he restricts the generalized concept by saying simply that "the most generic model of any socio-cultural phenomenon is the meaningful interaction of two or more human individuals." Upon introducing this concept of socio-cultural interaction, Sorokin is quick to point to three inseparably interrelated components—viz., "(1) Personality as the subject of interaction; (2) Society as the totality of interacting personalities; and (3) Culture as the totality of the meanings, values, and norms possessed by the interacting personalities and the totality of the vehicles which objectify, socialize, and convey these meanings."[6]

The process of interaction is seen to comprise three components: "(1) thinking, acting, and reacting human beings as subjects of interaction; (2) meaning, values and norms for the sake of which the individuals interact, realizing and exchanging them in the course of interaction; (3) overt actions and material phenomena as vehicles or conductors through which immaterial meanings, values, and norms are objectified and socialized."[7] The modality of a particular interaction depends on any one of three possible kinds of relationships between parties involved—

solidary, antagonistic, or mixed. Both antagonisms and solidarities very in intensity (from a mere coldness to the most intense hatred) and extensity (from a small fragment of one's personality to total involvement).

Sorokin classifies relationships into three types:

(a) *Familistic relationship*
As an "ideal" type based on mutual love, sacrifice and devotion, the familistic relationships are usually found among members of a devoted family and among close friends and have the following characteristics:

> (a) predominantly solidary; (b) total or broad in extensity; (c) of high intensity; (d) durable; (e) direct; (f) mutual, or two-sided; (g) marked by the fundamental, normative, and purposive types of motivation, all working harmoniously with one another; (h) based upon a deep sense of the socio-cultural oneness of the parties; (i) possessing leadership or government that is natural and spontaneous and truly paternalistic with a leader who is merely a *primus inter pares*.[8]

Such relationships are all-embracing, all-forgiving and all-bestowing and involve a fusion of the ego into "we".

(b) *Contractual relationship*
"In almost every contractual variety of mixed relationship the main motivation of solidarity is one of the purposive, implicitly egoistic, utilitarian type, often supplemented and moderated by the legal normative motivation."[9] The contractual relationship is limited and specified, covering only a portion of the lives of the parties concerned; the rights and duties of each party are specified by contract. It is self-centered and instrumental, each party trying to take maximum advantage of the relationship. Typical contractual relationships are those of the buyer and seller, employer and employee and the like.

(c) *Compulsory relationship*
This type of relationship is characterized by antagonism which may vary from some form of mild discomfort to the most intense hatred. "It may be rooted in the fundamental, the normative, or the purposive type of motivation or in a combination of all three."[10] An example of this kind of relationship would be des-

potic governments which use brute force and fraud to achieve
their goals.

Having identified the three types of relationships on the basis
of the nature of interaction, Sorokin hastens to add:

> The immediate and most decisive factors of either solidarity
> or antagonism of the interacting parties are (a) the character
> of their law and ethical convictions; (b) the concordance or
> discordance of the law and moral convictions of each party
> with those of the others; (c) the degree to which these norms
> are consistently and adequately practised by the overt actions
> and vehicles of the parties.[11]

Having differed from Durkheim on the role of the individual
personality as truly socio-cultural phenomena, he now differs
from Weber, rejecting any attempt to study human behavior without specific and intentional reference to norms, meanings and
values. "Stripped of their meaningful aspects," he protested to his
behavioristic colleagues in *Society, Culture, and Personality*, "all
the phenomena of human interaction become merely bio-physical
phenomena and, as such, properly form the subject of the bio-
physical sciences."[12] Therefore, Sorokin's definition of interaction
necessarily focussed upon human conduct that influences others
and may derive the proposition that any group of interacting
individuals is first of all a causal-functional unity in which all
components are mutually and tangibly interdependent. Every
social group then, as Pareto demonstrated, is a *social system*.
Because social groups in society form a system, the character and
quality of their interaction can be organized, unorganized, or
disorganized. And, for analytical purposes, Sorokin suggested
that these groups which honeycomb all of society fall into four
interrelated characteristics, viz., (1) each organized group is
characterized by a central set of meanings or ideas and values;
(2) the central set of ideas and values must be consistent within
itself—a principle closely approximating a theorem held by many
functionalists; (3) these consistent ideas and values assume the
form of norms to be followed by the group members; and finally,
(4) these norms, or "law-norms", must be effective and therefore
eventually enforceable. Within this framework of analytical constructs, Sorokin made much progress in his study of the concept
of interaction as a group phenomenon occurring within identifiable systems.

Culture and Change

Sorokin was not singularly concerned with an understanding of *personality* as the subject of social interaction, he was also involved in a study of *society* as the totality of those interacting personalities. And, culminating his grasp of interactional dynamics, Sorokin believed that both personality and society rested upon the foundation of culture. For, Sorokin took pains to explain, a culture consists of the totality of meanings, norms and values possessed by interacting persons and carried by material vehicles, such as ritual objects or works of art, which objectify and convey these meanings. While at Harvard, Sorokin's major sociological concern centered around the process of social organization, disorganization, and reorganization, within a panoramic view of history that stresses periodic fluctuations as the core component or characteristic of social change. His primary sociological presupposition was that of a 'social realism', a view of reality which postulates the existence of a supra-organic, supra-individual, socio-cultural reality. This presupposition runs throughout his analysis of socio-cultural systems.

In Sorokin's major study of social change, *Social and Cultural Dynamics*, 1937-1941, in four volumes, his position towards and analysis of socio-cultural phenomena are based on relatively coherent and integrated aggregates of cultural outlooks or in his words, "mentalities." These distinct and identifiable mentalities impress their meanings or meaning-systems upon definite time periods in the universal history of mankind. His quest, Sorokin explains in *Dynamics*, volume one, is "the central principle which permeates all the components (of culture), gives sense and significance to them, and in this way makes cosmos of a chaos of unintegrated fragments."[13] That no culture is ever fully integrated, Sorokin readily concedes. He argues, however, that each culture, so long as it survives, will reveal the functioning of a few major concepts or ideas or meanings which marks each culture's overall character or mood.

In his first volume of *Dynamics*, Sorokin offers his formal definition of culture as "the sum total of everything which is created or modified by the conscious or unconscious activity of two or more individuals interacting with one another or conditioning one another's behavior."[14] There are three components to this concept of culture, each related, yet each distinctively identifiable. They are: (1) "pure culture systems" which are systems of meanings or ideas in the most elementary sense—his illustration is $2+2=4$; (2) cultural systems are "socialized" by which he means operative in social interaction. Emerging from this is Sorokin's key concept, viz., the socio-cultural system. The sociocultural system, then, is a system of meanings that is expressed in communicable terms and that constitutes an important element of a specific area of interaction.

Amidst the development of this concept, Sorokin was led to another formulation particularly at the point where socio-cultural change encounters a shock from natural disaster or political revolution within interpersonal behavior. The concept, so formulated, was called by Sorokin the principle of polarization.' With this concept, Sorokin broke through an analytical barrier and gave to sociology another tool for its work. The principle of polarization holds that in the majority of actors the normal tendency to moral indifference in everyday, routine intersubjective behavior becomes intensified in times of acute crises such as political revolutions or natural disasters. The social majority then seeks only hedonistic, self-oriented gratification, while a significantly small number of social members become oriented to altruistic, religious, pietistic, and other-worldly activities. When the crisis passes, society resumes its normal distribution.

Throughout his career, Sorokin's thought was dominated by a concern for large super-systems. As we have mentioned, Sorokin believed that each super-system or socio-cultural complex was characterized by a central mood or idea which is the predominant view of truth in any specific culture. The three major "cultural mentalities" which Sorokin identified and studied in culture history were the Sensate, the Ideational, and the Idealistic. And, he pointed out, history suggests that the pattern or cycle of rise and fall of each is in this specific order—the sensate followed by the counterpoising ideational, followed by the synthesis of the idealistic. And these categories form the foundation for his theory of social change. Their characteristics are as follows:

1. *Ideational Culture*
"True value and true reality consist in a super-sensory, super-rational God." Reality here is felt to be disclosed only through a view that transcends the world of the senses and achieves a trans-

cendent vision of the eternal as in Platonic idealism; thus, people in this culture generally accept the truth of faith, believing that behind sense impressions lies another, deeper reality. Ideal culture is characterized by the following:

(1) Reality is perceived as non-sensate and non-material, everlasting Being (Sein); (2) the needs and ends are mainly spiritual; (3) the extent of their satisfaction is the largest, and the level, highest; (4) the method of their fulfilment or realization is self-imposed minimization or elimination of most of the physical needs, and to the greatest possible extent.[15]

Sorokin divides the Ideational culture into two sub-types: the ascetic ideational which involves a radical rejection of the Sensate world, and the active Ideational which involves an attempt to transform the Sensate world in the light of spiritual values.

2. Sensate Culture
In this system, "true reality and true value is sensory . . . beyond the reality and value perceived by our sense organs there is no other reality and no value." It is based on the belief that reality is directly accessible through the human senses; thus people, in this culture ascribe ultimate validity to their senses.

. . . the Sensate mentality views reality as only that which is presented to the sense organs. It does not seek or believe in any supersensory reality; at the most, in its diluted form, it assumes an agnostic attitude toward the entire world beyond the senses. The Sensate reality is thought of as a Becoming, Process, Change, Flux, Evolution, Progress, Transformation. Its needs and aims are mainly physical, and maximum satisfaction is sought of these needs. The method of realizing them is not that of a modification within the human individuals composing the culture, but a modification or exploitation of the external world. In brief, the Sensate culture is the opposite of the Ideational in its major premises.[16]

3. Idealistic Culture
"True value and true reality are an infinite manifold, partly supersensory and partly super-rational and partly sensory." A synthesis of Ideational and Sensate elements, the Idealistic culture represents a dialectically balancing tension. According to Sorokin:

Quantitatively it represents a more or less balanced unification of Ideational and Sensate, with, however, a predominance of the Ideational elements. Qualitatively it synthesizes the premises of both types into one inwardly consistent and harmonious unity. For it, reality is many-sided, with the aspects of everlasting Being and everchanging Becoming of the spiritual and the material, with the material, however, subordinated to the spiritual. The methods for their realization involve both the modification of the self and the transformation of the external sensate world: in other words, it gives *sum cuique* to the Ideational and the Sensate.[17]

It must also be remembered that Sorokin speaks of Mixed Cultures in which the elements of Ideational and Sensate cultures are combined but not integrated.

This, in summary, is Sorokin's unified theory of socio-cultural phenomena. With the aid of a research team, Sorokin amassed mountains of data to support his theory which, he claims, corresponds to empirical reality. Greek culture from the twelfth to the fifth century B.C. is regarded as Ideational while that from the fifth through the fourth century B.C. which included the Golden Age of Athens, was Idealistic. From the later part of the fourth century B.C. to the fourth century A.D. during which the Roman Empire emerged and flourished, Sensate culture held sway. The subsequent two centuries of mixed culture were followed by a long period of Ideational culture. The period from the end of the twelfth century to the early fourteenth which was the age of Gothic Cathedrals, of Dante, and of St. Thomas Aquinas, was Idealistic. Since the end of the fourteenth century, Sensate culture has been in the ascendancy, reaching the climax in mid-twentieth century.

Sorokin's theory of socio-cultural phenomena involves three fundamental principles which constitute the cornerstone of his theory of social and cultural change.

1. The Principle of Cyclical Change

Having rejected the unilinear view of socio-cultural phenomena which claims that history never repeats itself and that no two cultural objects are ever the same, Sorokin argued that the socio-cultural phenomena are always recurrent and that the process of social change is essentially cyclical. He writes:

> the great symphony of social life is "scored" for a countless number of separate processes, each proceeding in a wavelike manner and recurring in space, in time, in both space and time, periodically or non-periodically, after long or short

intervals. Briefly, or for an extensive time, in the same or in several social systems, a process moves in a certain quantitative or qualitative or spatial direction, or in all these directions, reaches its "point of saturation", and then often reverses its movements.[18]

Equipped with the classification devices of his conceptual system, Sorokin argued that the general trend of social change is that of a linear advance upto a certain point at which time either a reversal of cultural advance or the setting in of cultural stagnation occurs. In the case of the cultural reversal, the cultural movement is toward still another point of cultural advancement facing once again the inevitability of reversal. In this oscillating fashion, the pattern of culture change fluctuates between sensate mentalities on the one hand and ideational mentalities on the other. This oscillating action necessarily fosters at mid-way between the extreme of sensuality and spirituality the appearance of the synthesis of idealistic mentalities. Sorokin's study of cultural history throughout the world corroborated his theory of cultural change.

2. The Principle of Immanent Change

This principle explains why no social or cultural system is ever static but is in a process of eternal fluctuation. Sorokin writes: "Bearing the seeds of its change in itself, any socio-cultural system bears also in itself the power moulding its own destiny or life career. Beginning with the moment of emergence, each socio-cultural system is the main factor of its own destiny. This destiny, or the system's subsequent life career, represents mainly an unfolding · of the immanent potentialities of the system in the course of its existence."[19] Sorokin rejected the "externalistic theory of change" which attributes change within a particular social phenomenon to factors external to it. According to him, "The reason or cause of a change of any socio-cultural system is in the system itself, and need not be looked for anywhere else." However, he did not reject the impact of environment. "The environmental forces are not negligible, but their role consists essentially in retardation or acceleration; facilitation or hindrance; reinforcement or weakening, of the realization of the immanent potentialities of the system . . .. They cannot, however, change fundamentally the immanent potentialities of the system and its normal destiny in the sense of making the life career of an unfolding acorn that of a cow, or vice versa." Sorokin pointed out that in every culture, the predominant mentality carries within itself the demise of the dominant idea owing to the sheer exhaustion inevitable through history—thus, immanent change springs from each cultural idea. As cultural systems reach their peak of optimum dominance, Sorokin believed as he wrote in volume four of *Dynamics*, that these cultural systems "become less and less capable of serving as an instrument of adaptation, as an experience for real satisfaction of the needs of its bearers, and as a foundation for their social and cultural life." A cultural system, says Sorokin, when it presses to the limit its own premise from which it is derived, exceeds the point of social tolerance, distorts its grasp of truth by exaggeration, and anticipates its own decline. The decline ushers in a new and young mentality destined to reiterate the vicious cycle.

3. The Principle of Limit

There are definite limits to the possible variations that socio-cultural phenomena can assume. "Processes go on for some time without any appreciable change in their direction, but sooner or later the trend reaches its limit, and then the process turns aside into a new path."[20] Too much Sensate freedom and too much Ideational restraint will have the opposite effect. "When immobility persists too long, social systems generate forces working for differentiation." Moreover, there are limited possibilities for the variation of systems. For example, types of economic organization or political regimes rarely exceed six or eight in number; forms of marriage and family do not exceed ten.

In this regard, Sorokin was able to illustrate the dynamic rather than static quality of cultural change and cultural integration. Social reality, whatever else it may be, is a constantly oscillating process with anticipated uniformities and regularities. The process within socio-cultural systems is, necessarily, a dialectical one giving rise first to this perception of reality (weltanschaung) and then that one. This dialectic is at the heart of his concept of the "principle of limits"—the rhythmic periodicity of socio-cultural change, and the concept of the principle of immanent change—the location of the major causes of change within a socio-cultural system rather than being exterior to it. Sorokin was quick to mention that the highest level of integration of

socio-cultural meanings and values of a society were to be found
in the major social institutions. At given times in a culture's
history, the basic ideas or mentalities are in various stages of
internal development but at any given moment in the five basic
cultural components of a society—law, art, philosophy, science,
religion—there will be found a demonstrable effort toward consistency in each of its expressions of reality.

Theory of Social Mobility
Sorokin is recognized even now as a leading theorist in social
mobility in modern societies. His *Social and Cultural Mobility* is
a classic in the field and one of Sorokin's major contributions to
sociological literature. Mobility, Sorokin pointed out early in his
Russian period, is linked to the social stratification system of
every society. To understand the structural character of the stratification system is an essential prerequisite to an understanding
of social movements within social groups. For Sorokin, "Social
stratification means the differentiation of a given population into
hierarchically superposed classes. It is manifested in the existence
of upper and lower layers. Its basis and very essence consists in
an unequal distribution of rights and privileges, duties and responsibilities, social values and privations, social power and influences among the members of a society."[21] This stratification is
found in every society upon a tripartite structure consisting of
the economic strata (wealth), the political strata (power and
authority), and occupational strata (employment).

In addition to these three principal forms of stratification,
Sorokin also recognized two other dimensions—real and quasi-
real. The organized real strata are defined by the official law of
the group as in the case of the Pope-Cardinal-Bishop hierarchy
in the church or the Full Professor-Associate Professor-Assistant
Professor ranking in the university. The as-if, real and organized
stratum is made up of all those individuals occupying the same
position in the hierarchy of strata and also share similar rights,
duties, perceptions and behavior patterns because of the similarity of their stratum positions. Class subcultures provide a good
example.

Sorokin considers social inequality to be a universal phenomenon. According to him, there is no organized group which is
not stratified, where rights and privileges are always equally

shared among members of the group. However, stratification varies, both quantitatively and qualitatively, in different societies. The specific characteristic of a social class, Sorokin suggests, "is the coalescence of occupation and economic bonds plus the bond of belonging to the same basic stratum, whose properties are defined by the totality of its essential rights and duties, or by its privileges and disfranchisements, as compared with those of other classes. In this sense the social class differs fundamentally from all other groups."[22] Additionally, Sorokin attributes the following characteristics to social class:

> It is (1) legally open, but actually semi-closed; (2) 'normal'; (3) solidary; (4) antagonistic to certain other groups (social classes) of the same general nature ... (5) partly organized but mainly quasi-organized; (6) partly aware of its own unity and existence and partly not; (7) characteristic of the western society of the eighteenth, nineteenth, and twentieth centuries; (8) a multibonded group bound together by two unibonded ties, occupational and economic ... and by one bond of social stratification in the sense of the totality of its essential rights and duties.[23]

Within this framework, Sorokin defined social mobility in its broadest sense as "any transition of an individual or social object or value—anything that has been created or modified by human activity—from one social position to another." In other words, it meant the shifting of people in social space or as Sorokin put it, "to find the position of a man or a social phenomenon in social space means to define his or its relations to other men or other social phenomena chosen as the 'point of reference'." This concept or notion of the point of reference has flowed into standard sociological nomenclature as a basic stock-in-trade term in stratification studies. Sorokin suggested that what really needed careful and more representative analysis and exploration is "the relation of these groups to each other within a population, and the relation of this population to other populations."

In his study of human transitions from one social point to another, Sorokin discovered that social mobility through the stratified structures of society occur in two types—viz., horizontal and vertical. The horizontal movement concerns transitions from one social position to another situated on the same level as for example employment in comparable automobile manufacturing plants or membership in comparable religious tradition. Though

mobility has obviously occurred for the individual, there is no
obvious advance or decline in status. On the other hand, vertical
movement within society refers to transitions of individuals from
one social stratum to one higher or lower upon the social scale
such as an advance from the upper-working class to the lower-
middle class or vice versa. Such movement is qualitative and not
just quantitative as in the case of horizontal transitions.

Both ascending and descending movements in vertical transitions occur in two principal forms, Sorokin noted. First, there is
the penetration of individuals of a lower stratum into an existing
higher one, and second, there is the descent of individuals from
a higher stratum to a lower one. Both types are important for
an understanding of vertical mobility and each differs in cause
and characteristics. Sorokin's main focus here as elsewhere in his
theoretical development was with the collective group and not
the single individual. "The case of individual infiltration," he
explained, "into an existing higher stratum or of individuals
dropping from a higher social layer into a lower one are relatively
common and comprehensible. They need no explanation. The
second form of social ascending and descending, the rise and fall
of groups, must be considered more carefully."[24] Much of Sorokin's research in mobility centered around a quest to identify the
media of vertical mobility and the mechanisms of social selection
and distribution of persons in different social strata. Sorokin
identified what he called the "sieves" in society which sift individuals from one stratum and deposit them in another. The principal sifting media operative in vertical social strata movements
are the military, the church, the school, and political, professional, and economic organizations. For example, in times of war
or societal insecurity, army provides the "social stairway" through
which individuals born in the lower stratum achieve the highest
positions in society. Catholic church played a similar role for
individuals in Medieval Europe. Political organizations in a democracy and the school in an industrial society provide "elevators"
that enable individuals to climb up the social hierarchy.

Though much time was spent analyzing social mobility and
striving to understand strata movements, Sorokin was quick to
point to the positive as well as negative results of such movements in modern societies. Increased mobility "tends to reduce
narrowmindedness and occupational and other idiosyncrasies",

"facilitates an increase of intellectual life," and "a better and more adequate social distribution of individuals." However, its resulting dysfunctions have as great an impact on individuals and social structures as do its functional aspects. There is a heavy price paid for social, especially vertical mobility, Sorokin concludes. The price is the increasing of mental strain, mental disease, cynicism, social isolation, and loneliness of individuals cut adrift from their social moorings. "Mobility facilitates disintegration of morals," "diminishes intimacy and increases psycho-social isolation and loneliness of individuals."

Philosophical Orientation

Owing to his traditional training both at the Seminary and the Institute, Sorokin was earlier interested in philosophizing about the nature of man and reality. Total reality, he believed, is a manifold infinite which transcends any single perspective—thus he was an agnostic but not an atheist. Reality, he felt, encompasses the truth of the senses, of the rational intellect, and of suprarational, hyperconscious faith, intuition, or insight. All three modes of cognition, he was confident, must be utilized in the sociological endeavor to systematically study socio-cultural phenomena. Of course, this position won him no friends among the positivist or behaviorist camps, and certainly none among the communists. His sociological and philosophical position, described as the "integralist" school, was most cogently and exhaustively expounded in his *Society, Culture, and Personality* (1947). Here he argued that reality of a supra-individual socio-cultural sort is objectified in material and other "vehicles," but it cannot be reduced to the physical alone because the socio-cultural phenomena are integrated in cohesive fashion by their meaning-structure.

Here is how Sorokin himself describes his philosophy:

> Integralism is its name. It views total reality as the infinite X of numberless qualities and quantities: spiritual and material, ever-changing and unchangeable, personal and superpersonal, temporal and timeless, spatial and spaceless, one and many.... In this sense it is the veritable *mysterium tremendum et fascinosum* and the *coincidentia oppositorum* (reconciliation of opposites). Its highest center—the *summum bonum*—is the Infinite Creative X that passes all human understanding.[25]

Sorokin admits that he is in basic agreement with all true mystics and great logicians. Thus his ontology is a mere variation of the ancient and perennial stream of philosophical thought represented by Taoism, the Upanishads, and Bhagavad-Gita, brilliantly analyzed by the Hindu and the Mahayana Buddhist logicians, shared by all branches of Buddhism, and reiterated by the great Muslim thinkers and poets, Greco-Roman scholars, Christian mystics and the contemporary philosophies and moral teachings of the great minds of the East and the West.

Sorokin insists that in spite of the ever-increasing discoveries of science, it can hardly exhaust all the enigmas of total reality, nor can our language adequately define the supreme value. Empirical reality incessantly unfolds something new and there are no limits to the new objects, aspects, events, properties, relationships, etc. of this reality which is infinitely rich and inexhaustible in the forms of its Being and Becoming. To comprehend the whole plenitude of total reality, "man must become the omniscient God."

What are the key elements of Sorokin's philosophical system? First of all, integration is the keystone of Sorokin's philosophical system. Meaningful socio-cultural systems are integrated and they function and change in important parts as a whole and in "togetherness." In Sorokin's view, other conditions being equal, the highest amount of self-determination belongs to those social and cultural systems which are most perfectly integrated, causally and meaningfully.[26] This is true of philosophies, socio-cultural systems and human personalities. Anything that is unintegrated, be it a family, a government or a business enterprise, loses out and is short-lived in comparison with integrated ones.

In developing his integral theory of cognition and his integral systems of truth, Sorokin claims that there can be only five or six main integrated systems of truth. These are those based on (1) faith, (2) reason, (3) the senses, (4) their idealistic synthesis, and (5) an "integrated, sceptical and antagonistic, or critical system." The rest would be "merely an eclectic mixture of these systems. Since these are the only inevitable and logical possibilities, there can be no more than five possibilities of integrated forms, each based on a fundamental premise. They are: (1) the Ideational premise that true reality is super-sensory; (2) the Sensate premise, that is sensory; (3) the Idealistic premise that the two aspects are integrated and inseparable; (4) the skeptical premise that is unknown and unknowable; and (5) that it is "known only in its phenomenal aspect, while in its itranscendental aspect (if it has such an aspect) it is unknowable (the premise of Hume-Kant's Criticism and Agnosticism)." And precisely because the possibilities of integrated systems are limited, the three major systems of truth and reality—Ideational, Sensate and Idealistic—recur in any long-standing culture leading to the super-rhythms in historic social change. However, historical process of change is characterized by lack of direction or purpose. Sorokin likens the historical process to a man who is "circling in various directions without any definite goal or point of arrival."

Sorokin holds that none of the three major systems is entirely true or entirely false "but contains a part of truth and a part of error; and that with an increase of domination of each system its part of truth decreases while the part of error increases."[27] This is the only logical way to account for the capacity of major systems to recur, for, a completely false system could hardly dominate for any length of time whereas a completely true system would continue for ever. However, Sorokin hastens to add that Sensate systems are less viable and that "a considerable proportion of idealism is a prime requisite for the durable existence of society." This assumption, according to Sorokin, is supported by evidence that the "tide of materialism . . . almost always occurred before or during crises, hard times, social disintegration, demoralization, and other phenomena of this kind."[28]

In tune with the moral philosophies of great saints and mystics, Sorokin attests to the validity of the truth of faith. Indeed, he believes that the "truth of faith, derived from and based upon intuition, is the genuine truth as much as the truth of the senses and of reason."

This explains why the truth of faith has been able to dominate for centuries, and why the super-rational religions have been eternal cocomitants of the development of human culture. If the truth of faith (and intuition as its source) were entirely false, such a fact could not be. In the light of the above statement, the important and often indispensable role played by intuition in the cognition of true reality explains the perennial fact of the immortality of religion and arts, and the domination of the truth of faith over long periods; and this immortality of super-sensory religion and super-rational arts and ethics and domination of the truth of faith for long periods corroborates the important role of intuition as the source of truth, knowledge and creativeness.[29]

Yet, Sorokin laments that religion, philosophy and the fine arts have seldom attempted to test which of their intuitional insights have been genuine and which have been false; they have often failed to verify even the genuine intuitional "flash of enlighten-ment", "illumination", "revelation", or "mystic experience." Although science has somewhat grudgingly admitted the presence of primordial and other intuitional verities in its system of know-ledge, it has often intentionally denied the validity of intuitional cognition. In the present state of our knowledge, none of the branches of human cognition and creativity has fully realized the three-dimensional integral system of truth. "It is high time to realize that the terms of knowledge, cognition, and understanding mean much more than the purely logico-empirical knowledge of logico-empirical forms of being, and that this fuller and greater knowledge means a cognition and understanding of all possibly cognizable forms cf total reality, and particularly of its deepest and highest forms, through all channels of cognition and from all sources of knowledge available to man from science, philo-sophy, religion, ethics, fine arts, and other fields of man's creative and cognitive achievements."[30]

Sorokin: An Appreciation
One of the major criticisms of Sorokin's philosophical system per-tains to the consistency of his integralism with his metaphysics. On the one hand, Sorokin assumes that the nature of true reality is inexhaustible and unknowable and on the other hand, he claims that his system of philosophy—of truth and cognition—are based on empirical and rational methods. At the same time he admits that his meta-rational views are based primarily on faith and in this respect Sorokin is in the good company of saints and mystics. While critics characterize Sorokin's philosophical system as "metaphysical quest" or "mists of intuition," others see no inher-ent contradiction between Sorokin's positive sociology and a non-integralist philosophy of knowledge. For instance, Marquet thinks that Sorokin's integralism is consistent with his metaphysics.

Another criticism centers around Sorokin's moral judgment of systems and issues.[31] Critics charge that Sorokin has consistently slanted comparisons, always comparing the best in the Ideational and Idealistic cultures with the worst in the Sensate culture. While applauding the virtues of altruism, Sorokin has failed to see how the egoistic values of contemporary liberal society (Sensate culture) have been matched by massive controls ranging from the authority of the state to the authority of the conscience. Similarly, Sorokin's characterization of sexuality as an objectionable feature of the Sensate culture is considered nonsociological and value-laden. A far more serious criticism is that Sorokin has failed to see the changing meaning of sensuality in different cultural contexts. His inability to see the uniqueness of historical social structures led him to equate the modern Sensate period with the Greco-Roman Sensate period, a thoroughly misleading equation which blinded him to some of the essential empirical features of modern society.

However, unlike his sociological colleagues who chose to ignore the most important philosophical issues, Sorokin not only raised and faced them, he also demonstrated the inescapable presence of these issues in the scientific as well as philosophical study of man and society. And, unlike his philosophical collea- gues who would restrict the field, he developed comprehensive theories with implications in such diverse branches of philosophy as ontology, ethics, phenomenology, gnosiology, and the philo- sophy of science and of history.

Ford summarized Sorokin's major contributions to philosophy as follows:[32] Sorokin recognized the role of values and meanings *directly*. While holding to consistent concepts of "meaning" and "value" on a socio-cultural level, he has effectively demonstrated their use in widely varying empirical fields. Using his tremendous knowledge of the historical social theories and the empirical studies of the day, Sorokin was able to demonstrate to value-free and meaning-free scholars in social science that their paths are variously blind or circular, and their hopes of avoiding the cru- cial issues illusory. While the so called value-free social scientists may scoff at his hopes for "creative altruism" in the "reconstruc- tion of humanity," few would doubt today the depth and serious- ness of the "crisis of our age" which Sorokin delineated so ably.

It has been said that Sorokin is a true successor to the socio- logical masters—Comte, Durkheim, and Kroptokin—the first because of his interest in the social consensus, the second because of his work in social solidarity, and the last because of his research into the concept of mutual aid. Forever the emigre, Sorokin was a lonely and isolated man cut loose from his moor- ings in the Komi north country of the Russian wilderness of

forests and peasants. Though he had numerous American associates and colleagues, his true friends were old Russian emigres
from his Petrograd student days. Other than the enduring friendship of C.C. Zimmerman who joined Sorokin at Minnesota and
followed him to Harvard, he had no close American friends.
Always uneasy and never at home even in Harvard and Cambridge after thirty years, he was distant to his colleagues there,
defensive, insecure, and isolated.

In spite of such handicaps and personal idiosyncracies, Sorokin
made a great contribution to sociology in many ways. At the
University of St. Petersburg, he was the first professor of sociology and during his years at the University of Minnesota, he
taught many fine students destined to become distinguished
sociologists, such as T. Lynn Smith. In addition to extensive
writing, at Harvard he established the first department of sociology there and was that prestigious university's first professor of
sociology. And among other fine students, he taught Merton and
Loomis. From about 1940 until about 1965, Sorokin was ignored
by virtually all of sociology. Yet, in recent years, sociologists are
again coming to appreciate his systematic approach to the study
of social change and especially his recognition of the role of war
and revolution in such change. His work, Merton has suggested,
merits a place for him in the annals of the social sciences.

NOTES

CHAPTER I

1. Auguste Comte, Politique Positive, (Paris, Cres, 1912) Four volumes, IV; p. 9.
2. Auguste Comte, Positive Philosophy, trans. by Harriet Martineau, (New York, Calvin Blanchard, 1838 Four volumes, II: p. 14.
3. Ibid., p. 383-84.
4. Ibid., II, pp. 225-26.
5. Ibid., p. 225.
6. Auguste Comte, System of Positive Polity, (New York, Burt Franklin, 1966) Four volumes, IV, p. 27.
7. Ibid., p. 39.
8. Ibid., p. 47.
9. Positive Philosophy II, p. 219.
10. Ibid., p. 217.
11. Ibid. Quoted from J.H. Abraham, Origins and Growth of Sociology, (New York, Penguin Books, 1977), p. 111.
12. System of Positive Polity, IV, p. 52.
13. Positive Philosophy II, p. 251.
14. Ibid., p. 261.
15. Ibid., I, p. 14.
16. Ibid., II, p. 15.
17. Ibid., p. 22.

CHAPTER II

1. Randall Collins and Michaël Makowsky, The Discovery of Society (New York, Random House, 1972), p. 34.
2. Nicholas Timasheff and George Theodorson, Sociological Theory (New York, Random House, 1976), pp. 57-8.
3. Karl Marx, "German Ideology," pp. 197-216 in Erich Fromm, Marx's Concept of Man (New York, Frederick Ungar, 1961), p. 198.
4. Lewis A Coser, Masters of Sociological Thought (New York, Harcourt Brace Jovanovich, 1971), p. 74, 75.

5. Karl Marx, Selected Writings in Sociology and Social Philosophy (London, McGraw-Hill, 1964), p. 60.
6. Karl Marx and Friedrich Engels, Selected Works, 2 vols. (Moscow, Foreign Language Publishing House, 1962), p. 488.
7. Timasheff and Theodorson, op. cit., p. 61.
8. Calvin J. Larson, Major Themes in Sociological Theory (New York, David McKay, 1973), p. 40.
9. David Caute (ed.), Essential Writings of Karl Marx (New York, Macmillan, 1967), p. 32.
10. Calvin Larson, op. cit., p. 42.
11. As quoted by Jerome Balmuth in Marxist Social Thought (New York, Harcourt, Brace and World, 1968), pp. 7-11.
12. Timasheff and Theodorson, op. cit., p. 60.
13. As quoted by Jerome Balmuth, op. cit., p. xxi.
14. Ibid., p. 7-11.
15. Calvin Larson op. cit., p. 43.
16. Raymond Aron, Main Currents in Sociological Thought (Garden City, Doubleday, 1970), p. 154.
17. Selected Works I, p. 362.
18. Selected Works II, p. 51.
19. Doyle P. Johnson, Sociological Theory (New York, John Wiley and Sons, 1981), p. 133.
20. Ibid., p. 132.
21. Selected Writings, p. 223.
22. Ibid., pp. 79-80.
23. Reinhard Bendix and Seymour Martin Lipset, Class, Status, and Power (New York, Free Press, 1966), p. 7.
24. Ibid., p. 8.
25. Ibid., p. 11.
26. Karl Marx and Friedrich Engels, "The Class Struggle," in Amitai Etzioni and Eva Etzioni-Halevy (eds.) Social Change (New York, Basic Books, 1973), p. 102.
27. Lewis Coser, op. cit., p. 44.
28. Ibid., p. 49.
29. Selected Works II, p. 77.
30. Bendix and Lipset, op. cit., p. 9.
31. Raymond Aron, op. cit., p. 152.
32. Selected Writings, p. 223.
33. For a good discussion and critique of Marx's theory of class conflict, see Chapters 1 and 4 of Ralf Dahrendorf, Class and Class Conflict in Industrial Society.
34. Raymond Aron, op. cit., p. 174.
35. Ibid., p. 165.
36. Maurice Cornforth, Historical Materialism (New York, International Publishers, 1954), pp. 58-9.
37. See Bendix and Lipset, op. cit., p. 10.
38. Marx and Engles, in Etzioni, op. cit., pp. 36-7.
39. Ibid., pp. 37-8.

40. Irving Howe (ed.), Essential Works of Socialism (New York, Holt, Rinehart and Winston, 1971), p. 7.
41. Karl Marx, Early Writings (New York, McGraw-Hill, 1964) p. 39.
42. *Ibid.*, p. 39.
43. *Ibid.*, p. 156.
44. Early Writings, p. 124.
45. Marx and Engels, "On Alienation," in C. Wright Mills (ed.), Images of Man (New York, George Braziller, 1960), p. 498, 500.
46. As quoted by Richard Schacht, Alienation (Garden City, Doubleday, 1970), p. 95.
47. *Ibid.*, p. 110.
48. Images of Man, p. 505.
49. T.B. Bottomore, "Marxist Sociology," in the International Encyclopaedia of the Social Sciences (New York, Macmillan Company, 1968), p. 46.
50. T.B. Bottomore, "Karl Marx: Sociologist or Marxist?" in Serge Denisoff *et. al.* (eds.) Theories and Paradigms in Contemporary Sociology (Ithaca: F.E. Peacock Publishers, 1974), pp. 304-5.
51. Herbert Marcuse, "Re-examination of the Concept of Revolution," in Denisoff, *op. cit.*, p. 319.
52. His works represent the growing literature dealing with neo-colonialism and imperialism; see, for instance, Latin America: Underdevelopment or Revolution; Capitalism and Underdevelopment in Latin America; Dependence and Underdevelopment; Charles Wilber (ed.) The Political Economy of Development and Underdevelopment.
53. Marcuse, *op. cit.*, p. 320, 322.

CHAPTER III

1. Herbert Spencer, An Autobiography (New York, D. Appleton, 1904), Two volumes, II, p. 3.
2. Herbert Spencer, Principles of Sociology (New York, D. Appleton, 1896) Three volumes, I, p. 17.
3. *Ibid.*, Vol. II, quoted from J.H. Abraham, Origins and Growth of Sociology, (New York, Penguin Books, 1977), p. 217.
4. Robert L. Carneiro, The Evolution of Society: Selections from Herbert Spencer's Principles of Sociology (Chicago, The University of Chicago Press, 1967), p. 7.
5. Principles of Sociology, I, p. 479.
6. Herbert Spencer, Essays, Scientific, Political and Speculative (New York, Appleton, 1892), Vol. I, p. 35.
7. From J.H. Abraham, *op. cit.*, p. 223.
8. Principles of Sociology, Vol. I, p. 96 and Vol. III, p. 331.
9. See Herbert Spencer, First Principles of a New System of Philosophy (New York, DeWitt Revolving Fund, 1958).
10. Principles of Sociology, III, p. 331.

11. *Ibid.*, I, p. 96.
12. Don Martindale, The Nature and Types of Sociological Theory (Boston, Houghton Mifflin Company, 1960) p. 164.
13. Principles of Sociology, Vol. III, p. 331.
14. Herbert Spencer, The Study of Sociology (New York, Appleton, 1891), p. 43.

CHAPTER IV

1. Emile Durkheim, "Preface to the Second Edition," The Rules of Sociological Method (New York, Free Press, 1964), p. xliii.
2. *Ibid.*, p. 102.
3. Emile Durkheim, The Division of Labor in Society (New York, Free Press, 1965), p. 80.
4. *Ibid.*, p. 127.
5. *Ibid.*, p. 174.
6. *Ibid.*, p. 262.
7. Raymond Aron, Main Currents in Sociological Thought II (Garden City, Doubleday, 1970), p. 24.
8. Rules of Sociological Method, p. 103.
9. *Ibid.*
10. *Ibid.*
11. Emile Durkheim, Suicide, (New York, Free Press, 1951), p. 159.
12. *Ibid.*, pp. 209-10.
13. *Ibid.*, p. 225.
14. *Ibid.*, p. 252, 253, 254, 255.
15. Emile Durkheim, The Elementary Forms of Religious Life (New York, Free Press, 1965).
16. *Ibid.*
17. Robert Nisbet, The Sociology of Emile Durkheim (New York, Oxford University Press, 1974), 188.
18. George Simpson, Emile Durkheim (New York, Thomas Y. Crowell Company, 1963), p. 115.
19. *Ibid.*, p. 114.
20. Robert Nisbet, *op. cit.*, p. 200.
21. *Ibid.*, p. 204.
22. Division of Labor, p. 3.
23. *Ibid.*, p. 28.
24. *Ibid.*, p. 10.
25. Rules of Sociological Method, p. 67
26. *Ibid.*, p. 70.
27. *Ibid.*, p. 71.
28. Robert Nisbet, *op. cit.*, p. 219.
29. Rules of Sociological Method, p 72.
30. Robert Nisbet, *op. cit.*, p. 223.
31. Daniel W. Rossides, The History and Nature of Sociological Theory (Boston, Houghton Mifflin Company, 1978), p. 292.

CHAPTER V

1. Raymond Aron, Main Currents in Sociological Thought II, (Garden City, Doubleday, 1970), p. 128.
2. Vilfredo Pareto, The Mind and Society: A Treatise on General Sociology (New York, Dover, 1963), 4 volumes, p. 61.
3. Vilfredo Pareto, Cours d'economie Politique (Geneva, Droz, 1964), p. 12.
4. The Mind and Society, p. 51.
5. Ibid., p. 54.
6. R. Aron, op. cit. p. 137.
7. Ibid , pp. 137-38.
8. Ibid., p. 141 (quoted from Aron).
9. The Mind and Society, p. 54.
10. Ibid., p. 449.
11. Aron, p. 177.
12. Lewis A Coser, Masters of Sociological Thought (New York, Harcourt Brace Jovanovoich, 1971), p. 401, quoted.
13. Ibid., p. 399, quoted.
14. Aron, op. cit., p. 196.
15. Ibid., pp. 201-2.

CHAPTER VI

1. Kurt H. Wolff (ed.), Essays on Sociology, Philosophy and Aethetics by Georg Simmel et. al. (New York, Harper and Row, (1959), p. 141.
2. Georg Simmel, "The metropolis and mental life," pp. 47-60 in Richard Sennett (ed.) Classic Essays on the Culture of Cities (New York, Appleton-Century-Crofts, 1969), p. 48.
3. Ibid., p. 52.
4. Georg Simmel, Philosophie des Geldes (Leipzig, Duncker and Humblot, 1900), 2nd. ed. 1958.
5. Georg Simmel, Soziologie: Untersuchungen Uber die Formen der Verges ellschaftung (Berlin, Duncker and Humbolt, 1908) 2nd. ed. 1958.
6. Kurt Wolff, op. cit., p. 25.
7. G. Sotiroff, Georg Simmel, in David L. Sills (ed.) International Encyclopedia of the Social Sciences (New York, The Macmillan Company, 1968), 253.
8. Kurt Wolff, op. cit., p. 41.
9. Georg Simmel, "The Dyad and the Triad," in Lewis A. Coser and Bernard Rosenberg (eds.) Sociological Theory: A Book of Readings (New York, The Macmillan Company 1969) p. 60.
10. Ibid., p. 61.
11. Kurt Wolff, op. cit., p. 148.
12. Kurt Wolff, The Sociology of Georg Simmel (New York, Free Press, 1950), pp. 402-403.

13. Lewis Coser, Masters of Sociological Thought (New York, Harcourt Brace Jovanovich, 1971), p, 188.
14. Kurt Wolff, Essays on Sociology, p. 21.
15. Lewis Coser op. cit., p. 184.
16. James T. Duke, Conflict and Power in Social Life (Provo, Brigham Young University Press, 1976), p. 98.
17. Georg Simmel, Lebensanschaung: Vier Metaphysische Kapitel, (Munich, Duncker and Humblot, 1918).

CHAPTER VII

1. Peter L. Berger and Thomas Luckmann, The Social Construction of Reality (Garden City, Doubleday, 1966), p. 18.
2. Emile Durkheim, The Rules of Sociological Method (New York, Free Press, 1950), p. 14.
3. Max Weber, Theory of Social and Economic Organization (New York, Free Press, 1964), p. 101.
4. Berger and Luckmann, op. cit., p. 18.
5. Theory of Social and Economic Organization, p. 88, 90.
6. Hans H. Gerth and C. Wright Mills, From Max Weber: Essays in Sociology (New York, Oxford University Press, 1968) p. 55.
7. J. H. Abraham, Origins and Growth of Sociology (New York, Penguin, 1973) p. 207.
8. Daniel W. Rossides, The History and Nature of Sociological Theory (Boston Houghton Mifflin Company, 1978), p. 356
9. Theory of Social and Economic Organization, p. 99.
10. Calvin Larson, Major Themes in Sociological Theory (New York, David MacKay, 1973), p. 225.
11. Raymond Aron, Main Currents in Sociological Thought II (Garden City, Doubleday, 1970), p. 223.
12. Theory of Social Economic Organization, p. 90
13. George Simpson, Man in Society (Garden City, Doubleday, 1954), p. 52.
14. Calvin Larson op. cit., p. 123.
15. George Simpson, op. cit., p. 52.
16. Julien Freund, The Sociology of Max Weber (New York, Vintage Books, 1969), p. 77.
17. Theory of Social and Economic Organization, p. 115
18. Raymond Aron, op. cit., p. 224.
19. Don Martindale, The Nature and Types of Sociological Theory (Boston, Houghton Mifflin Company, 1960), p. 388.
20. Theory of Social and Economic Organization, p. 115.
21. Lewis A. Coser, Masters of Sociological Thought (New York, Harcourt Brace Jovanovivh, 1971), p. 219.
22. Theory of Social and Economic Organization, p. 89.
23. Daniel Rossides, op. cit., p. 363.

24. Raymond Aron, *op. cit.*, p. 234.
25. E. A. Shills and H. A. Finch (eds.), Max Weber on the Methodology of the Social Sciences (New York, Free Press, 1949), p. 54.
26. *Ibid.*, p. 72.
27. Lewis Coser, *op. cit.*, p. 220.
28. Max Weber, Basic Concepts in Sociology (New York, Citadel Press, 1964), p. 29.
29. Daniel Rossides, *op. cit.*, p. 380.
30. Gerth and Mills, *op. cit.*, p. 143.
31. J.H. Abraham, *op. cit.*, p. 210.
32. Peter Winch, "Max Weber," in Paul Edwards (ed.) The Encyclopaedia of Philosophy, (New York, Macmillan, 1967), Vol. 8, p. 282.
33. Raymond Aron, *op. cit.*, p. 229, 230.
34. Lewis Coser, *op. cit.*, p. 221.
35. Daniel Rossides, *op. cit.*, p. 357.
36. Robert M. MacIver, On Going to College (New York, Oxford University Press, 1938), p. 124.
37. Randall Collins and Michael Makowsky, The Discovery of Society (New York, Random House, 1972), p. 99.
38. Daniel Rossides, *op. cit.*, p. 377.
39. Lewis Coser, *op. cit.*, p. 245.
40. Reinhard Bendix, "Max Weber", The International Encyclopaedia, of the Social Sciences (New York, Collier Macmillan Company, 1968), p. 494.
41. Raymond Aron, *op. cit.*, p. 235, 240, 241.
42. Theory of Social and Economic Organization, p. 102.
43. Daniel Rossides, *op. cit.*, p. 376.
44. Shills and Finch, *op. cit.*, p. 99.
45. Lewis Coser, *op. cit.*, p. 223
46. Shills and Finch, *op. cit.*, p. 90.
47. Raymond Aron, *op. cit.*, p. 247.
48. Shills and Finch. *op. cit.*, p. 98, 68, 43, 93-94
49. Encyclopaedia of Philosophy, p. 283.
50. J.H. Abraham, *op. cit.*, p. 206-7.
51. Daniel Rossides, *op. cit.*, p. 372.
52. International Encyclopaedia of the Social Sciences, p. 496.
53. For a summary of Weber's theory see Robert Bierstedt, The Social Order (New York, McGraw-Hill, 1974). I am indebted to Bierstedt.
54. International Encyclopaedia of the Social Sciences, p. 497.
55. Collins and Makowsky, *op. cit.*, p. 100.
56. Reinhard Bendix and Seymour Martin Lipset; Class, Status and Power (New York, Free Press, 1966), p. 21.
57. Theory of Social and Economic Organization, p. 328.
58. Gerth and Mills, *op. cit.*, p. 214, 216, 228, 229.
59. Raymond Aron, *op, cit.*, p. 294.
60. Daniel Rossides, *op. cit.*, p. 378.
61. International Encyclopaedia of the Social Sciences, p. 500.

CHAPTER VIII

1. Edward Shills, "Karl Mannheim," in David L. Sills (ed.) International Encyclopaedia of the Social Sciences (New York, Macmillan Company, 1968), pp. 557-62.
2. Lewis A. Coser, Masters of Sociological Thought (New York, Harcourt Brace Jovanovich, 1971), p. 444.
3. Ibid.
4. Wenrer Stark, "Karl Mannheim," in Paul Edwards (ed.) The Encyclopaedia of Philosophy, (New York, Macmillan, 1967) Vol. 5, p. 151.
5. Nicholas S. Timasheff, Sociological Theory (New York, Random House, 1957), p. 306.
6. Lewis Coser, op. cit., p. 431.
7. Karl Mannheim, Ideology and Utopia (New York, Harcourt, Brace and Company, 1936) p. 244, 27, 26.
8. Peter L. Berger and Thomas Luckmann, The Social Construction of Reality (Garden City, Doubleday, 1967), p. 3.
9. Ibid., p. 7.
10. Karl Mannheim, Essays on the Sociology of Knowledge (London, Routledge and Kegan Paul), 1966, pp. 84-85.
11. Lewis Coser, op. cit., p. 452.
12. Ibid., p. 433.
13. International Encyclopaedia of the Social Sciences, pp. 557-62.
14. Berger and Luckmann, op. cit., p. 9.
15. International Encyclopaedia of the Social Sciences, pp. 557-62.
16. Berger and Luckmann, op. cit., p. 7.
17. Ideology and Utopia, 254, 2, 3, 278.
18. Karl Mannheim, Essays on Sociology and Social Psychology (New York, Oxford University Press, 1953), pp. 204-8 and 1.
19. Lewis Coser, op. cit., p. 430.
20. Ideology and Utopia, p. 3, 130, 245.
21. Nicholas S. Timasheff and George A. Theodorson, Sociological Theory (New York, Random House, 1976), p. 310.
22. Encyclopaedia of Philosophy, p. 151.
23. Lewis Coser, op. cit., p. 438, 437.
24. International Encyclopaedia of the Social Sciences, pp. 557-62.
25. Karl Mannheim, Essays on the Sociology of Culture (New York, Oxford University Press, 1956), pp. 171-2.
26. Karl Mannheim, Freedom, Power and Democratic Planning (New York, Oxford University Press, 1950), pp. 149-54.
27. Sociology of Culture, p. 181-2, 197, 218.
28. Karl Mannheim, Diagnosis of our Time (London, Routledge and Kegan Paul, 1966), p. 1
29. Freedom, Power and Democratic Planning, p. 23, 26, 27, 28, 29, xvii.
30. Essays on Sociology and Social Psychology, pp 260-1.
31. Diagnosis of Our Time, p. 7.
32. See Essays on Sociology and Social Psychology, Chapter 9.
33. Freedom, Power and Democratic Planning, p. 35, 36, 30, 175, 176.

34. Ideology and Utopia, p. xxi.
35. See Essays on Sociology and Social Psychology, especially pp. 29, 28, and 32.
36. Freedom, Power and Democratic Planning, p. VIII.
37. International Encyclopaedia of the Social Sciences, pp. 557-62.
38. Ideology and Utopia, p. 239.
39. Lewis Coser, op. cit., p. 434.

CHAPTER IX

1. Pitirim A. Sorokin, Society, Culture and Personality: Their Structure and Dynamics (New York, Harper and Brothers, 1947) p. 367.
2. Ibid.
3. Pitirim Sorokin, Socio-Cultural Causality, Space, Time. (Durham, Duke University Press, 1943).
4. Pitirim A. Sorokin, Social and Cultural Dynamics, 4 volumes. (New York, American Book Co., 1937-41), p. 5f.
5. Ibid , p. 8.
6. Socio-Cultural Causality, p. 49.
7. Pitirim A. Sorokin, Social Philosophies of an Age of Crisis (Boston, The Beacon Press, 1951), pp. 41-42.
8. Society, Culture and Personality, p. 99.
9. Ibid., p. 103.
10. Ibid., 106.
11. Ibid., p. 121.
12. Socio-Cultural Causality, p. 54.
13. Social and Cultural Dynamics, I, p. 23.
14. Ibid., p. 79.
15. Ibid·, pp. 24-28.
16. Ibid.
17. Ibid.
18. Ibid., p. 57.
19. Quoted from J. H. Abraham, Origins and Growth of Sociology (New York, Penguin Books, 1977), p. 439.
20. Social and Cultural Dynamics, pp. 63-4.
21. J.H. Abraham, op. cit., p. 416.
22. Society, Culture and Personality, p. 272.
23. Ibid., p. 271.
24. Social and Cultural Dynamics.
25. Philip J. Allen. Pitirim A. Sorokin in Review (Durham, Duke University Press, 1963), p. 372.
26. Ibid., p. 43.
27. Ibid., p. 47.
28 Ibid., p. 49.
29. Ibid., p. 52.
30. Ibid., p. 399.
31. Rossides, op, cit. pp. 461-5, paraphrased and summarized.
32. Allen op. cit., p. 64, summarized.

SELECT BIBLIOGRAPHY

Auguste Comte

(Works by)

(1819-1828) 1883 *Opuscules de Philosophie Sociale:* 1819-1828. Paris: Leroux.

(1830-1842) 1877 *Course de Philosuphie Positive:* 6 vols., 4th ed. Paris: Bailliere. Volume I: *Preliminaire Genereaux et Philosophie Mathematique.* Volume 2: *Philosophie Astronomique et philosophie de la Physiq.* Volume 3: *Philosophie Chimique et Philosophie Biologique* Volumes 4-5 *Philosophie Sociale.* Volume 6: *Complement de la Philosophie Sociale et Conclusions Generales.*

(1851-1854) 1875-77 *System of Positive Polity* 4 vols. London; Longmans.

(1855) 1889 *Appeal to Conservatives.* London: Trubner.

(1856) 1891 *Religion of Humanity: Subjective Synthesis,* or *Universal System to the Conceptions Adapted to the Normal State of Humanity.* London: Routledge.

(Works About)

Alengry, Franck 1900 *Essai Historique et Critique Sur la Sociologie Chez Auguste Comte:* Paris: Alcan.

Caird. Edward 1885 *The Social Philosophy and Religion of Comte.* NY Macmillan.

Ce Grange, McQuilkin 1923 *The Curve of Societal Movement: A Study of the Nature of Sociology in the Light of the Positive Politics of Auguste Comte.* Hanover, NH: Sociological Press.

Marjorie S. Harris 1923 *The Positive Philosophy of Auguste Comte.* Hartford, CT: Case.

Levy-Bruhl, Lucien 1900 *The Philosophy of Auguste Comte* NY: Putnam.

Mill, John Stuart 1865 *Auguste Comte and Positivism.* Ann Arbor: Univ. of Michigan Press.

Style, Jane. M 1928 *Auguste Comte: Thinker and Lover*. London. Paul.

Watson, John 1895 *Comte, Mill and Spencer: An Outline of Philosophy*. NY: Macmillan.

Karl Marx

(Works By)

1867, 1885, 1894 *Capital* 3 Vols. NY: International Publishers (1967).

The Eighteenth Brumaire of Louis Bonaparte. Chicago: Charles H. Kerr, 1913. (Orig. 1852).

Karl Marx: Selected Writings in Sociology and Social Philosophy. Edited by T. B. Bottomore and Maxmillien Rubel. NY: 1964.

(With Friedrich Engels) *The Communist Manifesto*. Chicago: Regenery, 1969 (Orig. 1848).

The Marx-Engels Reader. Edited by Robert C. Tucker NY: Norton, 1972.

(Works About)

Aiken, Henry D. *The Age of Ideology* NY: New American Library, 1956.

Lefebvre, Henri. *The Sociology of Marx*. NY: Random House, 1968.

Lichtheim, George. *Marxism: An Historical and Critical Study*. London: Routledge and Kegan Paul, 1961.

Tucker, Robert C. *Philosophy and Myth in Karl Marx*. London: Cambridge University Press, 1971.

Zeitlin, Irving M. *Marxism: a Re-Examination*. NY: Van Nostrand, 1967.

Herbert Spencer

(Works by)

(1850) 1954 *Social Statics: The Conditions Essential to Human Happiness Specified, and the First of Them Developed*. London: Routledge.

(1854-1859) 1963 *Education: Intellectual, Moral, and Physical*. Patterson, NJ: Littlefield.

(1855) 1920-1926. *Principles of Psychology*. 3d ed. 2 Vols. NY: Appleton.

1858-1874) 1915 *Essays: Scientific, Political, and Speculative*. 3 Vols. NY: Appleton.

(1862) 1958 *First Principles*. NY: DeWitt Revolving Fund.
(1864-1867) 1914 *The Principles of Biology*. 2 Vols. NY: Appleton.
(1873) 1961 *The Study of Sociology*. Ann Arbor: University of Michigan Press.
1873-1934 *Descriptive Sociology: or, Group of Sociological Facts, Classified and Arranged by Herbert Spencer*. 17 Vols. London: Williams & Norgate.
(1874-1896) 1925-1929 *The Principles of Sociology*. 3 Vols. NY: Appleton.
(1884) 1950 *The Man Versus the State* London: Watts.
(1892-1893) 1914 *The Principles of Ethics*. 2 Vols. NY: Appleton.
(1904) 1926 *An Autobiography*. 2 Vols London: Watts.
The Works of Herbert Spencer. 21 Vols. Osnabruck (Germany): Zeller, 1966-1967.
(Works About)
Duncan, David 1908 *The Life and Letters of Herbert Spencer*. London: Methuen.
Elliot, Hugh 1917 *Herbert Spencer*. London: Constable.
Ensor, R.C.K. 1946 *Some Reflections on Herbert Spencer's Doctrine that Progress is Differentiation*. Oxford University Press.
Hudson, William H. (1894) 1904 *An Introduction to the Philosophy of Herbert Spencer*. NY: Appleton.
Macpherson, Hector 1900 *Spencer and Spencerism*. NY: Doubleday.
Royce, Josiah 1904 *Herbert Spencer: an Estimate and Review*. NY: Fox, Duffield.
Rumney Jay 1934 (1966) *Herbert Spencer's Sociology: A Study in the History of Social Theory*. NY: Atherton.

Vilfredo Pareto

(Works By)
(1887- 1899a) 1965 *Libre-Echangisme, Protectionisme et Socialisme* Geneva: Droz.
(1887-1899b) 1965 *Le Marche Financier Italien, 1891-1899*. Geneva: Droz.
(1896-1897) 1964 *Course D'Economie Politique*. Oeuvres completes. Vol. 1 Geneva: Droz.
(1902-1903) 1965 *Les Systemes Socialistes*. Oeuvres completes. Vol. 5 Geneva: Droz.

(1906) 1966 *Le Manuel D'Economie Politique.* Oeuvres completes. Vol. 7 Geneva; Droz.
(1916) 1963 *The Mind and Society: A Treatise on General Sociology.* 4 Vols. NY: Dover.
1966 *Marxisme et Economie Pure.* Geneva: Droz.
(Works About)
Amoroso, Luigi 1938 "Vilfredo Pareto." *Econometrica* 6 : 1-21.
Bousquet, Georges H. 1925a *Introduction Aux Systems Socialistes de Pareto.* Paris: Giard.
Busino, Giovanni 1966 *Introduction a une Histoire de la Sociologie de Pareto.* Geneva: Droz.
Perrin, Guy 1966 *Sociologie ed Pareto.* Paris: Presses Universitaires de France.
Rocca, G. and Spinedi, V. P. 1924 *Bibliografia di Vilfredo Pareto.* Rome: Giornale degli Economisti e Rivista di Statistica.
Secretan, Philippe 1950 "Vilfredo Pareto et les problemes de la societe contemporaire." Etudes Sociales No. 2 : 10-26.

Emile Durkheim

(Works By)
(1893) 1960 *The Division of Labor in Society.* Glencoe, IL: Free Press.
(1895) 1958 *The Rules of Sociological Method.* Glencoe, IL: Free Press.
(1897) 1951 *Suicide: A Study in Sociology.* Glencoe, IL: Free Press.
(1898-1911) 1953 *Sociology and Philosophy.* Glencoe, IL: Free Press.
(1902-1906) 1961 *Moral Education: A Study in the Theory and Application of the Sociology of Education.* NY: Free Press.
(1903) 1963 With Mauss, Marcel. *Primitive Classification.* Chicago: The University Press.
(1912) 1954 *The Elementary Forms of the Religious Life.* London: Allen & Unwin.
(Works About)
Alpert, Harry (1939) 1961 *Emile Durkheim and His Sociology.* NY: Russell.
Bellah, Robert N. 1959 "Durkheim and History," *American Sociological Review* 24 : 447-461.

Davy, Georges 1960 "Emile Durkheim," *Revue Francaise de Sociologie* 1 : 3-24.

Gehlke, Charles E. 1915 *Emile Durkheim's Contributions to Sociological Theory*. NY: Columbia Univ. Press.

Merton, Robert K. 1934 "Durkheim's ᾿Division of Labor in Society," *American Journal of Sociology* 40 : 319-328.

Simpson, George 1933 "Emile Durkheim's Social Realism," *Sociology and Social Research* 18 : 2-11.

Wolff, Kurt H. (Editor) 1960 *Emile Durkheim, 1858-1917: A Collection of Essays with Translations and a Bibliography*. Columbus: Ohio State University Press.

Georg Simmel

(Works by)

(1890) 1910 *Uber Soziale Differenzierung: Soziologische und Psychologische Untersuchungen*. Leipzig. Duncker & Humbolt.

(1892) 1923 *Die Probleme der Geschichtsphilosophie: Eine Erkenntnis- Theoretische Studie*. Munich: Duncker & Humbolt.

(1900a) 1958 *Philosophie des Geldes*. Leipzig: Duncker & Humbolt.

(1908a) 1955 *Conflict and the Web of Group Affiliations*. Glencoe, IL: Free Press.

(1908b) 1958 *Soziologie: Untersuchungen Uber die Formen der Vergesellschaftung*. Berlin: Duncker & Humbolt.

(1910) 1964 *Hauptrobleme der Philosophie* Berlin: Gruyter.

(1917) 1920 *Grundfragen der Soziologie* Berlin: Vereinigung Wissenschaftlicher Verleger; Gruyter.

(1918b) 1926 *Dere Konflikt der Modernen Kultur: ein Vortrag*. Munich: Duncker & Humbolt.

The Sociology of Georg Simmel. Edited and translated by Kurt H. Wolff, Glencoe, IL: Free Press.

(Works About)

Spykman, Nicholas J. (1925) 1964 *The Social Theory of Georg Simmel*. NY: Russell.

Weingartner, Rudolph H. 1962 *Experience and Culture: The Philosophy of Georg Simmel* Middleton, CT: Wesleyan Univ. Press.

Wolff, Kurt H. (editor) 1959 *Georg Simmel: A Collection of Essays*. Columbus: Ohio State University Press.

Max Weber

(Works By)

1958 *The City*. NY: Free Press.

1968 *Economy and Society* 3 Vols. Totowa, NJ: Bedminister.

1946 *From Max Weber: Essays in Sociology*. NY: Oxford University Press.

1927 *General Economic History*. London: Allen & Unwin.

1954 *Max Weber on Law in Economy and Society*. Cambridge, MA: Harvard University Press.

1949 *The Methodology of the Social Sciences*. NY: Free Press.

1968 *On Charisma and Institution Building*. Chicago: The University Press.

1930 *The Protestant Ethic and the Spirit of Capitalism*. NY: Scribner

1963 *The Sociology of Religion*. Boston: Beacon Press.

1947 The Theory of Social and Economic organization. NY: Oxford University Press.

(Works About)

Bendix, Reinhard. *Max Weber: An Intellectual Portrait*. Garden City, NY: Doubleday, 1960.

Bendix, Reinhard, and Roth, Guenther. *Scholarship and Partisanship: Essays on Max Weber*. Berkeley: University of California Press, 1971.

Freund, Julien. *The Sociology of Max Weber*. NY: Random House, 1968.

MacRae, Donald G. *Max Weber*. NY: Viking, 1974.

Mitzman, Arthur. *The Iron Cage*. NY: Knopf, 1970.

Stammer, Otto, Ed. *Max Weber and Sociology Today*. NY: Harper & Row, 1972.

Weber, Marianne. *Max Weber: A Biography* NY: Wiley-Interscience, 1975.

Wrong, Dennis, ed. *Max Weber*. Englewood Cliffs, NJ: Prentice-Hall, 1970.

Karl Mannheim

(Works by)

(1922-1940) 1953 *Essays on Sociology and Social Psychology*. Edited by Paul Kecskemeti. London: Routledge.

(1923-1929) 1952 *Essays on the Sociology of Knowledge*. Edited by Paul Kecskemeti. NY: Oxford University Press.

(1929-1931) 1954 *Ideology and Utopia: an Introduction to the Sociology of Knowledge*. NY: Harcourt.

(1935) 1940 *Man and Society in an Age of Reconstruction: Studies in Modern Social Structure*. NY: Harcourt.

(1939-1943) 1950 *Diagnosis of our Time: Wartime Essays of a Sociologist*. London: Routledge.

1950 *Freedom, Power, and Democratic Planning*. NY: Oxford Univ. Press.

1956 *Essays on the Sociology of Culture*. Oxford Univ. Press.

(Works About)

Merton, Robert K.. (1941) 1957 "Karl Mannheim and the Sociology of Knowledge," pp. 489-508 in Robert K. Merton, *Social Theory and Social Structure* NY: Free Press.

Mills, C. Wright (1940) 1963 "Methodological Consequences of the Sociology of Knowledge," pp. 453-468, in C. Wright Mills, *Power, Politics and People: The Collected Essays of C. Wright Mills*. NY: Oxford Univ. Press.

Polanyi, Michael 1958 *Personal Knowledge: Towards a Post-Critical Philosophy*. Univ. of Chicago Press.

Pitirim Sorokin

(Works by)

1925 *The Sociology of Revolution*. Philadelphia: Lippincott.

(1927-1941) 1959 *Social and Cultural Mobility*. Glencoe, IL: Free Press.

1928 *Contemporary Sociological Theories*. NY: Harper.

1929 with Carl C. Zimmerman, *Principles of Rural-Urban Sociology*. NY: Holt.

(1937-1941) 1962 *Social and Cultural Dynamics*. 4 Vols. Englewood Cliffs, NJ: Bedminister Press.

1942 *Man and Society in Calamity: The Effects of War, Revolution, Famine, Pestilence Upon Human Mind, Behavior, Social Organization and Cultural Life*. NY: Dutton.

(1943) 1964 *Sociocultural Causality, Space, Time: A Study of Referential Principles of Sociology and Social Science*. NY: Russell.

(1947) 1962 *Society, Culture, and Personality: Their Structure and Dynamics: A System of General Sociology*. NY: Cooper.

1950a *Altruistic Love: A Study of American "Good Neighbors" and Christian Saints*. Boston: Beacon.

(1950b) 1963 *Modern Historical and Social Philosophies*. NY: Dover.

1954 *The Ways and Power of Love*. Boston: Beacon.

1956a *Fads and Foibles in Modern Sociology and Related Sciences*. Chicago: Regnery.

1956b *The American Sex Revolution*. Boston: Sargent.

1963 *A Long Journey: The Autobiography of Pitirim A Sorokin*. New Haven, CT: College and University Press.

1966 *Sociological Theories of Today*. NY: Harper.